T0110529

A Professional's Guide to Working with Vulnerable and Traumatised Children

This book presents "The Circle of Safety and Reconnection", a compassionate reflection model for working with vulnerable and traumatised children and young people in a nurturing way, providing hope for post-traumatic healing and growth.

The circle is a holistic and comprehensive framework for professionals working to create safety for children against violence and abuse. It takes into consideration a child's individual, intergenerational, and collective trauma also assessing their risk and protection factors and using different tools to regulate the nervous system and promote healing. A step-by-step guide, populated with practice examples and exercises to walk the reader through using and adapting the model in practice, the book discusses the nature, signs, and ways of trauma, the reasons for it, and the different ways of healing these wounds outside the therapeutic context. Additionally, as this field is high risk for secondary traumatisation, stress, burnout, and compassion fatigue, the author has dedicated a chapter focusing solely on the building of resilience in professionals.

This text is written for all professionals working in the field, including therapists and psychologists, social workers, educators, foster parents, nurses, day-care workers, and students.

Rikke Ludvigsen is a social worker, trainer, supervisor, family consultant, and therapist trained in safety planning, EMDR, SFBT, and stabilisation of chronically traumatised children. She has worked for over 20 years with children at risk, their parents, and their networks, and has trained over 1,000 professionals over the last decade.

A Professional's Guide to Working with Vulnerable and Traumatised Children

The Healing Circle

Rikke Ludvigsen

Routledge
Taylor & Francis Group

LONDON AND NEW YORK

Designed cover image: © Getty Images

First published 2024
by Routledge
4 Park Square, Milton Park, Abingdon, Oxon OX14 4RN

and by Routledge
605 Third Avenue, New York, NY 10158

Routledge is an imprint of the Taylor & Francis Group, an informa business

© 2024 Rikke Ludvigsen

The right of Rikke Ludvigsen to be identified as author of this work has been asserted in accordance with sections 77 and 78 of the Copyright, Designs and Patents Act 1988.

British Library Cataloguing-in-Publication Data
A catalogue record for this book is available from the British Library

Library of Congress Cataloging-in-Publication Data
Names: Ludvigsen, Rikke, 1974- author.
Title: A professional's guide to working with vulnerable and traumatised children : the healing circle / Rikke Ludvigsen.
Description: Abingdon, Oxon ; New York, NY : Routledge, 2024. | Includes bibliographical references and index. |
Identifiers: LCCN 2023059062 (print) | LCCN 2023059063 (ebook) | ISBN 9781032345369 (hardback) | ISBN 9781032345345 (paperback) | ISBN 9781003322672 (ebook)
Subjects: LCSH: Psychic trauma in children. | Psychic trauma in children--Treatment.
Classification: LCC RJ506.P66 L838 2024 (print) | LCC RJ506.P66 (ebook) | DDC 618.92/8521--dc23/eng/20240312
LC record available at https://lccn.loc.gov/2023059062
LC ebook record available at https://lccn.loc.gov/2023059063

ISBN: 9781032345369 (hbk)
ISBN: 9781032345345 (pbk)
ISBN: 9781003322672 (ebk)

DOI: 10.4324/9781003322672

Typeset in Times New Roman
by KnowledgeWorks Global Ltd.

To my beloved dad

If it wasn't for you, I wouldn't have known all this about trauma and trauma healing

Thank you!

Contents

Acknowledgements

When it comes to relational wealth and health, I am a very lucky and blessed person and I have so much and so many people to be grateful for.

I would particularly like to thank the people in my life who have supported me and cheered on me – and have always been there when I needed it the most. My dear family and close friends!

From near and far … here and beyond … always and forever in my heart.

You are all unique to me and carry a unique contribution to this creation.

Thank you!

Special thanks go to Arianne Struik and Sonja Parker for all that you have taught me and for showing me the way through the wilderness of trauma-informed safety work. Thanks also to Andrew Turnell, Susie Essex, Harvey Ratner, Chris Iveson, Evan George, and John Henden for your important teachings that have continuously inspired me over the years. Also, thank you, Denise Yusuf, Caara Goddard, and Cindy Louise, for your important contribution to making this book a reality – I am forever grateful!

Special thanks to Mette Guldfeldt for helping me find my new voice that led to the development of the Circle of Safety and Reconnection. Thanks also to Mette Vangsøe, Sandra Krebs-Hille, and Katrine Nordvig for proofreading the book – it was a safe experience to share it with you first.

Thanks to Kaya Flintholm for helping me with illustrations and Liv Søchting for carrying me the last half mile.

Also, thanks to Lillian Larsen, Steen Bager, Pernille Vestergaard Kleffel, and Julie Folke Jacobsen for your strong belief in safety planning and me over the years. Thanks to my former colleagues in Sikkerhedskonsulenterne for all I learned from our collaboration. To the board members of my NGO, Sisterpower International, and my "partner in social change", Heidie Graversen – thank you!

Thank you to all the beautiful people in the first batches of my 1-year training in Denmark for both being guinea pigs for my model and helping me learn how to teach it.

The same goes for the first batch of my Reconnect Trauma Release Practitioners. Thank you!

Most importantly, I'd like to thank all the children, young people, and their families and the child protection professionals who have helped me grow and learn all those years.

Without you, there wouldn't have been the learning journey that led to this book. Words will never be enough to express my gratitude.

Thank you!

Chapter 1

Introduction to trauma-informed work and the Circle of Safety and Reconnection

Introduction

Since the early beginnings of my work with vulnerable and traumatised children in January 2001, I have continuously sought to upgrade my knowledge and skill set to improve my work helping children and families in the best, fastest, and gentlest way possible. My teachers have inspired me to try new things, gain new skills, and bring new methodologies to the field, and I have learned from every child, young person, parent, professional, and person in the family private network I have met on the way. For the learning journey it has become, I am forever grateful.

This book will cover the essence of all the most important lessons that I have learned from working as a social worker, child protection worker, family counsellor, trauma therapist, trainer, supervisor, and consultant in high-risk and highly complex cases. Though the Danish social work context is very different from that of many other countries, I hope the content will make sense to other nationalities and in other contexts and will bring inspiration and insight of importance to the children, adolescents, and parents you are working with. In my opinion, the nature of trauma will be no different from one context to another, but the possibilities to work around it might be very different and will need some adaptation to the individual reader's work. Therefore, there will be small exercises at the end of every chapter to guide you in adapting the content to your individual practice.

The stories that I share are real-life cases, but I have changed all names, ages, and other information to protect their identities. The content of the stories might be overwhelming and triggering to read, and, as I warn you about this, I will also remind you that the stories have also been turned around into stories of safety and healing for the children and young people involved.

This is the reason for writing this book – to be able to help more children get the help they need.

I have worked with children of all ages and developmental stages exposed to traumatic experiences and life conditions. One child was beaten by a baseball bat while in her mother's uterus. Others experienced violence similar to torture, enduring intense pain applied from being whipped with wires, burned with cigarettes, beaten with hard objects, or confined. Some children suffered sexual abuse at the

DOI: 10.4324/9781003322672-1

hands of their parents, professionals, or other children and adolescents, and I have supported children who witnessed one parent expose the other one to brutal violence; some even witnessed one parent killing the other.

Many children and adolescents have also been exposed to psychological violence, degrading behaviour, and bullying in various contexts, including school, day care, and sports. Additionally, I have been engaged in helping refugees, children recovering from medical trauma, and victims of gender-based crimes. Regardless of the traumatic experience, the damage to their mental, emotional, and physical health has been severe, causing deep wounds to their development and well-being.

All their lives and stories have taught me a lot, and they have touched me, changed me, and created the person I am today. I usually tell people I train, "You should not do this work without doing your inner work, too". So, the next chapter is dedicated to sharing all that I have learned about staying strong and resilient after many years in this tough field.

My ambition has always been to change social and family systems and to empower all the people involved through the processes I facilitate. Ambition is one thing; reality is another, and I am painfully aware of the times when I, for different reasons, could not succeed. From these experiences, I learned my lessons by reflecting on what I could have done differently and needed to learn. This is what I call "the pain of learning", making me better, wiser, and more vulnerable while sharing my flaws and mistakes with others so they might not make the same mistakes in their work with vulnerable and traumatised children and families. This book is a product of this learning process and the know-how arising from all my reflection.

Often, I have been humbled deeply by the strength of the human spirit and the capacity to survive, adapt, and carry on despite the tremendous suffering people endure. Many of the people I have worked with are victims of cruel crimes, and acknowledging this is crucial. They deserve help that allows them, in a dignified way, to find safety, process their trauma, and build a better life for themselves, their children, and future generations. An essential part of the healing journey involves moving through three phases, from being a victim to becoming a survivor and, at last, a thriver (Dolan, 1998, p. 40). My continuous endeavour is always to help people find hope for a better future, help them find ways to achieve this, and support them in their choices to create that new and better future; this book aims to provide you with a GPS to guide the individual journeys of the traumatised children and young people you work with.

I also strive for people to learn to seek help and not suffer alone. "No man is an island, entire of its itself", as the poem John Donne wrote in 1624 reads (Donne, 2023), and we aren't supposed to face such difficulties on our own. A supportive network around us is crucial, but trauma can make it a frightening experience to trust and reconnect with others. As professionals, we may be the first to be trusted again, which is a huge privilege but also a significant responsibility.

I am very grateful for the trust people place in me when sharing their darkest moments and difficult feelings with me, and it's an honour every time I am allowed to help them heal and create important changes in their lives. Acknowledging that being a professional doesn't automatically grant us access to people's deepest and most intimate spheres and experiences is important. It sometimes takes so much more to earn people's trust, especially with people suffering from severe trauma caused by other people. I have developed the Circle of Safety and Reconnection and a trauma-informed mindset to support this process. These tools help us to be safe and trustworthy professionals for people embarking on the healing journey from being a victim to becoming a thriver. I will come back to the mindset after introducing you to the circle first.

The Circle of Safety and Reconnection

As my contribution to the professional field of working with vulnerable and traumatised children, I have developed a compassionate reflection model for practitioners to help them gain a holistic and comprehensive assessment tool to work with children's safety and trauma. This model considers their individual, intergenerational, and collective trauma, adverse childhood experiences (ACEs), risk factors, protective factors, and positive childhood experiences (PCEs). It provides various tools to regulate children's nervous systems and knowledge on the care needed to support their healing and engage private and professional networks in various ways. There will also be reflections on how to create the best and most healing intervention plans while ensuring that professionals and private networks support the healing process without re-traumatising the children. When it is used, the GPS will be set to find the way back home for the vulnerable and traumatised children and young people you are working with.

The model is called the Circle of Safety and Reconnection, and the book will guide you through its eight steps in a structured manner, providing a step-by-step process to adapt to your own work life. Reflection is essential to create practice depth in this field, and that is why I refer to the Circle of Safety and Reconnection as a reflective model. It covers information on crucial aspects of a vulnerable child's life, which we must gather and use wisely for the benefit of the child and their family. The model takes you through the essential elements of high-risk and high-complexity practice, requiring structure, strategy, knowledge, risk assessments, and engagement with all the important people around the child, including the child themself. Knowing what to work on next, whom to work with, and how to work with them effectively is crucial to creating meaningful and fast changes.

The rest of this chapter lays the foundation of mindset and knowledge about working in a trauma-informed way to support using the model. Chapter 2 focuses on your own state of mind as an important part of this work too. From Chapter 3 onwards, the book will follow this structure and provide knowledge, experiences, case examples, and exercises to give you a sense of how to use it in your practice. Chapter 11 will provide some final thoughts and conclusions and also gather your final reflections from reading the book and doing the exercises.

Illustration 1.1 The Circle of Safety and Reconnection

The model creates reflective practice depth in any context in which you work. While you may not be able to handle everything yourself, the model provides an overview of whom to reach out to for the best collaboration around a specific child. The approach may vary from child to child and over time, but the essential element involves forming close partnerships. When people come together to create change and healing for vulnerable and traumatised children, it becomes the most powerful way to achieve sustainable change for them.

A trauma-informed mindset for working with vulnerable children, adolescents, and their families

As a solid and powerful foundation for work with traumatised people, it's essential to have a certain trauma-informed mindset based on specific beliefs and values that qualify our assessments and help guide our actions. The mindset I have found most helpful is based on compassion, a calm brain, curiosity, courage, responsibility, respect, worthiness, and hope.

Compassion

Compassion is the ability to contain and be with another person in their pain without trying to fix things or being attached to a specific outcome. The intention is to reduce the other person's pain, and it's built on the power of empathic connection between two individuals (Halifax, 2009, 2010; Trzeciak, 2018). Cultivating compassion begins with creating a safe, non-judgemental space for others to share their deepest pain and vulnerability. It involves consciously acknowledging their suffering and being fully present with them while also intending to alleviate their pain through our supportive presence. A German research team defines empathy as experiencing suffering as happening to oneself, whereas compassion is characterised by feeling care, love, and warmth and developing a strong motivation to help the other (Singer et al., 2004). When working with traumatised children and their families, cultivating compassion helps people feel safe and acknowledged, enabling professionals to contain their pain without nervous system dysregulation. This will be covered in depth in Chapter 2.

A calm brain and the power of co-regulation

The growing understanding of the brain and nervous system has shown that we as human beings are very sensitive and attuned to each other. For better and for worse, we are automatically and constantly mirroring the states of other human beings through mirror neurons in our neocortex firing between us, making our individual states of mind very contagious (Porges, 2011; Siegel, 2020; Van der Kolk, 2015). Therefore, if someone has high arousal owing to an emotional outburst or stress, our nervous system will instantly register it and feel more dysregulated. Conversely, if someone is calm and relaxed, this will help us feel more regulated and calmer too. Being aware of this natural ability to read and mirror another person forms the basis for using our nervous system and brain to co-regulate with the children and young people we work with, providing them with a calm and regulated state to support their own regulation.

Co-regulation offers them a golden opportunity to learn how to be more regulated, recognise the difference between feeling calm and feeling stress in the body, and gradually become accustomed to it. To be able to lend them our nervous system, we must work on our own regulations skills, be aware of our own states, and learn techniques to regulate ourselves if we start to feel dysregulated when in contact with the children and their families. The book will explore these various aspects of maintaining a calm brain in more depth.

Curiosity

As a solution-focused practitioner, I am trained in facilitating conversations solely based on asking curious questions to help people reflect on and think themselves through their issues to find solutions based on their strengths, resources, and skills (Ratner et al., 2012). In order for the person to be the expert on their life and find their own answers to what are the best solutions for them, I am always cautious and mindful about choosing the next best, most helpful question for each person's unique situation. In the safety planning, family therapy/counselling, and trauma release sessions, I combine the questioning approach with bodywork, nervous system work, family counselling, guidance, and the use of different treatment tools, but always tailormade to the individual person and family based on their strengths, resources, skills, and best hopes.

In my trauma-informed work, the one question I am most curious about asking is what happened to the child. Inspired by Bruce Perry and other experts, I advocate shifting our perspective from "What is wrong with the child?" to "What has happened to the child?" (Perry & Winfrey, 2022) because, for us to understand their difficulties and how we can best help them, we need to know what they have experienced in their lives that might have caused these difficulties. This perspective will also enable children to understand themselves better, transform their negative beliefs about themselves into more positive ones, and replace feelings of shame, guilt, low self-esteem, and unworthiness caused by trauma with kindness and self-compassion. Sharing this understanding with parents, private networks, and professionals in the children's life also helps adults cope better with the children and, sometimes, understand themselves better.

From my experience, looking beyond people's seemingly meaningless, strange, and often harmful or destructive behaviours reveals a deeper story. When I observe this kind of behaviour, I always suspect it to be trauma-triggered, and I ask people, "What is this really about?" Without exception, their answer tells a story about the behaviour that serves as protection in the present and is rooted in past harmful experiences that have not been processed correctly. Viewing their reactions in this light helps me understand them better and leads them to understand their reactions better, promoting the healing of shame and the feeling of being wrong. As they realise that they did the best they could, to the best of their ability, they can now begin to deal with things differently and then do better. As Maya Angelou said, "When you know better, you do better" (Winfrey, 2011).

Courage

In the safety planning and trauma healing processes, some parents, people in the private network, and other professionals express concerns about talking with children about the tough details of all the bad things that have happened to them. Therefore, I reassure them that, if dealt with appropriately, it's not harmful to children to talk about the difficult things in their lives, and I continue engaging the children in conversation about their life, but with a sense of respect for their boundaries and vulnerability. These are their real-life experiences, and, if left unaddressed, they continue living or reliving them, and so it can be more damaging and traumatising for children *not* to talk about them and to be left alone with all these complicated things to handle (Glistrup, 2016; Struik, 2022). Thus, we need to dare to speak to them and develop the skills to do so in a safe and protective way.

Maintaining a calm brain, regardless of whatever overwhelming things they might share with us, is essential, as the professional's response to their disclosure and pain will influence the outcome of the healing process. Sometimes, children need someone to be with them in their distress, reassuring them that it's not their fault and that there isn't anything wrong with them. Providing an honest explanation about what happened in their life can correct the stories they might have formed in their minds. Without explanations from adults about what is going on in their life according to the actual incidents, they will make up their own stories in their mind for it to make sense, but, unfortunately, these stories are often about them being wrong, bad, and guilty (Glistrup, 2014, 2016), and this leads me to the following principle.

Responsibility

The responsibility for the incidents in a child's life and how they are influencing the present moment should never be placed on the child. Unfortunately, the child is often unintentionally held responsible for their issues when adults focus all their attention on trying to fix the child rather than addressing the contexts around them. When adults discuss how bad and wrong the child's behaviour is and how much trouble it's causing, they are unintentionally putting all the blame and responsibility on the child, leading to a damaging sense of shame and being wrong and affecting their self-esteem and self-worth. Unless the child has a genetically predisposed diagnosis, for which they can never be blamed, their behaviour is shaped by the different environments they grow up in, and it's always adults' responsibility to create safe and caring environments that support the child's healthy development and well-being. Therefore, a trauma-informed mindset involves removing the responsibility from the child and transferring it to the adults, where it truly belongs and where changes can be made. Children are too young and undeveloped to handle this level of responsibility, and they rely on adults for regulation, setting boundaries, and understanding right from wrong, among other things.

The neocortex isn't fully developed until the early 20s (Perry & Szalavitz, 2007), and, as a result, children and young people may struggle to predict the consequences of their actions. This is even more difficult for traumatised children owing to the impairment of normal brain development caused by trauma (Perry & Szalavitz, 2007). Be mindful that I am talking about responsibility, not blame, as there is a difference between the two. Helping vulnerable and traumatised children isn't a blame game, and blaming only leads to resistance and conflict. Instead, we should be curious about everybody's perspective and intentions to understand what happened, not to accept it but to engage in a partnership to create the needed change for the child to ensure it will not happen in the future.

This part of the mindset must be communicated with the most profound respect for all parties involved in the child's life. We should acknowledge that everybody did their best for the child, to the best of their abilities, but sometimes this may not have been enough. Throughout my years in child protection, I have carried with me the belief that, if the adults around the child could have done things differently and better, they would have done so. So, with respect, we need to engage them in the hard work to learn and grow from the past and use the present to create change and a better future for all.

Respect

Respect for everyone engaged in the collaboration around children and the children themselves is an essential aspect of the trauma-informed mindset, including when we disagree with each other about our different perspectives on a child's situation. My general rule of thumb is that the more we disagree, the more mindful and aware we must be of respectful communication with each other. To foster such communication, I have found the use of nonviolent communication developed by Marshall Rosenberg (Rosenberg, 2015) beneficial in my practice. It serves as a foundation of my communication, enabling me to address difficult matters honestly and with compassion and respect while minimising feelings of shame and guilt.

Shame is a complicated emotion for many people (Brown, 2013), and toxic shame is a significant component of developmental trauma (Heller & Lapierre, 2014). It plays a crucial role in forming a person's negative self-image and often leads to overwhelming sensations and reactions when it is triggered. This creates a significant risk of professionals activating trauma responses and survival behaviours if we aren't careful in communicating challenging aspects of a child's safety and well-being in a respectful way.

From my training with Susie Essex, the founder of the Resolutions approach, I have learned that, in denied child abuse cases, building partnerships with parents based on openness and respect is crucial to create the best and safest outcome for children (Turnell & Essex, 2006). In my work with perpetrators, I strive to meet them with compassion and respect for them as human beings, even when it's challenging. During these times, I find it helpful to remind myself that no child is born evil, and the harm people cause to others is often linked to the damage they have suffered themselves, and they, too, require to be met with compassion and respect from professionals. This understanding is supported by research on adverse childhood experiences which reveals that many incarcerated people are among the most traumatised people, having experienced six or more ACEs (Felitti et al., 1998). This topic will be revisited in Chapter 6.

Dignity and worthiness

Article 1 of the Universal Declaration of Human Rights states that all humans are born equal in rights and dignity, underscoring the importance of treating each other in dignified and respectful ways. To me, dignity is very closely connected to worthiness and how all humans are born worthy of love and belonging and must have these two basic needs met to be healthy and thrive. Childhood trauma often involves undignified treatment leading to struggles with self-worth and self-esteem, feeling the need to become someone other than who they are to be loved and be a valued part of the community. These deep wounds from growing up in traumatising living conditions need healing.

As professionals, we can support this healing process for traumatised children, adolescents, and their families in how we talk to, engage with, believe in, see, and acknowledge them. I once worked with a young woman in her 20s who engaged in extreme self-harm and severe suicidal thoughts owing to childhood emotional neglect and psychological violence in childhood. This caused her to hold a negative belief about herself, saying, "I don't deserve to be alive", because she didn't feel worthy of love and belonging in the world. I challenged this belief by highlighting that she, like all humans, was born into this world as a part of humanity, making her equally worthy of love and belonging. There may be other self-harming and suicidal children and young people who also need to hear that they are worthy of love and belonging and that their presence matters to support their healing journey.

Hope

Speaking of self-harm and suicide, hope can be a lifesaving force. In Viktor Frankl's book *Man's Search for Meaning*, he shows us the power of hope by describing how fellow inmates in concentration camps during the Second World War would die within days after losing the last bit of hope (Frankl, 2006). This is how powerful hope is. From workshops with the solution-focused brief therapist John Henden about severe trauma and suicide prevention, I have learned that hope can make it virtually impossible for people to commit suicide when they believe things can get better and they can overcome their struggles. Hope plays an essential part in the solution-focused approach and, therefore, it can be very valuable in trauma work, too (Froerer et al., 2018).

In my practice, I explicitly focus on hope, starting by asking people the best hopes questions that I have learned in solution-focused brief therapy (Ratner et al., 2012), being either "What are your best hopes for our collaboration?", "What are your best hopes for the trauma therapy?", or "What are your best hopes for the training/supervision?" Through the many conversations with people I have had over 20+ years, I have realised that one of my most significant tasks in working with both families and professionals is to be vicarious hope when they have lost it themselves.

In my trauma release sessions, when other professionals have made children and youth believe their condition to be chronic, I am very aware of daring to give them hope for healing. I draw upon my experiences with all the people doing trauma work who have recovered but also the message of hope for healing from experts such as Arianne Struik, Peter Levine, and others. Their insights have made me aware that severe trauma and PTSD can be healed under the right circumstances and with the right framework and methodology (Levine, 1998; Struik, 2019).

Attachment and connection – a critical need to survive, develop, and thrive

Before writing more about trauma and its cause, I will briefly introduce the most crucial aspect of a child's healthy development. This is to establish a deeper understanding of where it goes wrong when the development is impaired owing to violence, abuse, inadequate care, or emotional neglect causing developmental trauma to the child.

Basic human needs and brain development

Human beings need love and belonging to secure their survival in the same way a plant needs water or animals need a pack to belong to, and one of the greatest threats you can experience in life is a lack of attachment and care as an infant, because this will leave you very vulnerable, with little chance of survival. From the moment we are conceived and start developing in our mother's womb, we are vulnerable to a potential lack of care and connection from our mother and, after birth, from our father and likely other caregivers (Maté, 2019; Perry & Szalavitz, 2007; Szalavitz & Perry, 2010; Van der Kolk, 2015). The attachment and prenatal attachment between a child and its caregivers are essential for the healthy development of the brain and all the aspects of human development connected to the brain, such as our capacity to connect and attach, self-regulate, develop empathy, mentalise, and so much more (Perry & Szalavitz, 2007; Perry & Winfrey, 2021; Van der Kolk, 2015). In Chapter 5, attachment and prenatal attachment will be described in more detail, but it all starts with and goes back to the development of the brain.

The first 3 years are the most critical, where the child's brain develops the most and forms the building blocks for its further physical, emotional, social, and cognitive development (Hart, 2009; Perry & Szalavitz, 2007; Siegel, 2020). This period is called the "preverbal" stage, where the child experiences the world through its senses and feelings and gradually learns to recognise language, which will enable it to speak between 2 and 3 years old (Hart, 2009). The infant is born with the ability to sense and react to sensory impulses from its surroundings, but feelings, thoughts, and the ability to talk, memorise, and mentalise must be developed and learned through interactions with caretakers and other children and adults in a continuous process, until the brain is fully developed at around 23 years old (Hart, 2009; Perry & Szalavitz, 2007; Siegel, 2020). Every child grows and matures step by step, according to their own individual "zone of proximal development", the term the Russian child psychologist Lev Vygotsky coined for the natural and ideal place for all learning. This place is where we find the balance between building on what we already know and being challenged enough to struggle but still succeed and have fun while learning (Smith et al., 1997).

Our brain is divided into three parts that build on each other from the bottom up, respectively, the reptilian brain at the brainstem, the mammalian brain being the limbic system, and the human brain, called the neocortex (Perry & Szalavitz, 2007; Perry & Winfrey, 2021; Siegel, 2020; Szalavitz & Perry, 2010; Van der Kolk, 2015).

The reptilian brain is the sensory brain that supports the development of autonomous regulation and the senses that from birth help the infant make sense of the world and be in contact with the surroundings for it to survive. Whenever the infant experiences something, it will try to make sense of it, and, when it succeeds, the nervous system will relax, the child will experience that it can trust its senses, and, from there, it starts building resilience and the ability to regulate stress. From birth, babies lack the ability to self-regulate stress and rely on their primary caregivers to co-regulate them by soothing and providing a sense of calm using their own regulated state of mind (Struik, 2019).

The mammalian brain is then built around the reptilian brain and has to do with the child's feelings, moods, and expectations about others and the experience of someone being significant to them and vice versa. This forms the most important building block for the child's attachment system, and, around the age of 12–18 months, the child has developed their attachment pattern based on the quality of contact with their caregivers, which then will determine the pattern they use to build relationships through the rest of their life.

The last part of the brain to develop is the neocortex, which is the home of rational thinking, imagination, reflection and planning, our ability to mentalise and build empathy, compassion, and states of mindfulness. The three parts need to be connected to each other to function in a healthy way, creating connections between our senses, feelings, and thoughts to achieve coherent and meaningful understanding of our experiences in life, which helps us understand and handle these situations in a way that builds resilience. If the links are missing, disruption will happen – for example, if a child senses something is wrong around them, but the adults assure them everything is all right when it's not. This creates a disruption of the link between the three and will leave the child alone with the task of trying to make sense of the divergent information between what they sense and what they are being told (Glistrup, 2016, 2021). On the other hand, when being able to talk about difficult things that are appropriate for their age, the child will experience that it's okay to talk about them, it's okay to sense and feel as they do, and there isn't anything wrong with them, helping them to build resilience instead of becoming vulnerable (Levine & Kline, 2012).

Providing the infant with good, attuned contact following, and adjusted to, the child's lead concerning eye contact, touch, positive interactions, and mirroring is also of great importance to the healthy development of the child and their ability to feel safe in themselves and the world and thereby thrive and develop healthily (Levine & Kline, 2012; Perry & Szalavitz, 2007; Siegel, 2020; Van der Kolk, 2015). Also, the caregivers need to be able to read the child's basic needs and know the difference between the child's cries and signals to understand whether it's time for food, a nappy change, or sleep or whether, for example, the child is in pain. This enables the parents to provide the appropriate care for the right basic need at the right time, supporting the development of healthy physiological regulation as a foundation of the child's brain development and a sense of safety and contentment to help support the child's safe attachment to the parents (Perry & Szalavitz, 2007;

Siegel, 2020; Van der Kolk, 2015). It's perfectly normal and safe for the child to experience some disruption in the relationship between parent and child, and it's through the repair of these disruptions that safe attachment and resilience will be built. This will be described in more detail in subsequent chapters, along with mentalisation in Chapter 5 and emotion regulation in Chapter 4.

The nature of different kinds of trauma and traumatic experiences

A recent study by the National Survey of Children's Health Research has shown that almost 50 per cent of all children in the United States have experienced at least one significant traumatic event in their life (Perry & Winfrey, 2021). This doesn't necessarily mean that they will all become traumatised from these events, as it's not the traumatic experience itself that is traumatising for a person. Whether it becomes a trauma or not is determined by how overwhelming the experience is to the individual person and how it's processed and stored in the brain afterwards. This processing can be done by the person either on their own or with the help of friends, family, or professionals after the incident, so that it will not impact them in the long term (Levine, 1998; Perry & Winfrey, 2021). To understand this in more depth, it's vital to understand more about how the nervous system works.

The nervous system and the "windows of tolerance"

From a nervous system perspective, trauma arises when an individual encounters an overwhelming experience or living conditions that can't be naturally digested and processed. The inability to process the experience leads to ongoing distress and disruption within themselves, their relations, and their overall sense of being in the world (Levine, 1998). As a foundation of trauma-informed work, I will introduce you to the understanding of the nervous system developed by the American professor of psychiatry Daniel Siegel (Siegel, 2020), also inspired by Arianne Struik's way of communicating this to children and their families (Struik, 2019).

Every human being has a defence nervous system to ensure their survival, and it has evolved over millions of years, being connected to all three parts of the brain described earlier. When the three parts of the brain work together, we are within our "windows of tolerance" to sense, feel, think, and be social using all our human capacities, such as speaking, planning, reflection, mentalisation, self-control, and so on. The nervous system is influenced by the area in our brain, called the amygdala, that registers fear and is located in the limbic brain, which constantly scans our surroundings for signs of danger, just like a smoke detector scans for signs of smoke and fire to protect us (Van der Kolk, 2015). During the day, we experience different levels of arousal within our windows of tolerance, depending on what we experience, who we engage with, and what the amygdala, as the smoke detector, scans. When the amygdala detects danger, it signals this strongly to us, making the human brain shut down in favour of our instincts. Here, our survival mechanisms take over, leaving us in a state of survival outside our windows of tolerance. Depending on how severe the danger detected is, we can either get into a state of hyperarousal controlled by the sympathetic nervous system – being the fight, flight, and hide response to ensure our survival – or a state of hypo-arousal, involving collapsing and freezing, controlled by our parasympathetic nervous system.

The fight is like the lion out on the savannah that attacks, the flight is the gazelle that runs when the lion attacks, and hiding is the hare that sits still, hides, and waits for the fox to pass by. In this state, the brain pumps cortisol and adrenaline into the body, and the heart beats faster, resulting in the blood pumping more quickly around the whole body and making the muscles tense and ready to flee, fight, or actively freeze, while maybe feeling angry, scared, and agitated. If these instincts are blocked and not experienced as sufficient to overcome the danger, the brain shuts down completely into a state called hypo-arousal. This is characterised by shock or a state of collapse where the blood flows from the limbs into the vital organs, and the legs and arms become limp and rubbery, accompanied by a slow heart rate and shallow breathing. One might experience this as a state of submission, surrendering to anything that might happen, or the body can also stiffen as if you feel completely paralysed.

The purpose of this state is to use as little energy as possible to survive, only utilising breathing and the vital organs at the same time as the brain begins to secrete pain-relieving substances. Back on the savannah, this process of playing dead both helps to ensure the best possible chance of survival, as lions prefer fresh meat and might not eat a dead animal, and, at the same time, also helps to not feel any pain as a preparation to die if the lion eats it anyway. This automatic reaction happens because, when in danger, our only task is to ensure our survival and get out of there as fast as possible. We would act too slowly to protect ourselves if we first had to reflect on and discuss how to run if there was a lion after us.

When it's all over, and we're safe, the human brain operates again, and we can get back into our window of tolerance, shaking off the experience, maybe talking it through with others, and then moving on with the day. However, for traumatised people, this natural process of processing the traumatic event has somehow been blocked by the overwhelming experience of danger in the nervous system, and this means that they have not yet realised that the traumatic event is over and they have survived it, but, instead, it has left them in a chronic state of survival. Chronic stress makes the window of tolerance smaller and the amygdala more active, scanning for danger where there is none and leaving the person more sensitive to stressful situations and triggers of the traumatic incident.

The nervous system isn't only influenced by the amygdala but also by the vagus nerve, the body's longest cranial nerve, connecting the brain to all the internal organs. Stephen Porges has developed the polyvagal theory (Porges, 2011), which describes the connection between the vagus nerve and the nervous system reactions described above. It also describes the connection between us and our relationships, as Porges considers our nervous system to be social. This means that we impact each other constantly, enabling us to co-regulate each other, so that the people around us can either calm us down or maintain or increase stress, depending on how they respond to us. Again, this highlights the importance of having a calm brain when working with traumatised children and young people. Porges calls the state of being safe and relaxed within the window of tolerance social bonding, hyperarousal is called mobilisation, and hypo-arousal is called immobilisation.

From his understanding, only 20 per cent of the sensations about signs of danger and signs of safety come from the brain, while 80 per cent come from the body. A well-functioning vagus nerve promotes psychological stability and stress resilience, but, if you have trauma or chronic stress, the vagus nerve might send incorrect impulses between the two and register dangers where there are none or make things feel safe when they aren't. By engaging in activities such as breathing exercises, yoga poses, and specific exercises that stimulate the vagus nerve, we can actively influence the body's relaxation and help calm a hyperaroused or mobilised state. Similarly, these techniques can also be used to activate people to get them out of a hypo-aroused or immobilised state. This offers multiple perspectives for working with children and young people through somatic approaches instead of relying solely on talk therapy.

From traumatic experience to trauma

A traumatic experience is defined as an experience that consists of the following elements: (1) causing severe damage to a person or threats of it, (2) causing other people's death or threatening others' or one's own life, or (3) grossly exceeding one's own or others' personal boundaries, both physically and mentally, or threats of it. These elements include violence, assaults, rape, sexual violence, torture, war, bullying, loss of a caregiver or loved one, accidents, natural catastrophes, discrimination, racism, surgery, homelessness, imprisonment, removal into care, and more (Levine & Kline, 2012).

These different types of traumatic events can either be single incidents causing shock trauma – for example, surgery, a rape, an assault, a visit to the dentist, or a parent's death, or they can show up as clusters of traumas when the same incidents happen several times, such as violence in a relationship happening repeatedly, medical interventions involving several incidents, repeated incidences of bullying at school, and so on. Developmental trauma is the severe trauma that comes from living in traumatising conditions with your caretakers, exposing you to harm, and also the damage from emotional neglect consisting of the lack of care, connection, and safe attachment described above. This accounts for most of the children I have worked with and is the primary reason for writing this book.

Trauma can also be characterised as individual, intergenerational, collective, or secondary trauma. This chapter will cover individual trauma, whereas intergenerational and collective trauma will be covered in depth in Chapter 5, and secondary trauma in Chapter 2. The child can be exposed to individual trauma in the preverbal age, called preverbal trauma, and trauma experiences later can either be defined as awake dogs or sleeping dogs, depending on the level of awareness and readiness to process it (Struik, 2019). The term "awake dogs" represents the trauma that the child remembers, can put words to, and wants to process to feel better, and "sleeping dogs" represents the trauma the child avoids, suppresses, or dissociates from. Arianne Struik has developed the "sleeping dogs method" to work with the stabilisation of these children to get them into trauma therapy and process the memories when they are stable and safe enough (Struik, 2019). I won't be able to cover this in depth here, but in Chapter 10 I will get back to the different phases of trauma treatment: stabilisation, processing, and integration.

As described above, not all traumatic experiences become trauma, and other experiences that are apparently not traumatic can become so because they were experienced as dangerous to the person – for example, falling in the street, feeling your legs being swept away underneath you (Levine, 1998). So, in other words, trauma is the personal impact on your nervous system from experiencing a situation that is so overwhelming that the standard processing of memories in the brain gets disrupted and it leaves you stuck in the state of survival, storing the memories in a frozen state with the same sounds, visions, smells, bodily feelings, other sensory impressions, and feelings as when it happened (Levine, 1998; Shapiro & Forrest, 2001). This means that, when thinking of it or experiencing a trigger, the person will feel like it's happening again in the present moment, because they will be back at the time of the trauma, and the activation of the nervous system described around the windows of tolerance will automatically happen with no control over it. Because this happens automatically and very fast, and the memories often are unconscious, it can be difficult for the traumatised person to understand that it's the memories from the past causing the reaction in the present, which can be very scary.

Understanding the triggers and their responses to them will be necessary and helpful for them to feel safer. Therefore, it's important for professionals working with traumatised people to learn to understand trigger behaviour. When becoming aware of it and understanding the connection, they can learn to regulate themselves better when triggered and experience a more significant sense of control of their mind and body and ability to cope in everyday life. A child who shows signs of being affected, seemingly without a clear reason, can indicate that trauma is being activated even if the initial traumatic situation has ended. Despite being safe in the present moment, the child may not perceive this as such owing to unprocessed distressing memories that continue to resurface. These memories mislead them into believing that the past danger is reoccurring, triggering their survival response repeatedly as a means to protect themselves from the danger. This can reinforce the feeling of being unsafe and create more and more stress inside the child, as traumatised children can be triggered in their memories many times a day and be constantly stuck in a state of survival without other people knowing this because of their sleeping dogs (Struik, 2019).

The human ability to dissociate when experiencing extreme and traumatic events and living conditions is a survival mechanism that can be activated when the intensity of the experience overwhelms the child's ability to regulate and deal with it or make sense of it. In response, the child may dissociate, withdraw inward, and appear mentally absent for a brief period. Dissociation involves a disconnection from normal consciousness, and, when a child dissociates during an event, they often lack conscious memory of that event, experiencing amnesia (Struik, 2019). There are different versions of dissociation; for example, a person can dissociate the whole experience, not remembering anything, or can dissociate the emotion, remembering the event but not the emotion associated with it, or can use structural dissociation to the extent that it becomes dissociative disorder (Struik, 2019).

People with dissociative identity disorder (DID) have developed parts within themselves to adapt to threatening circumstances. There might be no awareness between these personality parts, or they might partly be aware of another part, which can cause fear and phobic avoidance of the other parts (Knipe, 2018). These different parts all have different adapted behaviours to the extent that they can appear to be different personas, with different expressions in voice, language, and body. It's a rare condition, but it does exist and represents the ultimate adaption and defence mechanism to endure being in the world. Since dissociation in any of its conditions is a defence mechanism, it's meant only to be used briefly to get through the problematic episodes and have these episodes processed and integrated into consciousness. Still, if the conditions do not stop and the experiences aren't processed, it can become a chronic condition creating a massive disturbance in the present, without people understanding the cause of their suffering.

Case example: Mary-Ann

Mary-Ann was in her late 30s and, in many ways, she functioned and behaved well, but at times she would behave in ways that reminded her of her abusive mother, the reason for her wanting to do trauma processing and deal with her traumatic upbringing. She had grown up in a very dysfunctional family, with massive psychological and physical violence as well as emotional and physical neglect. From the trauma map of her many traumatic events, she identified the worst experience as the weekly interrogations orchestrated by her mother after her parents' divorce. During these sessions, her mother would force her and her siblings to listen to her scolding their father, manipulating them into believing he was evil, and play recorded conversations of the children talking with their father while cross-examining them. Mary-Ann described how, during these sessions, she had imagined herself flying out of the room to stand outside the window and look at them from out there. This enabled her to endure being in the room physically. During the trauma treatment, it became clear that she was still emotionally dissociated from the experience and struggled to talk about it without losing contact with me. In her everyday life, she would also experience dissociative conditions when triggered by memories of it. The processing of other traumas first and stabilising her psyche, in general, helped her integrate this part and process the memories, so that she no longer needed to dissociate but became more integrated with herself, no longer feeling trapped in the shadow of the past but feeling freer to be who she is and proud of it.

Extreme living conditions characterised by violence, abuse, emotional neglect, and a lack of care and connection, as described in this case, can cause severe damage to a child's health, development, and well-being, resulting in developmental trauma and impairment of the brain. The younger children are, the more profound the damage can be, as an infant's lack of care and connection in the early years can be perceived as life-threatening. Research indicates that different brain areas can be affected depending on the trauma's timing, type, and intensity (Perry & Winfrey, 2022). Still, there is hope, because our brains possess a remarkable capacity for healing and can form new and healthier neural networks to support our development. This can happen if we change the care situation and offer appropriate treatment to process and release the traumatic experiences of the past that have impacted development.

Bruce Perry's highly successful neurosequential model is designed to systemically rebuild the brain as much as possible for each traumatised child and young person by stimulating the brain areas that are assessed to be impaired (Perry & Dobson, 2013; Perry & Szalavitz, 2007). Researchers and therapists continually discover new approaches to work with and address early childhood trauma to transform the development and well-being of children and adults affected by severe traumas, rather than treating them as sufferers of chronic conditions. Even for adults, it's never too late to start this healing process of working with the emotional, psychological, and neurological damage they might have suffered in childhood and adolescence owing to neglect, abuse, and lack of care and connection with their caregivers. Among other things, brain scans of clients at their first and after their last eye movement desensitisation and reprocessing (EMDR) sessions have shown that the brain changes and evolves during trauma processing (Pagani et al., 2012, 2015). For this healing to happen, it's crucial to understand the impact of trauma on the brain and how important it is to adopt a trauma-informed approach to help survivors of traumatic events and living conditions to feel safe again. Failing to do so may keep the entire nervous system in a state of alarm and survival mode, leading to severe damage to the body, mind, and soul (Levine, 1998).

To explain the effect of trauma processing, I often use the analogy of thawing frozen energy in the nervous system, which, similar to frozen seawater in wintertime, returns to its original state as it thaws. When the memories are processed, the energy associated with them typically returns to its original condition. They will become memories without overwhelming feelings and sensory inputs, weakening the sensory impressions connected to the traumatic experiences. After the processing, critical work may be needed to restore the brain, depending on how early in life the trauma happened. For example, a little boy named Anthony had been exposed to trauma during infancy. After the trauma had been processed, all the adults around him actively supported the development of all the ordinary skills he didn't develop in his first years owing to his being in survival mode and unable to develop normally. For Laura, however, it was different because she was older when traumatised.

Case example: Laura

Laura was in her late teens and had suffered from anxiety and panic attacks since she was in her early teens. She came from a good family background and generally had a good, safe life, with only one traumatic incident in her life showing up in our conversation about her trauma history. The incident was her boyfriend being in a car accident, which led to the hospitalisation of the boyfriend. This was such a shock to Laura that she started to change and feel different afterwards. She started to experience anxiety as well as panic attacks, leading to experiencing "fear of the fear", which had continued for many years. After only one session of the traumatic incident being processed and a new, positive belief about being in control being installed, for the first time in several years, she felt utterly calm and safe. After the session, she was hopeful that it had all been processed, and the anxiety and panic attacks would not come back, but she was also somewhat sceptical since she had lived with them for so long. I explained to her that trauma processing, in many ways, will change how we react to experiences in life, but there will still be challenging and fearful times. Feeling fear in dangerous situations is healthy, but there is a difference between this and being afraid all the time owing to past events. At a follow-up meeting 1 month later, she had experienced arousal in some situations but not once to the extent of experiencing anxiety and panic attacks, because she now felt in control of herself. In the integration phase, her job was to trust this sense of being in control of herself, believing it was not coming back, and then start acting from the new and safe state instead of out of fear. As a part of writing this book, I asked her if she would get back to me 6 months later and let me know if the change was still accurate. When I heard from her, she felt great, was sharing life with a new boyfriend, and was still in the process of being in the world in a new and better way, with no anxiety or panic attacks.

In various professional contexts, you meet many children who may not have access to trauma treatment, like Laura and Anthony, because it's still not widely used worldwide. Still, that doesn't mean we can't make a difference in their lives. On the contrary, it makes a crucial difference to children that professionals in their lives know about trauma and can provide a trauma-informed environment in their everyday life. When potentially traumatising events occur, it's essential not to leave the child processing the experience alone, but to stand with them in their pain and help them gradually digest and release the overwhelming sensations arising from traumatic incidents.

Also, you can always bring the trauma-informed mindset to action and try to understand what happened to the child. Once you know this, passing this understanding on to the child, parents, colleagues, and other professionals is beneficial to show new and better ways for the child to cope and providing support to help them find healthier coping strategies, but it's also important to acknowledge that it was not their fault and that there isn't anything to be ashamed of or feel guilty about. They are okay as they are.

Every way to resolve and heal trauma will be different. The more complex the trauma, the more time and resources it will require, and the more we must work on stabilisation and creating changes in the contexts around the child rather than trying to fix them. Some children will heal from only a short period of therapy, and, in those cases, the contents of this book will not need to be considered. It's mainly for the highly complex work needed to prevent, understand, assess, and heal developmental trauma that I have developed the Circle of Safety and Reconnection model. The model is described in detail, going through one step at a time from Step 1 in Chapter 3 to Step 8 in Chapter 10.

Trauma work with children in different contexts

Outside the therapeutic setting, professionals meet children in several contexts, such as foster family/residential homes, school/day care, hospital/psychiatry, or family therapy/help in the home, or as a legal authority in custody or child protection cases. There are different perspectives on working with traumatised children depending on the context. I want to highlight these differences to acknowledge the many diverse aspects of this topic and help you get the most out of the book, depending on which context you find yourself in.

Trauma in the foster family, adoptive family, and residential homes

Children in care and adopted children face very different systems around the world, but they share a common experience of having been raised in traumatising conditions and being exposed to traumatising events. Their biological parents were unable to provide adequate care for them to secure their health, development, and well-being. Even though the removal was likely in their best interest, it could have contributed to further traumatisation. The children adopted or taken into care from birth can also be at risk of prenatal trauma due to lack of prenatal attachment or the mother's stress levels, as well as postnatal trauma from the sudden loss of and abandonment by the mother.

As a result of their traumatic experiences, these vulnerable children may not be responsive to love and belonging to the extent that attachment work will be enough for them to develop and thrive healthily. They may need additional knowledge and professional skills to deal with their trauma in everyday life. Their trauma might manifest as intense conflicts, aggressive behaviour, and rejections as they push adults away because it's unsafe to attach to them. Alternatively, they develop a need to please others out of fear of being abandoned again. Other challenging issues could be sexualising or violent behaviour, creating safety issues that adults might not be equipped to handle and potentially putting other children at risk.

At the beginning, the new carers may not initially grasp the full extent of the developmental damage these children have endured. As time passes and the children settle into their new homes, their true emotional state emerges, often leaving many adults shocked about the unexpected behaviour and feeling lost and in need of tools, knowledge, and support to properly care for these children. When working with these severely traumatised children in these settings, in many ways, the task is to provide unconditional connection and care for them because they might not give much in return regarding contact and relationships.

The key is to be there, still standing and willing to connect with them, even if they reject you, don't connect with you, or aren't behaving appropriately. It's also essential to consider the trauma they have experienced and their developmental stage at the time of the trauma. Sometimes 14-year-olds are only as emotionally mature as a 2-year-old, and it's crucial to be able to tell the difference and to know when it's necessary to treat the child as a child of 2 years or 14 years.

Generally, there is a belief that it's most appropriate for a child to grow up in a loving and caring family. Using foster or adoptive families is preferred, depending on how the social system functions in different counties. However, in some cases of severe developmental trauma, a residential home might be a more suitable placement for a child. The shift in professionals and the less intimate setting of an institution can help them settle better, as being in a family setting might be too overwhelming and scary for them (Struik, 2019). This could lead to collapses in placements. There are a lot of children in care that experience one or more collapses, and this can be even more traumatising for them (Egelund, 2006).

Foster parents and residential staff may advocate for reducing contact with the child's biological family if the child's emotional reactions are strong after contact visits. However, it's important to be mindful that such reactions can also be a sign of attachment to the parents and a natural response to missing someone they are attached to, rather than necessarily indicating a harmful situation. Sometimes, increasing contact visits with the biological family may help support and strengthen the attachment to their new carers. Either way, assessing and making decisions in these situations can be very challenging and highlight the complexity of working with children in such contexts.

A couple of years ago, I was asked to help assess how to better support a child who had just experienced a collapse in a foster care placement after less than a month. One task was to evaluate the child's attachment to the biological family to determine if we could use them to stabilise the child in a crisis. During the transition from his previous institutional placement into the foster family, the contact visits with his mother decreased as a part of his settling with the new foster family. This, instead, increased his stress level significantly, to the extent that he became like a wild lion in the new setting. After getting him back to the institution and re-establishing the contact visits with his mother, he became his true self again. Through the process, it became evident that his mother might be able to create the necessary change to get him back home, and, after months of hard work by all the adults around him, it succeeded, and he is still home with his mother.

The Circle of Safety and Reconnection might help you reflect on the characteristics of the trauma that the children you care for are experiencing, understand their triggers, identify patterns, assess their attachment to their biological families, and gain insight into trauma responses and healing processes. By reading the book and doing the exercises, you will gain more tools, knowledge, and support to assist these children better.

Family therapy/family counselling and support of parents

In many ways, trauma shows up in the biological parent's home in similar ways to those described above while professionals are working with them as a family therapist/counsellor or other support people. In work with parents, issues around the parents taking responsibility for the trauma may arise if they are the ones causing it. Some parents are willing to take on full responsibility for their children's safety and well-being without hesitation and work with their own trauma to become better parents in the present moment and be part of their child's healing journey. Others will refuse to admit to having done anything harmful or wrong in the child's care and want the child to be "fixed", causing an even more significant risk to the child's well-being and development.

As a family therapist and counsellor, you might be working with the child and parents in the family setting, witnessing and experiencing what it's like to be the child in their home. This is extremely powerful for creating the needed change because you see it and hear it all. But it also puts you in a position full of dilemmas, and it's a huge responsibility to describe and assess the care situation and whether it's good enough. Going through the Circle of Safety and Reconnection might help you get an overview of all the information and create a well-structured process, prioritising the most urgent things and making the most suitable treatment plan according to the balanced risk assessment and goal-setting process.

Trauma in school and day-care settings

As a professional in the school and day-care system, you may encounter many vulnerable and traumatised children daily without even knowing it, as their stories might not be shared with you, and they can be challenging to spot. Many children find that school and day care are their sanctuary from all the difficult things happening in their lives. They enjoy their time in the safe space and can keep up appearances while being there so they will go under the radar. Some of them are easier to spot: they display outgoing and aggressive behaviour and struggle to concentrate. They demand much attention from the adults and can't sit still, concentrate, or take in information in class, making it challenging for educators to handle and deal with them.

Managing multiple children with special needs in a class/group makes sustaining engagement challenging. This leads to dilemmas of what to do, how to do it, and whom to choose to focus on. Assessments in school and in day care about whether a child should be submitted to a psychiatric examination or whether something is wrong at home can be challenging to make, and there might be conflict between parents and professionals in determining the problem and the solution to the problem. Discussions about who needs to do what often cause even more stress for the child, and valuable time goes by without any change happening. I have often been a part of building bridges between parents and professionals in this context, and it's so powerful to see the difference in the child when we start talking about what we can all do together to support the child in all areas, where things make it tricky for them to thrive. Often, there are issues at both school/day care and home, and we must be aware of the need to solve the problems wherever they are situated, not being a matter of either/or.

In Denmark, in recent years, there has been an extreme rise in children avoiding going to school. The many processes I have been engaged in look similar, showing a pattern over time where the child increasingly isn't showing up because it's getting more and more challenging to go to school, and then, one day, they give up and stop coming. All of them, without exception, have believed that they couldn't do it, even if they wanted to, and, from my perspective, this is a sign of stress and burnout, in the same way adults might experience in their job situation. In other countries, other specific conditions might call for a more trauma-informed stance regarding schools and day care, such as the heart-breaking rise in school shootings in the United States.

The use of the model in this context might help to create a broader perspective on the child's situation and what happened to the child, providing a better understanding of the situation and giving new views on how to deal with the issues appearing in this context, in collaboration with parents and other professionals around the child.

Trauma in physical and mental health institutions

Trauma also shows up differently in the physical and mental health sectors, some occurrences more apparent than others. In the psychiatric system, when someone is diagnosed with PTSD or complex PTSD, it's evident that the person suffers from trauma, but becoming aware of many other areas can be more challenging. The ACE studies mentioned earlier show the direct link between adverse childhood experiences and mental and physical health issues. There may be signs such as psychosomatic pain or other diagnoses such as ADHD, autism, personality disorders, anxiety, depression, and so on. Substance abuse, alcohol abuse, and addictions of all kinds are also highly correlated with trauma, and Dr Gabor Maté is trying to raise awareness of this (Maté, 2010; Maté & PESI, 2014, 2020).

Treatment in the psychiatric system can also be traumatising, unintentionally – for example, if a patient must be held down by force because they are causing harm to themselves or others or they are forced to stay in the hospital without consent. These situations can be traumatising and re-traumatising, making their recovery more complex.

Children and parents might also show up in the ER with injuries, once or more often. If they have been subjected to medical investigations and surgery, it can also unintentionally cause trauma, as has been the case for several small children I have done trauma therapy with after they finished their cancer treatment. Their stories look similar in the way the signs of trauma showed up in different situations at home and at day care afterwards, but also in the way they had already shown trauma responses and signs of being triggered during their stay in hospital in such a way that the professionals thought they were overreacting and being hysterical. Their parents didn't believe this but also didn't understand their behaviour as it was so unlike their natural way of being. When getting help from me to identify the trauma and triggers, the child's reaction suddenly made so much sense to the parents, and they were all very relieved that they trusted their instinct and gut feeling that something was wrong.

Trauma therapy was needed for these children to move on from the traumatic experiences paradoxically caused by saving their lives. Others might not require treatment, but we must be aware of, and interested in understanding, why children suddenly react differently after medical procedures and take this seriously to ensure it doesn't impair their future development.

Trauma in child protection and custody cases

From my many years working in the child protection context, with hundreds of children and their families, I have been shown the need to work in a trauma-informed way with children in general, but in particular with vulnerable and at-risk children. Many of them are born into traumatic living conditions that can cause developmental trauma, and so the more we know about it, the more we can use this knowledge in our risk assessments and action plans and provide the needed help to recover.

Regarding custody cases, many children might experience their parents' divorce as traumatic. Besides this, they might also be caught in a custody fight between their two parents and, in the worst cases, they are being forced to choose whom of the two to love. So, if they aren't traumatised by the divorce, there is a significant risk that their nervous system will be activated by the conflict often arising from the court case supporting the settlement of custody, and this also might leave the child with chronic stress and trauma from the situation.

The tricky part for the professionals in these contexts is that they have the authority to decide important things concerning the child's life and welfare, which is a huge responsibility. Still, they are also often the person furthest away from the child. Hopefully, the Circle of Safety and Reconnection will help them to get a comprehensive view and make an assessment of the individual child's situation; this will allow them to make the best possible, balanced risk assessments and the best possible action plan to engage everybody involved in creating sustainable changes for the benefit of the child's health, well-being, and development.

References

Brown, B. (2013). *The gifts of imperfection.* Hazelden.

Dolan, Y. (1998). *One small step – moving beyond trauma and therapy to a life of joy.* Authors Choice Press.

Donne, J. (2023). "No man is an island." www.poemhunter.com

Egelund, T. (2006). *Sammenbrud i anbringelser – En forskningsmæssig belysning.* B. A/S.

Felitti, V. J., Anda, R. F., Nordenberg, D., Williamson, D. F., Spitz, A. M., Edwards, V., Koss, M. P., & Marks, J. S. (1998). Relationship of childhood abuse and household dysfunction to many of the leading causes of death in adults. The Adverse Childhood Experiences (ACE) Study. *American Journal of Preventive Medicine, 14*(4), 245–258. www.ncbi.nlm.nih.gov/pubmed/9635069

Frankl, V. (2006). *Man's search for meaning*. Beacon Press.

Froerer, Adam S., von Cziffra-Berg, Jacqui, Kim, Johnny S., & Connie, Elliott E. (2018). *Solution-focused brief therapy with clients managing trauma*. Oxford Univeristy Press.

Glistrup, K. (2014). *Hvad børn ikke ved ... har de ondt af – bryd tavsheden*. Gyldendal.

Glistrup, K. (2016). *Snak om det ... med alle børn – En bog om følelser i familien* (3rd ed.). PsykoInfo Midt.

Glistrup, K. (2021). *Snak om det ... med alle børn*. Learn X. https://zevio.com/da/event/snak-om-det-med-alle-boern-513

Halifax, J. (2009). *Being with dying: cultivating compassion and fearlessness in the presence of death*. Shambhala.

Halifax, J. (2010). Compassion and the true meaning of empathy [video]. TEDWomen.

Hart, S. (2009). *Den følsomme hjerne: hjernens udvikling gennem tilknytning og samhørighedsbånd* (1st ed.). Reitzel. https://doi.org/9788741253428

Heller, L., & Lapierre, A. (2014). *Udviklingstraumer* (Healing developmental trauma). (M. Chack, Trans.). Hans Reitzels Forlag.

Knipe, J. (2018). *EMDR toolbox. Theory and treatment of complex PTSD and dissociation* (2nd ed.). Springer.

Levine, P. A. (1998). *Væk tigeren – helbredelse af traumer* (Waking the tiger – healing trauma) (F. R. Pedersen, Trans.). Borgens Forlag/Gyldendal.

Levine, P. A., & Kline, M. (2012). *Traumer set med barnets øjne – heling af traumer hos børn og unge* (Trauma through a child's eye. Awakening the ordinary miracle of healing. Infancy through adolscence) (H. T. O. E. M. Thomsen, Trans.). Dansk Psykologisk Forlag.

Maté, G. (2010). *In the realm of hungry ghosts: close encounters with addiction*. North Atlantic Books.

Maté, G. (2019). *When the body says no – the cost of hidden stress*. Vermillion, Penguin Random House UK.

Maté, G., & PESI. (2014). *Dr. Gabor Maté on addiction: from heroin to workaholism - a biopsychosocial perspective*. Eau Claire, WI: PESI.

Maté, G., & PESI. (2020). *The seven myths of addiction* Eau Claire, WI: PESI.

Pagani, M., Di Lorenzo, G., Monaco, L., Daverio, A., Giannoudas, I., La Porta, P., Verardo, A. R., Niolu, C., Fernandez, I., & Siracusano, A. (2015). Neurobiological response to EMDR therapy in clients with different psychological traumas. *Frontiers in Psychology, 6*, 1614. https://doi.org/10.3389/fpsyg.2015.01614

Pagani, M., Di Lorenzo, G., Verardo, A. R., Nicolais, G., Monaco, L., Lauretti, G., Russo, R., Niolu, C., Ammaniti, M., Fernandez, I., & Siracusano, A. (2012). Neurobiological correlates of EMDR monitoring – an EEG study. *PLoS One, 7*(9), e45753. https://doi.org/10.1371/journal.pone.0045753

Perry, B. D., & Dobson, C. L. (2013). The neurosequential model of therapeutics. In J. D. Ford & C. A. Courtois (Eds.), *Treating complex traumatic stress disorders in children and adolescents: scientific foundations and therapeutic models* (pp. 249–260). Guilford Press.

Perry, B. D., & Szalavitz, M. (2007). *The boy who was raised as a dog and other stories from a child psychiatrist's notebook: what traumatized children can teach us about loss, love, and healing*. Basic Books.

Perry, B. D., & Winfrey, O. (2021). *What happened to you? Conversations on trauma, resilience, and healing* (1st ed.). Flatiron Books.

Perry, B. D., & Winfrey, O. (2022). *What happened to you? Conversations on trauma, resilience and healing*. Bluebird.

Porges, S. (2011). *The polyvagal theory: neurophysiological foundations of emotions, attachment, communication, and self-regulation*. W. W. Norton.

Ratner, H., George, E., Iveson, C., & ProQuest. (2012). *Solution focused brief therapy: 100 key points and techniques*. Routledge.

Rosenberg, M. (2015). *Nonviolent communication: the language of life* (3rd ed.). Puddledancer Press.

Shapiro, F., & Forrest, M. S. (2001). *EMDR: eye movement desensitization and reprocessing*. Guilford Press.

Siegel, D. J. (2020). *The developing mind* (3rd ed.). Guilford Press.

Singer, Tania, Seymour, Ben, O'Doherty, John, Kaube, Holger, Dolan, Raymond J., & Frith, Chris D. (2004). Empathy for pain involves the affective but not sensory components of pain. *Science, 303*, 1157–1162.

Smith, L., Dockrell, J., & Tomlinson, P. (1997). *Piaget, Vygotsky and beyond: future issues for developmental psychology and education*. Routledge. Publisher description www.loc.gov/catdir/enhancements/fy0649/98107787-d.html

Struik, A. (2019). *Treating chronically traumatized children: the sleeping dogs method* (2nd ed.). Routledge.

Struik, A. (2022). *Eksklusivt intervie with Arianne Struik* [Interview].

Szalavitz, M., & Perry, B. D. (2010). *Born for love: why empathy is essential – and endangered* (1st ed.). William Morrow. Contributor biographical information www.loc.gov/catdir/enhancements/fy1011/2010280500-b.html; Publisher description www.loc.gov/catdir/enhancements/fy1011/2010280500-d.html

Trzeciak, S. (2018). Want a happier life? Be more compassionate [video]. TED x UND.

Turnell, A., & Essex, S. (2006). *Working with 'denied' child abuse. The resolutions approach*. Open University Press.

Van der Kolk, B. A. (2015). *The body keeps the score: mind, brain and body in the transformation of trauma*. Wellbeing Collection, Penguin Books.

Winfrey, O. (2011). *The powerful lesson Maya Angelou taught Oprah*. Harpo Productions, Oprah Winfrey Network.

Chapter 2

Preventing stress, burnout, and compassion fatigue

Putting the oxygen mask on first

Working with vulnerable and traumatised children is rewarding and meaningful but also very demanding and challenging owing to the intense daily exposure to people's overwhelming emotional states. In order to stand our ground and be resilient enough to keep doing this year after year, the safety rule from aircraft about putting one's own oxygen mask on first before helping others applies, just as on a flight. I have supervised numerous professionals from different backgrounds in this field and noticed a pattern of putting themselves aside to be there for others, which I used to follow myself – a tendency that seems both natural and honourable, and maybe, for many, also the most reasonable when working with people in pain and suffering. Nevertheless, it isn't the best strategy to keep going on and on, year after year.

If you are reading this book, chances are that you are a dedicated person with a passion for your work who wants to know and learn more and continue to grow and develop your skills without any consideration of changing your career. However, if you are considering changing your career, you may be heading towards a state of burnout. Either way, this chapter is for you, in honour of your deep devotion and the sacrifice you have made, and I hope that my perspective will help you stay connected or reconnect with yourself and your passion, regaining the energy to keep going.

I have done all the don'ts, made my way through the wilderness of child protection doing my inner work, trying to become wiser and care for myself better because I was the kind of social worker who would almost run from meeting to meeting with a cup of coffee in my hand and forget to eat all day. When I left that job and started my own business, I felt a continuous sensation of running in my nervous system for several weeks after leaving my workplace. I had to take a serious, hard look at myself and how I had driven myself to the state of exhaustion. I also realised that it was my luck that I decided to start my business and move on with my vision and mission for the vulnerable and traumatised children because I still had my passion and my energy, but I wouldn't have lasted a lifetime in this field running like that. Looking back on those days, I have done my inner work,

DOI: 10.4324/9781003322672-2

learned the lessons, and am taking my own medicine today, knowing that I need to put the oxygen mask on first for me to be the best version of me and be of the best service to the people I work with, both the professionals and the families, adolescents, and children.

It takes one to know one, and now I see people like the old me every time I provide training and supervision. Previously, I was preoccupied with implementing methodology and solely focused on the well-being of the children and their families. However, I've shifted my focus to also being deeply concerned about the professionals. There are two reasons for this shift. First, I genuinely want your work life to be rewarding, meaningful, and passionate. I want you to be happy and thrive as you help others and hold vulnerable and traumatised children's lives and healing in your hand, in collaboration with all the other significant adults around them. Second, the children and their families need you to be at your best, with a calm brain, enabling you to work with them in the safest and most suitable manner for their safety, health, development, and well-being. Returning to the aircraft metaphor, pilots are only allowed to fly after taking a certain amount of time to rest and recover. Also, the people in the control towers guiding the planes have very strict work rules for safety reasons. In the same way, the children need us to care for ourselves and our colleagues in a collaborative effort for them to be safe.

The risk of developing compassion fatigue and burnout in working with traumatised children

Chapter 1 described how the nervous system reacts to being overwhelmed by external experiences in life or internal re-experiences of past traumas. Now, let us look deeper into how these processes naturally affect professionals working with vulnerable and traumatised children in their daily life. Let's also look at what we need to be aware of to help regulate ourselves and each other when we get either hyper- or hypo-aroused in our work. It isn't a question of whether it's happening or not, but more about how we deal with it when it happens, because our autonomic nervous system constantly influences us.

The autonomic nervous system consists of the sympathetic and parasympathetic nervous systems. The sympathetic system relates to activity, and the parasympathetic system relates to calm, rest, and recovery. It automatically regulates many of the body's functions by constantly sending signals to the body in an automatic process that we can't control, but yet we can become better at consciously regulating it (Hart, 2009; Porges, 2011; Siegel, 2020). As described in Chapter 1, the vagus nerve is a significant player in relation to both the activation and regulation of the sympathetic and parasympathetic nervous systems. It's very helpful to regulate the body's state of calm, rest, and recovery, for example, by using breathing exercises that are deep enough to achieve the needed regulation. Later, I will provide you with an exercise to support this regulation, as I have become a yoga teacher trainer in order to be able to use these old techniques to regulate clients' nervous system, no matter the context, or in supervision with professionals when they have become significantly dysregulated and need to come back to their body and connect to a sense of safety, calm, and rest.

In a professional context working with vulnerable and traumatised children, we are constantly influenced by things that might activate a stress response, either as an immediate survival response in a specific situation or as a prolonged stress response over time. Robustness can't solely be attributed to an individual but must be understood as an interaction between a person and their specific context and how they support each other to be either sensitised or resilient to a given pressure over time (Perry & Szalavitz, 2007). An overwhelming work context significantly heightens the risk of compassion fatigue and burnout. The context in our field, no matter if you are a teacher, social worker, family therapist, health nurse, nurse, foster parent, or any other professional working with children, has been increasingly challenging for a long time, and it seems like it's caused by a combination of a rise in demands and lack of organisational and individual resources to meet these demands. Pressure emerges from families, workplaces, politicians, relatives, and the media, while ethical standards and best practice must be upheld. Moreover, the increasing demands from children, who are more frequently experiencing anxiety, depression, and vulnerability, and families, facing more challenges in times of one global crisis arising after another, also contribute to this complex scenario (Lebrun-Harris et al., 2022).

Recent statistics in Denmark from 2022 reveal that social workers have the second-worst overall working environments (Arbejdstilsynet, 2022). Another piece of research indicates that around 5–15 per cent of therapists experience an impact that affects their functionality and quality of life to the extent that they need help themselves (Bercier & Maynard, 2015). A third study discovered that 55 per cent of the therapists asked felt burdened, with 27 per cent experiencing an extreme burden (Meldrum et al., 2002). Similarly, US nurses working with children with chronic diseases encountered periods of compassion fatigue and actively needed coping strategies to prevent burnout (Maytum et al., 2004). At the same time, Bruce Perry underscores the declining level of personal contact across children's different arenas, resulting in relational poverty that threatens their brain development and well-being (Perry & Winfrey, 2021; Szalavitz & Perry, 2010). The special needs arising from this make it increasingly challenging for caring professionals to provide sufficient service, care and contact, often leading to feelings of inadequacy followed by shame and guilt.

The professionals I have worked with have generally appeared to be highly responsible individuals, taking their job and responsibility very seriously. However, they are consistently influenced by the overwhelming feelings of the children and families and by the high complexity of finding the right solution for each child within the given structure of the welfare system. Often, the burden becomes too heavy to carry on their shoulders, leading to feelings of inadequacy. From the many times I have helped people overcome this, I have come to realise that the feeling of inadequacy is an inherent aspect of working with vulnerable and traumatised children. Therefore, it's important to create awareness of it and to be able to talk about it, handle it, and transform it into something more supportive of our health and well-being because, otherwise, it's very harmful for us professionals to experience this long term.

One consequence of the demanding nature of our field of work is the frequent overactivation of the amygdala. I have witnessed professionals constantly scanning for potential dangers, automatically focusing on all the things they couldn't do or accomplish, what was not functioning, and where they fell short, rather than acknowledging their achievements and successes. This behavioural pattern significantly impacts the nervous system, and, over time, it will start to react as if the workplace is a dangerous environment to be in. In the state of survival, people start to disconnect from their surroundings and begin to run faster to get more work done, as I experienced during my time in child protection in Copenhagen. The encouraging and hopeful news is that there is something we can do to prevent this, but, before going into this, let's do a brief exercise to create awareness of the survival states of stress and burnout in your work.

Exercise on three ways the activation of survival states appears

I see three main things coming into play when professionals are overwhelmed and are becoming either hyper- or hypo-aroused in their jobs:

1 They experience something dangerous or threatening to themselves, others, or their organisation in the present moment.
2 They experience something that triggers a memory of a traumatic experience/overwhelming feeling or family pattern from their own past that hasn't been processed in their nervous system and becomes activated in them in the present moment.
3 They experience the overwhelming emotional states of the children and their families as being their own feelings, even though they aren't. Just as we can use our nervous system to co-regulate others, we can be dysregulated by others' stressed nervous systems, we need to be fully aware of using our regulations skills as protection when in contact with overwhelmed people.

One of the most important things to register when feeling overwhelmed is which of the above has been activated. So, take some time now and think for a moment about a given situation that is stressing you and think about the following questions:

1 Is there a given threat against you or anybody else occurring in this situation? If yes, share it with your team and managers, as it's a situation that must be dealt with in your organisation and not on your own.
2 If not, then ask yourself: where do I know these feelings from, and what do they trigger in me from my past or dysfunctional family pattern?
    If you have experienced something similar in your own life, now is the time to look at it with caring eyes and self-compassion and process this old memory and emotion by doing your own inner work. To support this, it can be helpful to recognise that it belongs to the past and that you are in a different position

to help and manage this in a professional way in the present context. People might bring these triggers into our supervision sessions. Our focus isn't to go into the details of their own story but is more on helping them to comprehend themselves and their reaction to the situation better and find ways to engage and deal with the children in a healing manner that is also empowering for them.

3   If there is nothing in your past that is triggered, then ask yourself: whose feelings am I overwhelmed by?

This helps distinguish between what is yours and what is others'. It doesn't necessarily have to be the children or their parents who overwhelm you; it can also be other professionals who are triggered or experience things differently, maybe even as a life-threatening situation.

The benefit of distinguishing between what is yours and what belongs to others lies in the ability to differentiate between the two, which enables you to consciously start protecting yourself against being overwhelmed by others. For instance, you can structure your time schedules based on your tolerance for being in conversations with highly overwhelmed people who challenge you. You can proactively regulate yourself better before meeting with people overwhelmed by emotions or arrange to debrief with a colleague afterwards to restore your balance after being overwhelmed. If other professionals' emotions overwhelm you, you might even put words to it by having a conversation with them about dysregulation and co-regulation and how to mindfully support each other better in collaboration when situations are overwhelming. In this way, you help the other professional, yourself, the child, and all stakeholders in the collaboration.

Case example: Larry

Larry, a teacher with over 20 years of experience working at a special needs school, encountered a threatening incident between two children. Despite handling the situation adequately and ensuring both children's safety effectively, Larry's nervous system did not register that he handled it successfully and safely for all. Overwhelmed by fear and a sense of danger, he had to take sick leave from work. In our first session, he couldn't see himself returning to the same workplace but, after gaining a deeper understanding of the nervous system's response and processing trauma, Larry could envision returning to work again, and he approached his employer and discussed a safe way for him to return. In a subsequent session, he confirmed that he had successfully accomplished this.

The neurobiology of compassion fatigue

Stress and burnout

From a nervous system perspective, stress and burnout are two different reactions to being overwhelmed by sensations for an extended period. Stress manifests as the hyperaroused and mobilised state, while burnout is connected to the hypo-aroused and immobilised state. Initially, as you start working in this field, you are most likely operating within your windows of tolerance, described in Chapter 1. However, you will most likely start to feel overwhelmed by all the demands and the children's trauma and pain after some time. You might increasingly feel the hyperaroused state while trying to deal with it the best you can. You begin to work more, you run faster at work, you might take work home with you, your body starts pumping cortisol and adrenalin out into the system, and you start to get the bodily feeling of being stressed, irritated, and maybe anxious. Suppose this process continues without you getting the sense of resolution to the problems you are trying to solve; from a survival perspective, the hyperarousal state is no longer enough for you to survive in this context, and the nervous system closes down even more and enters the hypo-aroused state. In this state, you have given up, maybe lost meaning, and started to not care about the task and people any more, and your body has collapsed into a state of burnout. This is a state of physical, mental, and emotional exhaustion that builds up over time, where you might feel depressed and inefficient or even cynical (Maslach et al., 2001), and it is also assessed to find the basis of compassion fatigue, together with secondary traumatisation (Isdal, 2018).

Secondary traumatisation

One particular challenge arising from the complex task of helping traumatised children, young people, and their families is the high risk for professionals to be secondarily traumatised by the stories of the people they work with, which plays an essential part in the development of compassion fatigue (Figley, 1995; Isdal, 2018). Secondary traumatisation is different from compassion fatigue in the sense that it can be experienced more like a shock trauma with symptoms of PTSD, such as flashbacks and re-experiencing other people's stories, or experiencing avoidance behaviour in similar situations (Isdal, 2018). It can also lead to heightening states of arousal, either the hyperarousal state of being constantly alert or the numbness from the hypo-aroused state; if not dealt with appropriately, it can have a long-term effect on the nervous system of which compassion fatigue is an expression (Figley, 1995; Isdal, 2018). It is different from PTSD in that the exposure is indirect, being heard about from someone else. Therefore, it might not be as overwhelming as the client's experience, but it will infect you enough to impact your nervous system, particularly when you hear multiple stories of the same nature (Isdal, 2018).

Maybe you recall someone telling you a story that left disturbing images in your mind that you couldn't get rid of afterwards, and they kept coming back as flashbacks with an unpleasant rush in your nervous system. You might have felt the urge to shake those images off your retina. Then you have experienced how contagious human trauma can be between people engaged in empathic connection with each other because the mirror neurons in the brain mentioned earlier activate and recall the same state of mind that the other one is experiencing, enabling us to be empathic and share strong emotional moments with each other (Høgsted, 2018).

Compassion fatigue

The term "compassion fatigue" was introduced by the American professor of psychology Charles Figley to describe the state where professionals' capacity to feel compassion and contain and tolerate other people's strong feelings and painful stories has been undermined (Figley, 1995). This arises from the neurological processes linked to empathy that make us experience another person's pain as if it were our own, because the area of the brain related to pain is activated in the empathic response (Singer et al., 2004). Understanding this helps us become aware of the power of human nature, enabling us to connect to each other and allowing us to supportively contain and even alleviate each other's pain to some degree. However, we have to be mindful that there is a downside to it, as empathy isn't an endless resource available to us, causing dilemmas and challenges for professionals to deal with when the pain of the people we are here to help exhausts our empathy (Isdal, 2018). Acknowledging that this is an inherent aspect of working with traumatised people and people suffering deep pain will hopefully help us talk about it and deal with it in ways that will remove the shameful feeling of inadequacy and not being good enough at doing our work.

Compassion fatigue contains elements of both secondary traumatisation and burnout (Paiva-Salisbury & Schwanz, 2022). Symptoms of compassion fatigue can be physical symptoms such as being exhausted, getting headaches, tension in the body, and becoming nauseous just at the thought of hearing more about other people's problems. Symptoms can also be more emotional and mental, such as being overwhelmed by feelings of powerlessness, meaninglessness, hopelessness, helplessness, anger, and fear; maybe even feeling restless and irritable; experiencing depression; using substances excessively; and experiencing poor concentration and memory issues (Lombardo & Eyre, 2011). Workwise, it can show up as avoidance of working with certain people or tasks, the feeling of a lack of empathy and inability to relate to other people's feelings, thoughts, and energy anymore, or having more days off sick (Lombardo & Eyre, 2011). In general, many people find it more challenging to go to work and engage in social relations at work, and so they withdraw relationally from colleagues (Isdal, 2018). Compassion fatigue might also show up differently, as overinvolvement with clients and their situation is a powerful player at work, being unable to keep a good work–life balance.

The appearance and nature of compassion fatigue vary depending on each situation, including a person's coping skills, triggers from their own trauma, lack of emotional support from their social network, and how they personally deal with feelings, among other things (Paiva-Salisbury & Schwanz, 2022). Often, people show more than one symptom, but any given symptoms described in the references provided in this section can be a sign of compassion fatigue (Eyre, 2011). Therefore, if you are experiencing any of the symptoms mentioned or feel called to dig deeper into the topic for details on more symptoms, don't ignore it but acknowledge that you are here right now and, by facing it and dealing with it, you can change it. The faster you see and act on it, the easier it becomes to heal it, and the first step is to acknowledge and name it. Later, we will be looking more into how to find the balance between giving and taking, caring and providing self-care, feeling compassion for others and self-compassion, being involved but not over- or uninvolved, and how to do our own inner work and do some work with our colleagues to secure our passion and the joy of going to work year after year.

Shame

The feeling of shame and not being enough significantly influences the development of these emotional states in our work with vulnerable and traumatised children because it takes vulnerability to share the feeling of inadequacy and overwhelm with other people (Brown, 2013). As every emotion serves a purpose, shame is crucial for a child to learn to self-regulate their state of mind and also to control their behavioural impulses when growing up (Siegel, 2020), but toxic shame represents the feeling and belief of not being good enough and the fear of not being worthy of connection and has a damaging impact on our self-worth and self-esteem (Brown, 2011, 2013). Brené Brown distinguishes shame from guilt in the sense that shame focuses on the self – "I am bad/wrong" – and guilt focuses on behaviour – "I did something bad/wrong" (Brown, 2012).

I have had the honour of working with numerous professionals who courageously put words to these feelings of shame and inadequacy with their colleagues and me. This has revealed to me that this underlying stressor is constantly present one way or the other in this work, adding to the already high levels of stress. From these experiences, I have learned that the most helpful approach for transforming this state involves providing a safe space for people to feel it, name it, and share it and be met with "me too" from me and their colleagues. When everybody in the room understands that we are all in the same boat and "it isn't just me" but it's part of the highly complex work, there is an energetic sigh of relief in the room, which alone reduces the stress level.

Shame is highly related to self-criticism and is a destructive feeling also correlated to low self-esteem, violence, addiction, depression, anger, suicidal thoughts, and much more (Brown, 2012; Xie, 2019). Neurobiologically, shame and self-criticism shrink our neocortex's capacity to maintain attention, increase impulsivity, and can lead to mental challenges similar to those caused by sleep deprivation (Xie, 2019). However, if we start viewing it as a collective challenge and dare to share our vulnerability with each other and help each other grow and stay strong, we can continue to build resilience and post-traumatic growth after secondary trauma, burnout, and compassion fatigue.

Case example: Ingrid

Ingrid, a middle-aged family therapist with 18 years of experience working with vulnerable children, began experiencing unsettling dreams. In these dreams, she felt disconnected, lacking energy and walking around like a zombie. Overwhelmed and fed up with her job, Ingrid contemplated leaving to find peace and tranquility for a while, but she did not.

One dream stood out to her. In a semi-awake state, she entered a shop and inexplicably stole hand soap, concealing it in her pocket. As she stepped back into the street, she felt a hand on her shoulder, waking her from her slumber, and she looked up into the face of a security guard asking her, "Why did you do that?" Overwhelmed with emotion, Ingrid broke down in tears, confessing, "Because I couldn't save him or his children". She woke from the dream at this moment and realised that not only had the situation with the family she was referring to in her dream overwhelmed her in her professional life, it had also triggered childhood trauma, leading to burnout. Seeking help, Ingrid reached out to me to process the overwhelming state of her nervous system and, through trauma processing, she regained her energy and reconnected with her true self and her passion for her job.

Mindset and principles to stay resilient

To maintain a balance and stay in our window of tolerance, we must cultivate self-awareness and stay connected to our bodily sensations, thoughts, emotions, and sense of who we are (Høgsted, 2018). Achieving this often requires consistent effort to regulate ourselves and stay grounded while being exposed to the intense feelings of the children and their relatives. The mindset and principles that I will now introduce to you help me and others to keep our hearts warm and our minds sharp in highly stressful situations where we need to maintain an overview and stay on track with the safety and well-being of the child and where the stakes are high. These principles help us, as professionals, remain safe, calm, and hopeful in a job characterised by great fear of making mistakes and feelings of hopelessness and powerlessness when things aren't turning out as planned and hoped for.

Keeping a reflective mind to achieve practice depth

Over many years, Professor Eileen Munro has investigated child protection practices in depth, and one conclusion of her extensive work is that "the single most important factor in minimising error is to admit that you may be wrong" (Munro, 2002, p. 141). Thus, if you want to have a safe level of practice depth in this highly complex, high-risk work with traumatised and vulnerable children, it's recommended to be open to feedback and embrace a stance of uncertainty instead of trying to find the truth (Ferguson, 2004).

To me, doubt is one of my best friends in this work because it keeps my mind flexible and open to feedback, and I constantly question myself to ensure that I will get all the crucial details to the best of my ability. If we become too certain about ourselves and that our perspective is the "right" perspective, we will become narrow-minded, experience tunnel vision, and start to argue with people about who is right and wrong instead of reflecting on different perspectives and dilemmas that might broaden everybody's views on the situation. Creating room for reflection may even enable us collaboratively to find new ways and build new solutions as it's constructive and helps all involved be in a position to learn, which everybody can gain from, not least the children. Space for discussion, on the other hand, can be dangerous and isn't helpful to keep brains calm in a field where we really need it. If we argue about conflicting perspectives, the discussion is more likely to be centred around the professionals' viewpoints rather than the children's circumstances, creating a risk of losing the children's position as being at the centre of the collaboration. If we instead listen to everybody's perspective and value them as being equally valid with sincere curiosity, honesty, dignity, humility, respect, responsiveness, and propriety, so that we see all the nuances between black and white, including when we disagree the most, we are more likely to create the best and safest solution for the child because we help each other to shed light on our blind spots, respectively.

Pulitzer Prize-winning journalist and author Kathryn Schulz has been researching and writing about the topic of being wrong. She argues that making mistakes and being wrong are part of the human condition (Schulz, 2011a, 2011b), and there is no such thing as being able to make no mistakes in life or in our jobs. Despite this, there is a tendency to aim to make no mistakes in work with vulnerable and traumatised children in many different parts of the world, which is definitely not helpful for the level of stress in organisations. Kathryn Schulz sheds light on how it feels to be wrong, and her answer is that, until we realise that we are wrong, the feeling is to "be right" (Schulz, 2011b). Adopting this viewpoint could potentially shift our perspective on errors, because we might never actually know when we are right or wrong. So, instead of arguing about it, the most beneficial action for all would be to listen and learn and use other people's perspectives to create the best and most sustainable solutions for the children and young people.

Acknowledging everybody's perspective would be the safest strategy for all involved, including yourself, as it will foster a sense of security in your job, leaving you less vulnerable to stress and burnout. In the spirit of embracing the human condition of making errors, Maya Angelou's "Do the best you can until you know better, then when you know better, do better" is also relevant to mention here (Winfrey, 2011). Inspired by this, I once said to a team of social workers working with safety planning, "We know what we know when we know it … and when we know better, we can do better", when they were questioning themselves about why they had not got to know important information about a child's life earlier. We can keep our eyes wide open and learn as much as possible about a child's life, and the better we know the children and families, the more will be disclosed, but it won't be disclosed all at once. As soon as new information appears, we can deal with it. Therefore, I have continued to use this phrase, and many professionals after them have found these words helpful on their learning journey.

Sharing is caring

My best advice for securing your long-term well-being in this field of work is to be vulnerable, not to hesitate to share your flaws and insecurities, and to ask for help if needed. When you do this, you open yourself to getting the support needed and also show the way to others so they will allow themselves to do the same. This will create space for imperfection, vulnerability, and a safe learning environment that might improve the overall working environment, as it will leave people capable of being raw and authentic with each other and showing up with honesty and integrity as the basis of a safe relationship and connection (Brown, 2013, 2015, 2017, 2018). Brené Brown explains that "empathy is the antidote to shame" (Brown, 2012), meaning that, if you talk to somebody about your shame and the things that make you feel shame and are met with empathy, the shame can't survive.

A working environment where colleagues could hold that caring and empathic space for each other when working with vulnerable and traumatised children could prevent many of the nervous system reactions discussed earlier in this chapter. As mentioned, concerning shame, this could "just" be the words "me too" that enable the body to release some painful feelings, help you think differently about the distressing situation, and even think differently about yourself. Instead of you beating yourself up with self-criticism, this could see the birth of more self-care and self-compassion, which are the antidotes to compassion fatigue and burnout.

So many of the professionals that I work with are hard on themselves in a way that isn't reasonable when I know how much heart, time, and effort they put into the children and families they are working with. If they overheard their colleagues talk to themselves like this, I am sure they would stop them immediately. Therefore, I am mindful of helping them see themselves with more caring eyes, and I love seeing the change happen in them when they realise they can be proud of themselves for showing up and giving it all they have. This is one of the best parts of my work life. Are you, too, being hard on yourself? If so, I hope you will accept the invitation to see yourself with the same caring eyes, and I would like you to stop reading now and do a little exercise. It doesn't have to take long.

Solution-focused exercise

Think back on the last week at work and list 20 things you are proud of that *you* did. If you start to think about what other people did that you are proud of, ask yourself, "What did I do to make this happen?" in order to bring it back to yourself and your own effort and actions. Take a piece of paper, make a list of answers to the following questions, and save it for a rainy day:

- What did you do last week that you are proud of?
- What else?
- What else? And another 17 times.

You might find it difficult or ridiculous, and you aren't the first, but I will still encourage you to keep trying to find these 20 things and see how you feel about yourself afterwards. I will go into the theory behind the exercise later in this chapter to explain why I find it very valuable. But, for now, try it out.

The power of teamwork

During challenging times, I have helped several teams of colleagues realise the significance of fostering deeper connections on a professional and personal level. This helps them build trust in each other and achieve the feeling of being able to rely on each other for support when things get tough. So, don't underestimate the power of getting to know each other through bringing more humour into play, sharing some of your favourite music, and telling stories about your children or what you did last weekend, and don't underestimate the routine of prioritising eating lunch together or drinking morning coffee before it all takes off. This could also involve asking a colleague if they would go to a meeting with you that you find very difficult or offer the same to a colleague if you see the need for it.

Sometimes, these little examples of care and self-care will be helpful to alleviate pressure on the nervous system and create space to deal with other important stuff afterwards. These are some of the small things you and your colleagues can do in everyday life to stimulate a supportive and caring working environment in a high-risk field, as we are hardwired for connection. Basically, adults also need love and belonging to be healthy and thrive (Brown, 2011; Perry & Winfrey, 2021; Szalavitz & Perry, 2010). One way to look at it is to see it as investments that will come back to you tenfold; it only takes 5 minutes to stop and connect with others for us not to feel alone and to get help to regulate if we have been experiencing something that was dysregulating for us. To many, taking time to connect feels like a waste of time in the here and now when the workload is high, and we need to run faster, but it's one of the most important steps to take daily to stay connected, grounded, and well regulated in a context with increasing demands. From my experience, the difference between well-functioning groups and others that are less well functioning lies in their interpersonal relationships, support and help in the daily work life, and a sense of "we" compared with an isolated "I". These are some of the differences that make the difference, as Gregory Bateson called it (Bateson, 2010).

In the act of self-care, you can engage in activities that are good for you and make a list of these things to save them for a rainy day, so that you remember how to take care of yourself when you need it most. I recently talked to a retired man who used to be a director in a big business with more than 600 employees, and he said to me that his recipe for managing great responsibility was "the bigger the responsibility, the more meditation". This is a fascinating perspective for professionals working with vulnerable and traumatised children with the immense responsibility that this work entails.

Feelings of hope and meaning

He who has a *why* to live for can bear almost any *how*.
Friedrich Nietzsche (Frankl, 2006, p. 76)

Another thing making a difference is the power of faith, hope, and meaning, leading me back to Viktor Frankl and his book *Man's Search for Meaning* (2006), previously mentioned in the section on hope (Chapter 1). These aspects are also essential to prevent compassion fatigue and burnout because, even though we don't have the power to change the structural context of the work, we can find ways to cope with this that empower us instead of burning us out. As we explored the power of hope earlier, the focus here will mainly be on meaning. Frankl categorised prisoners into two different types, those who had lost faith, meaning, and hope and those who saw life as a challenge and had a very strong *why* to live for, the latter being more likely to survive (Frankl, 2006). To have a strong why is to find meaning in life, meaning in suffering, meaning in experiences in a way that will make reason out of them and will help one gain strength to endure and overcome. Burnout is often related to loss of meaning, underscoring its significance, as emphasised in Viktor Frankl's research (Cohut, 2019).

Aaron Antonovsky also developed his "sense of coherence" theory during his stay in the concentration camps in the Second World War. He found three factors enhancing people's ability to endure and cope with these extreme challenges: comprehensibility, manageability, and meaningfulness (Antonovsky, 1982). As you can see, here also is the meaning central to developing coping strategies. I have not yet met any professionals working with vulnerable and traumatised children who did not have a strong why. Still, I have met people who had lost or were at risk of losing it and were suffering in many ways. Therefore, the reconnection to meaning is the centre of attention here in this chapter. It's excellent news if you have not disconnected from your sense of purpose in your work. However, I will still invite you to do this exercise so you keep connecting to your why as a prevention strategy.

Exercise: reconnecting to the big why

Take 5 minutes to invest in your well-being and self-care by leaning back and thinking about why you chose to do what you do workwise. Reflect on the following questions, write your answers down, and save them for a rainy day with your other list.

- What is it about working with vulnerable and traumatised children that is meaningful to you?
- What is the purpose of your choosing this work?
- What difference are you here to make for others, and how did you succeed today?
- What do you feel most passionate about concerning your work?
- Why is it important for the children and their families that you showed up to work today?
- Why is it important for the local community and society that you showed up today?
- What are the bigger purpose and meaning of your daily work?

When in concentration camps during the Second World War, Viktor Frankl concluded that, when you can't change a situation, you are forced to change yourself (Frankl, 2006). He taught us that we always have a choice of how to respond to a given situation, and, when we can't change situations or contexts, we can change how we react to them, how we want to cope with them, find meaning in them, and move forward with more strength. In your context, this could mean developing better coping skills and changing the inner state to create more hope, meaning, pride, and self-compassion in your work and your effort. Therefore, I recommend you do the exercises in this chapter and invest a little time and effort to see what difference they create in your work-life experience.

Emotional agility

As humans, we feel strongly about things that matter to us, and, if we have a meaningful job of great importance to us, then strong feelings will be a part of this job, and so the better we become at acknowledging and dealing with them and regulating/co-regulating them, the more resilient we become. Thus, to create resilience in our work life, we must continuously work on our ability to deal with intense and difficult emotions instead of trying to ignore them and push them away when they show up as a natural element of the work with vulnerable and traumatised children.

Suppressed emotions don't disappear but grow bigger and become more disturbing to the point where they will start to control us more than we are controlling them. We then lose the ability actually to deal with things, but, if we allow and accept our true and accurate feelings, we activate a readiness potential in the brain that helps the brain to take concrete steps to solve the problem in the right way for us (David, 2016, 2017). Susan David, a psychologist at Harvard Medical School, states that allowing ourselves to feel our true emotions is the birthplace of innovation, engagement, and creativity, just as Brené Brown, in her research, has shown that vulnerability is the birthplace of creativity and innovation (Brown, 2012; David, 2017). These are traits that I see are necessary to help vulnerable and traumatised children most successfully. In recent years, within the child protection field, I have noticed an increasing need to have ongoing conversations about finding new and better ways to co-create working environments based on curiosity and support for each other – environments that nurture individual and collective resilience and build on the same principle of curiosity and care that Susan David has found to be essential for building emotional agility (David, 2016, 2017).

The use of solution focus to create resilience and well-being

As a solution-focused practitioner, I value this approach's remarkable effectiveness in connecting people with their resources, strengths, skills, and coping strategies to empower them quickly. Research from 2014 on the implementation of solution-focused work in child protection in Tenerife even shows that the implementation enhanced the social workers' resilience as a byproduct (Medina & Beyebach, 2014).

With teams I meet regularly, I often start by asking them to do an exercise in pairs reflecting on their achievements and successes since our last meeting. They are often reluctant to do this, as they don't like to brag about themselves. Still, I continue to ask them because I have seen the benefits of it so many times. In just 5–10 minutes, their state of mind has changed for the better, the energy in the room has changed to a higher vibration, and they appreciate it when it's done. If the whole group is feeling low, stressed, and under great pressure, I like to do it all together, asking them about their collective successes in times of adversity. As they start to articulate the strengths, resources, and skillful behaviour inherent in the team, it contributes to collective resilience and influences all group members individually. Sometimes, if more intervention is needed, I will also take them through a group process of reflection about what they need to do differently in the future to be able to take better care of themselves and each other. It will likely lead to some agreements on what to do to get through the hardship in a good way and also how to do it. This brings hope, a feeling of community, and confidence that they, as a group, can get through this too. In general, it adds to the positive emotions as an antidote to the difficult ones.

Professor Barbara Lee Fredrickson's research demonstrates that cultivating positive emotions profoundly impacts our resilience and our ability to bounce back after adversity. This is partly because it enhances our ability to expand our perception and creativity and imagine new and alternative solutions, strengthening flexible thinking. Also, it enhances the ability to collaborate more openly with others and strengthens and maintains relationships (Fredrickson, 2009, 2011). One way to gain access to these benefits is to start sharing good stories and successes with your colleagues and making it a habit to do this on a daily or weekly basis, as well as starting to acknowledge each other's contribution both to the people you work with and the working environment. For a manager or an organisation, it's a good investment to start cultivating a culture like this and investing time and energy in acknowledging your employees. As you see, the outcome will be better results and greater well-being and productivity.

Exercise: solution-focused debriefing of stressful situations

I learned this exercise from the solution-focused therapist Dr Jacqui von Cziffra-Bergs. I am very grateful for her permission to use it in this chapter, as it's a potent tool for debriefing after difficult and overwhelming incidents or stressful periods (Cziffra-Bergs, 2015).

Look inside the box in Illustration 2.1 and notice what you are seeing.

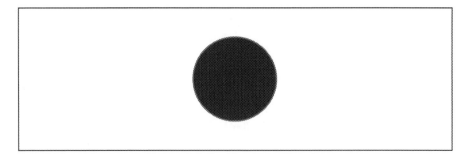

Illustration 2.1 Black circle in white space

While it's obvious to see the big black circle, most people tend not to notice all the white around the black circle. The same thing happens when we are overwhelmed by, for example, a traumatic event or stress from our workload: we get tunnel vision, focusing only on overwhelming things, but, if we also look around and see all the white too, it will most likely transform the overwhelming sensation into resilience. As the facilitator of a conversation, you have to be mindful of selectively focusing on the behaviour related to strength, resources, coping, and signs of resilience in the situation for this to happen (Froerer et al., 2018).

Now, choose one overwhelming situation causing you stress at the moment, and let's try to investigate the white area curiously by asking some or all of the following questions about what you have done in this situation that you can be proud of:

• In this situation, what have you done that you are proud of?
• How did you manage to do this?
• What would your colleagues say they are proud of you doing?
• What are your managers proud of you doing?
• What would the children/adolescents/family say that they are satisfied with you doing?
• What more did you do that you are proud of? How did you manage to do that? What other strengths, resources, and skills were you using to deal with this challenging situation? How are you coping, despite it being difficult? What else?

You can ask "What else?" as many times after each question as you like and continue until you have a complete picture around the black circle that shows you your skillful behaviour resources, strengths, and power to deal with this and until you feel a change in your mood from overwhelmed to calm.

If you find it challenging to do this on your own, ask your colleagues to do it with you and then, afterwards, do it with them, so you can help each other cope with particularly difficult situations or the general work overload.

Case example: Jack

Jack was a young social worker in his early 30s, with some years of experience in child protection, when his manager contacted me to get help to deal with a threatening situation. Jack expressed a lack of confidence and a feeling of inadequacy after he had experienced being thrown out into the practice field with no introduction, support, or feedback other than criticism at his former workplace. So he never knew if he was doing anything right. Although his current workplace offered a much better environment, the consequences of the long-term stress were now showing up as feelings of being inadequate, insecure, and unsafe in the position. Using the solution-focused approach, I helped him integrate all the valuable lessons he had learned from his past years, acknowledging all the coping strategies he used during these stressful times and making him realise he was a competent social worker. By recognising his core values and skilled ways of working with children and families, Jack began to take pride in his abilities. After two sessions, he did not feel the need for further support. He now felt capable of dealing with the workload, navigating the demands of child protection work, and handling the threatening situation that caused his manager to contact me.

Compassion and self-compassion as the antidote to compassion fatigue

> It takes tremendous strength of the back to uphold yourself in the midst of conditions. And that is the mental quality of equanimity. But it also takes a soft front – the capacity to really be open to the world as it is. To have an undefended heart.
>
> Roshi Joan Halifax (Halifax, 2010)

Cultivating compassion is, for many, associated with Buddhism, but, scientifically, it has proven to be a significant professional skill to develop to prevent stress, burnout, and compassion fatigue (Trzeciak, 2018). As humans, we generally feel strongly about things that are important to us. Research has shown that people who cultivate compassion feel pain more deeply in the moment but return to baseline faster, with a long-term positive effect on their resilience (Halifax, 2010).

First, let's start with differentiating compassion, empathy, and sympathy from each other.

Sympathy is understanding another's feelings, empathy is feeling what another person feels, while compassion involves both feeling their pain and also wishing to alleviate the emotional or physical pain that this person is experiencing (Laursen, 2021). Thus, compassion always stems from an empathic response that is cultivated into an intentional wish to reduce the other person's pain and then transforms into an act of care, love, and warmth based on the intention to help the other person (Halifax, 2009, 2010; Trzeciak, 2018). This activates the brain regions for love and belonging, becoming a factor that protects against compassion fatigue as it creates safety and connection between ourselves and others. This is instead of being affected by the automatic biological response to someone suffering where we feel the same pain as the other (Singer et al., 2004). The activation of compassion leads to more energy, greater self-esteem and inner peace, better neuro-integration of both sides of the brain, a stronger immune system, and a feeling of helpers' high that activates endorphins and the reward centre in the brain that triggers positive emotions such as happiness (Trzeciak, 2018).

The American professor and doctor Stephen Trzeciak developed an entire theory of "compassionomics" and promotes knowledge about the proven scientific effect of cultivating compassion after he studied thousands of research documents. One of his messages is that cultivating compassion in the health care system results in better health for patients, better-quality treatment, and lower cost, and health care professionals thrive better and have a higher resistance to burnout (Trzeciak, 2018). Stephen Trzeciak defines compassion as an emotional response to another person's pain and suffering that involves an authentic desire to help, including taking action to relieve the pain (Trzeciak, 2018). Joan Halifax, a social activist, Buddhist teacher, and pioneer in working with end-of-life care, describes compassion as including the ability to let go of attachment to a specific outcome. She believes that it's an inherent human quality that needs the right conditions to grow (Halifax, 2009, 2010). Another aspect of the cultivation of compassion involves connecting to the nature of human suffering, understanding that we all want to free ourselves from pain and suffering and experience happiness. In this way, we aren't very different from each other, and we use the ability to understand this to actively transform suffering through actions and activities (Brach, 2019).

Self-compassion, much like compassion, involves three components, accordingly, (1) self-kindness, (2) common humanity, and (3) mindfulness (Neff, 2013), focusing on including ourselves in the circle of people that we are compassionate towards. Self-compassion helps us be more caring and kinder towards ourselves instead of being self-critical. Self-criticism is found to have a positive intention to function as motivation to achieve our goals. Still, in contrast, it activates the nervous system to respond to danger, as described in Chapter 1, and doesn't support our well-being. So, if we can befriend ourselves instead of fighting, we can have a kinder and more caring relationship with ourselves and grow experiences with self-compassion, enhancing our capacity for feeling compassion (Neff, 2013).

To practise self-compassion is to build self-care skills, be less self-critical, and be present and meet one's own suffering and difficult feelings with genuine care, kindness, interest, curiosity, and self-caring eyes. Self-compassionate people are better at coping with difficult emotions and dealing with negative thoughts. They are more flexible in their response to change, with lower degrees of depression and anxiety, lower cortisol, and a higher heart rate. Hence, they are calmer and more relaxed and feel safe (Xie, 2019). Thus, a healthy relationship with ourselves not only cultivates compassion for others but also makes us more resilient (Neff, 2021).

The Chinese proverb "Not to act is also to act" comes to my mind in relation to compassion, reminding us that, instead of trying to fix things, it can be a powerful support to be present with people in their pain, helplessness, suffering, and frustration, with only the intention of containing it to soothe it. Many people have a perception that they can only be valuable and helpful to others by fixing things or situations for them, leaving them powerless or helpless if they cannot, but, in these moments, we can still be of help by being available for others with a compassionate presence. Often, the most healing thing we can offer people is a safe and calm space to share the most difficult, shameful, and horrible experiences and meet them with loving eyes and kind, soothing words, helping them to be regulated and find the strength and possible solutions to their challenges.

Exercises: breathwork and compassion

I want to share more of the tools and techniques I have used with myself and others over the years. There are many more to choose from in mindfulness, meditation, self-compassion work, solution-focused work, breathwork, yoga, other bodywork forms, and so on.

Breathing exercise

Breathing exercises help regulate the nervous system, and so, if you are hyperaroused, you can take immediate control of the situation by using your breath. Deep breathing into your stomach will help you become calm, so try to see if you can manage a slow count of 5. If you can't, don't blame yourself; continue from where you stopped.

- Take a deep breath in for a count of 5: slowly count 1, 2, 3, 4, 5.
- Hold your breath for a count of 5: slowly count 1, 2, 3, 4, 5.
- Breath out again for a count of 5: slowly count 1, 2, 3, 4, 5.
- Hold your breath for a count of 5: slowly count 1, 2, 3, 4, 5.

Please do this at least five times, or as long as you need, and slowly register how relaxation is taking over your body, instead of fear, stress, and overwhelming feelings, and let it slowly enter your consciousness that you are in control, right here and right now.

I suggest using this exercise at least twice a day to prevent stress, burnout, and compassion fatigue and keep us connected to our bodies. I do it myself every morning before getting out of bed, in the evening before going to sleep, and during the day when I need regulation, but also before training, supervision, meetings, and therapy to ground myself so that I am able to hold the space with a calm brain.

Meditation for grounding and expansion of compassion

Sit quietly with your eyes closed and take deep breaths into your stomach.

Slowly, for a count of 4, breathe in; for a count of 4, breathe out.

Then, imagine a bright light running down your body, from your heart all the way into the Earth, connecting with the core of the planet. In your own time, think to yourself, "I now connect with the heart of the Earth", and feel how you connect from your heart to the heart of the Earth while you still breathe deeply and slowly. You may feel the grounding in your body of being connected to Mother Earth in this way. You may feel your energy system opening up more or feeling stronger. It may differ from day to day and from experience to experience, so mindfully investigate the impact on your body and energy system.

Then, imagine a bright light running from the heart of the Earth back to your heart and all the way through the top of your head to reach a place high up in the sky that we call the heart of the sky. Quietly, in your own time, think to yourself, "I now connect with the heart of the sky". Breathe slowly and notice how it feels to be connected to the heart of the Earth and the heart of the sky simultaneously, while you go back to your own heart and softly open your heart to the world around you, imagining you are radiating the bright light running through you into the world and saying quietly to yourself "I now connect to my own heart and the heart of humanity".

Exercise to reconnect to your body in a safe way

Sit with a straight back against a chair and your feet on the ground and take deep breaths into your stomach. While breathing deeply, try to notice where you feel safe, calm, and relaxed in your body. Carry on breathing and notice how the relaxed state slowly becomes bigger while you breathe for at least five breaths, and then continue with the following. If there is tension in your body, discomfort, or a stressed state, notice it while you focus on the feeling of safety, calm, and relaxation, experiencing simultaneous dual attention in your body. Allow both states to be present while holding space for the stress to release and increase the relaxation while you keep breathing deeply. If you need more support to connect to your body, you can also place one hand over your heart and the other on your stomach to feel your belly moving in and out while you do the breathing exercise above.

References

Antonovsky, A. (1982). *Health, stress, and coping*. Jossey-Bass.

Arbejdstilsynet. (2022). *National Overvågning af Arbejdsmiljøet blandt Lønmodtagere NOA-L*.

Bateson, N. (2010). *An ecology of mind. The Gregory Bateson documentary*. N. Bateson.

Bercier, M. L., & Maynard, B. R. (2015). Interventions for secondary traumatic stress with mental health workers: a systematic review. *Research on Social Work Practice*, *25*(1), 81–80.

Brach, T. (2019). *Radical compassion: learning to love yourself and your world with the practice of RAIN*. Viking.

Brown, B. (2011). The power of vulnerability [video]. TEDxHouston.

Brown, B. (2012). Listening to shame [video]. Ted2012.

Brown, B. (2013). *The gifts of imperfection*. Hazelden.

Brown, B. (2015). *Rising strong*. Ebury Digital.

Brown, B. (2017). *Braving the wilderness: the quest for true belonging and the courage to stand alone*. Random House.

Brown, B. (2018). *Daring greatly: how the courage to be vulnerable transforms the way we live, love, parent and lead*. London: Penguin.

Cohut, M. (2019). Burnout: facing the damage of "chronic workplace stress". MedicalNews-Today, Healthline Media.

Cziffra-Bergs, J. v. (2015). *Re-creation of a trauma session*. SolutionFocused Institute of South Africa.

David, S. (2016). *Emotional agility: get unstuck, embrace change, and thrive in work and life*. Avery.

David, S. (2017). The gift and power of emotional courage [video]. TEDWomen 2017.

Ferguson, H. (2004). *Protecting children in time: child abuse, child protection and the consequences of modernity*. Palgrave Macmillan.

Figley, C. R. (1995). *Compassion fatigue: coping with secondary traumatic stress disorder in those who treat the traumatized*. Brunner/Mazel.

Frankl, V. (2006). *Man's search for meaning*. Beacon Press.

Fredrickson, B. (2009). *Positivity: top-notch research reveals the 3-to-1 ratio that will change your life*. Harmony.

Fredrickson, B. (2011). Positive emotions open our mind [video]. Greater Good Science Center.

Froerer, Adam S., Cziffra-Bergs, J. v., Kim, Johnny S., & Connie, Elliott E. (2018). *Solution-focused brief therapy with clients managing trauma*. Oxford Univeristy Press.

Halifax, J. (2009). *Being with dying: cultivating compassion and fearlessness in the presence of death*. Shambhala.

Halifax, J. (2010). Compassion and the true meaning of empathy [video]. TEDWomen.

Hart, S. (2009). *Den følsomme hjerne: hjernens udvikling gennem tilknytning og samhørighedsbånd* (1st ed.). Reitzel. doi.org/9788741253428

Høgsted, R. (2018). *Grundbog i belastningspsykologi – Forebyggelse af primær og sekundær traumatisering ved psykisk krævende arbejde*. Forlaget Ictus.

Isdal, P. (2018). *Medfølelsens pris – når professionelle hjælpere får brug for hjælp* (Smittet av vold. Om sekundærtraumatisering, compassion fatigue og utbrenthet i hjelpeyrkene). (J. Wang, Trans.). Akademisk Forlag.

Laursen, H. (2021). Empati og medfølelse er svaret på empati-udmattelse. https://nordic-compassion.dk/empati-stress/empati-sympati-medfoelelse/

Lombardo, Barbara, & Eyre, Caryl. (2011). Compasson fatigue: a nurse's primer. *The Online Journal of Issues in Nursing, 16*(1).

Lebrun-Harris, Lydie A., Ghandour, Reem M., Kogan, Michael D., & Warren, Michael D. (2022). Five-year trends in us children's health and well-being, 2016–2020. *JAMA Pediatrics, 176*(7).

Maslach, C., Schaufeli, W. B., & Leiter, M. P. (2001). Job burnout. *Annual Review of Psychology, 52*(1), 397–422.

Maytum, Jennifer C., Bielski Heiman, Mary, & Garwick, Ann W. (2004). Compassion fatigue and burnout in nurses who work with children with chronic conditions and their families. *Journal of Pediatric Health Care, 18*(4), 171–179.

Medina, A., & Beyebach, M. (2014). The impact of solution-focused training on professionals' beliefs, practices and burnout of child protection workers in Tenerife Island. *Child Care in Practice, 20*(1), 7–36.

Meldrum, L., King, Robert, & Spooner, Darren. (2002). Secondary traumatic stress in case managers working in community mental health services. In C. Figley (Ed.), *Treating compassion fatigue*. Brunner-Routledge.

Munro, E. (2002). *Effective child protection*. Sage.

Neff, K. (2013). The space between self-esteem and self compassion [video]. TedX.

Neff, K. (2021). *Fierce self-compassion*. Penguin Life.

Paiva-Salisbury, Melissa L., & Schwanz, Kerry A. (2022). Building compassion fatigue resilience: awareness, prevention, and intervention for pre-professionals and current practitioners. *Journal of Health Service Psychology, 48*(1), 39–46.

Perry, B. D., & Szalavitz, M. (2007). *The boy who was raised as a dog and other stories from a child psychiatrist's notebook: what traumatized children can teach us about loss, love, and healing*. Basic Books.

Perry, B. D., & Winfrey, O. (2021). *What happened to you? Conversations on trauma, resilience, and healing* (1st ed.). Flatiron Books.

Porges, S. (2011). *The polyvagal theory: neurophysiological foundations of emotions, attachment, communication, and self-regulation.* W. W. Norton.

Schulz, K. (2011a). *Being wrong: adventures in the margin of error.* Ecco.

Schulz, K. (2011b). On being wrong [video]. TED2011.

Siegel, D. J. (2020). *The developing mind* (3rd ed.). Guilford Press.

Singer, Tania, Seymour, Ben, O'Doherty, John, Kaube, Holger, Dolan, Raymond J., & Frith, Chris D. (2004). Empathy for pain involves the affective but not sensory components of pain. *Science, 303,* 1157–1162.

Szalavitz, M., & Perry, B. D. (2010). *Born for love: why empathy is essential – and endangered* (1st ed.). William Morrow. Contributor biographical information www.loc.gov/catdir/enhancements/fy1011/2010280500-b.html. Publisher description www.loc.gov/catdir/enhancements/fy1011/2010280500-d.html

Trzeciak, S. (2018). Want a happier life? Be more compassionate [video]. TEDxUND.

Winfrey, O. (2011). *The powerful lesson Maya Angelou taught Oprah.* Harpo Productions, Oprah Winfrey Network.

Xie, W. (2019). Dare to rewire your brain for self-compassion [video]. TEDxUND.

Chapter 3

The Circle of Safety and Reconnection, Step 1

Assessing the current risk to the child's safety, health, development, and well-being

Different aspects of defining safety

Defining safety in the context of working with vulnerable and traumatised children involves several aspects concerning their health, development, and well-being. The definition and understanding of safety I use in my practice and throughout this book is "Safety is strength demonstrated as protection over time" (Turnell & Essex, 2006, p. 114) taught to me by Susie Essex and Andrew Turnell. In my trauma-informed safety work, I am concerned about physical, emotional, as well as therapeutic safety. Physical safety refers to the violence and physical and sexual abuse witnessed or experienced by the child in their family or the harm and self-harm to which some children and young people expose themselves and others. Emotional safety refers to neglect, psychological abuse, and traumatic experiences in the past that the child might not have been able to process, which leaves them in a state of fear and feeling unsafe in the here and now. Sometimes, assessing current physical safety can be challenging when past trauma continues to affect the child and leaves them re-experiencing it as if it's still happening in the present moment. This can lead them to talk about it or react to it as if it's ongoing.

The reflections occurring from using the Circle of Safety and Reconnection will hopefully clarify and address safety issues by investigating different aspects of risk behaviour that children might be exposed to and be impacted by in their life. The differentiation between risk factors and risk behaviour allows us to distinguish between potential long-term risk factors and the immediate risk arising from concrete harmful actions and behaviour in the present moment. In this chapter, we will go into more detail about risk behaviour, and we will dig deeper into risk factors in Chapter 6.

Physical and psychological violence

Violence is defined by the World Health Organization (WHO) as

> The intentional use of physical force or power, threatened or actual, against oneself, another person, or against a group or community, that either results in or has a high likelihood of resulting in injury, death, psychological harm, maldevelopment or deprivation.
>
> (Krug et al., 2002, p. 5)

DOI: 10.4324/9781003322672-3

The UN Convention on the Rights of the Child Article 19 defines it as "all forms of physical or mental violence, injury or abuse, neglect or negligent treatment, maltreatment or exploitation, including sexual abuse" (United Nations Committee on the Rights of the Child, 2011, p. 4). As you see, neglect and deprivation are also part of this definition, and these will be investigated in more detail later too.

Physical violence

Physical violence can be expressed as either shaking, pushing, punching, pulling hair, beating with a flat hand, beating with fist, striking with an object, or kicking (Børns Vilkår, 2021). It can already be experienced by a fetus in the uterus. A Danish research paper from April 2022 by Mary Fonden shows that violence against women increases during pregnancy because of jealousy felt by the partner, who must now share attention with the fetus (Mary Fonden, 2022). One of the most severe examples of violence against a fetus I have worked with was a child exposed to violence involving a baseball bat during pregnancy, resulting in severe brain damage and lifelong special care needs. As a fetus has no right to protection, the only option is to advise women exposed to violence about safeguarding themselves and their unborn child, as many are unaware of the potential consequences. This awareness is crucial when going through the child's trauma history in a family with violence issues, to help understand the child's symptoms and special needs from a trauma perspective and to avoid overlooking important details about the child's health and development. We will dig deeper into this topic and the prenatal aspects of a child's life in Chapters 4 and 5.

In Denmark, physical violence against and abuse of children and adults are criminalised. However, in other countries, violence against children remains legal, and it's widely used to discipline children. "Ninety per cent of the world's children live in countries where corporal punishment and other physical violence against children is still legal" (Humans Rights Watch, 2014). In my view, violence being legalised doesn't make it less damaging to a child. On the contrary, children are protected against violence under international law, with the UN Convention on the Rights of the Child stating that all children should be protected from all forms of violence; there is also focus on the family in Article 19 (Naughton et al., 2017), which requires states to protect children from all the forms of violence defined above while in the care of parent(s), legal guardian(s), or any other person who has the care of the child (United Nations Committee on the Rights of the Child, 2011). Even though it's illegal in Denmark, a report came out in November 2021 that showed that every fifth student in the eighth grade had been subjected to physical violence at the hands of their parents one or more times within the previous year; in most cases, it was several times. Of these, 9 per cent were cases defined as more severe violence, and 55 per cent were girls. Mothers and fathers exposed their children to violence equally (Børns Vilkår, 2021).

In the United States, 60 per cent of all American children experienced direct or indirect exposure to violence as a witness within the year preceding a survey, with 40 per cent being victims of multiple incidences (Finkelhor & Office of Juvenile Justice & Delinquency Prevention, 2009). It's crucial to raise awareness that witnessing domestic violence is considered as psychologically harmful to a child as being a direct victim of it (Kitzmann et al., 2003; Ottosen et al., 2020; Sudermann & Jaffe, 1999). When a child witnesses violence between parents, not only does the violent parent become unsafe for the child, but also the parent who was supposed to be a safe parent and safeguard the child becomes unsafe, as the parent shows the child that they can't protect themselves. From a child's perspective, it leaves them with no safe adults to rely on. The home and the world become very unsafe places where the child might only be able to rely on themself, with too much responsibility for a child to carry.

Signs of physical violence include bruises, branding marks, bone fractures, shaken baby syndrome, or frequent ER visits (Schweitzer, 2019), but often they are hidden and won't be detected. A recent study carried out in a collaboration between the University of Copenhagen, Københavns Politi, and Børnehus Hovedstaden systemically screened children for signs of physical violence with a forensic medical examination after children had been referred to Børnehuset, a child protection department to which children get referred when there are allegations of violence or abuse towards them. These examinations showed signs of physical violence in one-quarter of the children, signs that wouldn't normally be discovered as only 3.8 per cent of the children referred to Børnehuset would have been examined by a GP and 2.3 per cent by a forensic doctor (Bugge et al., 2022). This means that many children carry evidence of being exposed to violence and abuse but will never be examined and may not get the help needed for them to be safe and well.

Signs of psychological violence are trickier to spot compared with physical violence. In general, for both types of violence, if no physical signs are available, indicators that something is wrong might be shown by psychosomatic symptoms such as stomach pains, headaches, or sleeping problems, or emotional issues such as low self-esteem, behavioural and relational challenges, suicidal thoughts and self-harm, depression, and anxiety (Oldrup et al., 2016). It's always important to carry out an individual assessment as signs and reactions depend on the specific child, and every child must be considered independently.

Psychological violence

In 2019, psychological violence was criminalised in Denmark alongside physical violence to recognise that a child's exposure to such violence can be equally as damaging as, or even more damaging than, physical violence. Research conducted in the United Kingdom has demonstrated that growing up with psychological abuse has a longer-term impact on children's well-being than growing up with physical violence (Naughton et al., 2017). Psychological violence is the most common form of violence. It degrades the child's fundamental core of worthiness, dignity, and self-esteem and threatens the child's healthy development, leaving the child feeling unsafe, unhappy, confused, and unable to trust others (SafeLives, 2019).

Often, the children struggle to have positive beliefs about themselves and, instead, feel unwanted and unloved. Like any abuse, a huge amount of shame and guilt is also correlated with it, which can lead to the sense of being a "bad" child, feeling like a failure and that everything is their fault. This can potentially lead to developmental trauma that persists into adulthood if left untreated. In the same research in Denmark from 2021 about physical violence, almost every fourth student in eighth grade had been exposed to psychological violence in the home, most often being called something that made them sad (Børns Vilkår, 2021).

Psychological violence aims to control and limit a person, and it happens when a "person repeatedly degrades, humiliates, violates, dominates, manipulates, threatens or isolates another person" (Lev uden vold, 2018, p. 3). More concretely, the child might be experiencing scolding, criticism, and degrading comments on their looks, personality, and feelings, or they aren't talked to and are given the silent treatment. Also, they might be experiencing one parent talking negatively about the other or be prevented from seeing the other parent or other important people in their life. There are many other different ways it can be expressed.

An aspect of psychological violence involves exerting control over the other person (SafeLives, 2019). In certain families, adolescents' social life can face excessive control that violates their freedom to choose clothing, friends, education, hobbies, and social engagements and is termed negative social control. This level of control is often targeted at girls by one or both parents, family members, or entire communities and can raise concerns for the children's safety, health, development, and well-being among the professionals around the child. The parents often feel that their influence is undermined by the culture of young peers in the given country, and their family values, norms, and religion are challenged. They might be genuinely worried about Western youth engaging in behaviours such as alcohol consumption, drug use, and premarital intimate relationships leading them to control their children to protect them from this (Friberg & Bjørnset, 2019).

For young people in these families, this control can be experienced as psychological violence, impacting their self-esteem and well-being. The dilemmas arising from navigating the two different worlds might force them to lead a "double life", acting as one person at home and another outside the house and, potentially, facing the threat of being caught and punished (Friberg & Bjørnset, 2019). The issues of negative social control can also escalate to more severe problems, such as honour-related punishments and crimes. The United Nations Population Fund (UNFPA) estimates that, globally, 5,000 women and girls are killed annually in honour killings, while other NGOs estimate the number to be as high as 20,000 (D'Lima et al., 2020).

Parenting control demonstrated with a higher level of social control might not always be harmful. It depends on a concrete individual assessment of whether there is enough room for the child's self-expression and whether the relationship with the family is safe enough not to harm the young person's health, development, and well-being. However, if change is needed, there are also ways to work around this issue as a professional.

Case example: Alisha

Once, as a child protection worker, I suddenly had a young teenage girl, Alisha, standing in my office, so affected by drugs that she could hardly stand. Still, she could tell us her fear of going home. Her family had threatened her life when they discovered she was using drugs and was leading a double life to deal with the identity of both being Arabic and Danish. She was immediately placed in a safe house, but, after a little while, she missed her family badly and wanted to return home. So, we engaged in a safety planning process with the parents and extended family, unsure if we could succeed. We did end up returning her home with a safety plan assessed to be safe enough for her, and it turned out to be the best thing for her, but it called on all my courage and that of my colleagues to help the girl in this way.

Sexual abuse

The definition of violence used by the WHO mentioned above does include sexual abuse as it's considered to be the use of physical force or power (Krug et al., 2002). Also, sexual abuse is defined in Article 18 of the Council of Europe Convention on the Protection of Children against Sexual Exploitation and Sexual Abuse (Council of Europe, 2007) as

> (a) engaging in sexual activities with a child who, according to the relevant provisions of national law, has not reached the legal age for sexual activities (this doesn't apply to consensual sexual activities between minors), and (b) engaging in sexual activities with a child where use is made of coercion, force or threats; or abuse is made of a recognised position of trust, authority or influence over the child, including within the family; or abuse is made of a particularly vulnerable situation of the child, notably because of a mental or physical disability or a situation of dependence.
>
> (Radford et al., 2015, p. 10)

Sexual abuse takes many forms and happens in different settings, including homes, schools, streets, war zones, and sex clubs, involving elements of either touching and/or showing or looking at body parts, images, or videos. This also enables it to happen online in the modern world.

Similar to psychological violence, signs of sexual abuse is difficult to spot. It will mainly be shown as behavioural, emotional, and developmental challenges for children (Wurtele, 2009). Additionally, they might also show sexualising behaviour themselves, as numbers show that 35 per cent of children with worrying sexualising behaviour have been exposed to sexual abuse themselves (Pedersen et al., 2017). From training with specialists at Januscentret in Denmark working with children who become perpetrators themselves, I have learned that the younger children are when exhibiting inappropriate sexual behaviour and displaying knowledge regarding sex and sexual language that's not appropriate to their age, the greater the cause for concern. This could indicate potential sexual abuse. To have something with which to make a comparison, it's helpful to gain knowledge and understanding of children's sexuality in general.

In the natural exploration of sexuality during childhood, there exists a sense of playfulness, curiosity, and spontaneity devoid of any sense of shame or anxiety. This exploration unfolds through equal, voluntary, and mutual interactions with friends and peers of the same age, development, and size (Stop It Now!, n.d.). Physical signs of sexual abuse such as wetting and soiling accidents unrelated to toilet training, persistent or recurring pain during urination and bowel movement, or bleeding or discharges in the genitals, anus, or mouth aren't very often seen. However, if they do appear, the children will need to be investigated by a doctor to test for sexually transmitted diseases and signs of damage to the genitals, anus, or mouth (Stop It Now!, n.d.). Forensic doctors advise conducting these examinations within 48 hours of discovery to be able to find evidence of sexual abuse. Often, disclosure of sexual abuse won't happen unless the child shows sexualising behaviour or says something about it, but, in many instances, the child will backtrack and deny that anything happened for fear of the consequences. Speaking up can lead to being punished by their parents or family members for telling and being blamed for all the distress the disclosure causes. So, they might feel guilty about it and think it's safer to withdraw the statement.

In Denmark, a study conducted in 2016 by the former National Research Center, called SFI, on violence and sexual abuse asked 2,000 young people in the eighth grade about their experience of unwanted sexual incidents with peers, family members, and other adults. They categorised the assaults into three groups: exposure, touch, and intercourse (Oldrup et al., 2016). Of the respondents, 12 per cent had experienced exposure to incidents where they either were exposed to others or were forced to expose themselves to others; 12 per cent also had experienced unwanted incidents with touch, defined as either someone touching the young person sexually or having the young person touch themselves or another person in a sexual way, more than twice as many girls as boys. In addition, 7 per cent of the girls and 5 per cent of the boys had experienced attempted or completed intercourse, and, of these cases, 0.6 per cent were illegal completed intercourse with an adult (Ordrup et al., 2016). In 2014, research carried out by UNICEF found that approximately one in ten girls under the age of 20 experienced forced sexual intercourse or other forced sexual acts worldwide, amounting altogether to 120 million girls. This research also found that boys are subject to sexual violence as well, but the numbers are difficult to obtain from most countries (United Nations Children's Fund, 2014).

Most perpetrators sexually abuse children for other reasons than having a diagnosis of paedophilia, which is a psychiatric diagnosis showing "sexual predilection for children, often in late childhood or early puberty", according to WHO ICD-10 and DSM-5. This diagnosis only accounts for around 1 per cent of the male population and significantly fewer females (Bengtson et al., 2020), but be mindful that one study shows 5 per cent of sexual assaults are carried out by women, and other research suggests the number is higher (McLeod et al., 2021; Tardif &

Spearson-Goulet, 2012). Most diagnosed paedophiles can control their predilection for children and be ordinary citizens (Bengtson et al., 2020). Still, at a workshop with a Danish expert from Save the Children Denmark many years ago, I learned that people with intentions to act on their sexual fantasies involving children are more likely to seek opportunities to be close to children in contexts such as day-care centres, leisure activities, sports clubs, schools, and homes for children in care and disabled children. Research indicates that children in care and disabled children are more vulnerable than ordinary children when it comes to sexual abuse (Radford et al., 2015). Besides paedophilia, other factors contributing to child sexual abuse may include alcohol consumption and various emotional, social, and mental difficulties.

When we look at the characteristics of children and young people exhibiting sexually disturbing behaviour towards other children, it might provide insight and a better understanding of this topic, as they may continue such behaviour into adulthood if they don't get the right help. Of these children, 35 per cent have been exposed to sexual abuse themselves, 51 per cent have been exposed to physical violence, 45 per cent to psychological violence, 46 per cent to bullying, and 85 per cent to emotional neglect. In addition, 60 per cent have a psychiatric diagnosis, 24 per cent have signs of an autism diagnosis, 54 per cent have a cognitive level of functioning below normal (IQ < 85), and 67 per cent have other social problems. Additionally, they show some developmental defiance/challenges, such as weakened self-regulation skills, social skills, and empathy, and the risk is higher when they enter the developmental stage of puberty (Januscentret, 2021). So, the combination of these three risk factors – (1) exposure to violence, abuse, and neglect; (2) unsafe attachment and weakened affect regulation; and (3) neuropsychiatric disturbances – contribute to risk behaviour.

Most sexual abuse of children happens after the perpetrator has groomed the child. For children, it's most likely to be a person known to them, usually an adult or older child, whereas, for adolescents, it's most likely to be their own intimate partner (Radford et al., 2015). Grooming happens both in the physical world and online and is a process where the perpetrator gets to know the child well and then manipulates and seduces them to be able to exploit and abuse them sexually afterwards. As professionals, we must find ways to help parents and children be aware of the risk, handle it, and protect themselves as best as possible. Many parents are unaware of their children's interactions with other people online and would be terrified to know that Danish police recently warned about a new global tendency of children as young as 6 years old voluntarily sharing videos with sexualised content online. The reason has not yet been discovered, but the risk of the material being abused and misused in ways that are harmful for the children has made Save the Children Denmark propose to start offering guidance to children as early as kindergarten about the code of conduct on social media to help them protect themselves. This example shows why we must relate to the child's entire life when assessing their safety. As we see here, the safety issues apply not only to the home but to all the contexts of the child's life, because it can obviously be traumatic and harmful for a child to be subjected to sexual or other kinds of abuse, violence, and bullying in contexts other than the home.

Bullying

When it comes to bullying, many of my clients in trauma therapy, both adults and children, have been traumatised by overwhelmingly harmful experiences at school caused by their peers and, occasionally, also their teachers. I consider this a very serious matter. In the United States alone, a study conducted in 2017 showed that 20.2 per cent of all students reported being bullied at school, and 41 per cent suspected it would happen again (Seldin & Yanez, 2019), but, getting a view of the different statistics, other estimates are higher. I most commonly use the following definition of bullying:

> A person is bullied when he or she is repeatedly and over time exposed to negative actions by one or more people […] A negative action takes place when a person intentionally causes, or attempts to cause, another person harm or discomfort.
>
> (Stephensen and Møller, 2004, p. 7)

Dan Olweus divides bullying into two categories: either direct bullying – taking the form of direct assaults such as pushing, calling someone degrading things, rolling eyes, pulling a person's clothes, or buckling someone's legs – or indirect bullying – causing social isolation by gossiping, starting rumours about other people, isolating people from the community, not talking or responding to people, and so on (Stephensen and Møller, 2004).

The harmful effects of bullying are shown in mental health issues and, among others, feelings of anxiety, unworthiness, loneliness, isolation, low self-esteem, shame, and being unsafe. At its worst, it can end in suicide, homicide, and school shootings (Wang et al., 2020). In the 2020s, it's crucial for parents, teachers, or other adults dealing with young people to be aware that digital bullying, also called cyberbullying, is widespread online; with 24/7 access to mobile phones, emails, and social media, young people can't turn off the bullying, and neither can it be regulated by adults in the same way as it used to be in, for example, the schoolyard. Instead, young people are at risk of receiving hurtful and harmful messages at home, without anybody knowing, or they can be humiliated and ridiculed in groups and on the wider internet. In that sense, young people today are way more vulnerable because there is always a camera present and videos can catch moments to be used for the wrong reason.

Case example: Lisa

In second grade, Lisa's mother contacted me to do trauma processing with Lisa after she had been exposed to severe bullying by different kindergarten and school kids. She had nightmares and flashbacks and was avoidant of going to school and needed to change schools. She did the trauma processing during the transition between schools, and, before she started in her new class, all her symptoms had almost disappeared. Then, one day at the new school, a boy asked her a question out of curiosity, to get to know her better, but Lisa was triggered somehow and thought the boy was bullying her, and the old symptoms came back. Lisa's mother told me that the other boy was a nice kid who did not want to harm Lisa, but she experienced it this way. Therefore, we worked on processing more trauma, and I helped her to separate the new boy in the present moment from those who had bullied her in the past, so that she could see him in the right light and start to connect with him in a safe way for both.

After covering different forms of abuse that we are trying to keep children and young people safe from by taking them into care, I must state very clearly that removing children isn't equal to safety. As mentioned above, these children are vulnerable to abuse, and Danish research from 2017 showed that 22 per cent of 15-year-old children in care had been subject to abuse in a broader sense, including bullying, within 6 months of being asked. This was mainly from other young people outside the placement, but also from adults inside and outside the placement (Olsen & Laustsen, 2017).

Considering their family conditions, it's also essential to be aware that contact visits must be safe because, if they return to unsafe environments for weekends and holidays, it might be further traumatising and re-traumatising for them and cause significant damage to their development and well-being. Whether it's traumatising and/or re-traumatising or a supportive thing for the child's growth to see their parents without a support person present must always be an individual assessment based on the quality of attachment, contact, and care between child and parents.

Self-harm and suicide

Children and youth may also pose a risk to themselves if they are suicidal or self-harming. Whenever we are worried about a child or young person exhibiting self-harm, suicidal thoughts, plans, or even attempts, we must also make a risk assessment. In your country, most likely, there are clear guidelines that show which national authorities have the responsibility to help suicidal people and determine whether they need protection from harming themselves by being hospitalised. As a professional, it's always good to know these guidelines, and, when in doubt, it's important you ask and seek information about them. We must take these cries for help seriously, as suicide is preventable, but, for people who see it as the only way out of the pain or a hopeless situation, it's difficult to see that there are other ways to deal with it. From my perspective, suicide isn't to be considered as a wish to die but as a solution to a problem to which the person can't see any other solutions. They need our help as professionals to understand what they are trying to solve with these thoughts, plans, or attempts and to be guided towards alternative avenues.

According to the guidelines and helplines in your country, you can seek assistance from NGOs specialised in suicide prevention and contact psychiatric hospitals to consult with professionals in this field. While doing this, it's still critical that you make a risk assessment of the danger that the suicidal person is exposing themself to. One way to get this information could be using a scaling question presenting a continuum of varying levels of suicidal behaviour. The safest end of the scale represents thoughts such as "life isn't worth living" as non-specific ideation. The middle of the scale represents suicidal ideas with the intent to die and/or a plan to fulfil, and the other, most dangerous end of the continuum represents actions of self-harm, suicide attempts, and suicide (Henden, 2008). Depending on where they are at on this scale, we must act accordingly. As professionals, we need to take their calls for help seriously and dare to engage in open and honest conversations with those we work with, to recognise and understand that the power of connection between humans and the power of hope are pivotal in preventing suicide. This is why, when working with suicidal people, whether children, young people, or adults, I start by asking them what their best hopes are for their future. I make agreements that they won't harm themselves while they are in therapy because they will need to give us a chance to be able to achieve these hopes. In Chapter 9, I will return to this topic in more depth.

Critical neglect endangers the child's health, development, and well-being

In addition to the various risk that we have now covered, vulnerable and traumatised children can also be exposed to different kinds of severe neglect and deprivation so harmful to their health, development, and well-being that neglect and deprivation were also covered in WHO's definition of violence shown above (Krug et al., 2002). The difference between abuse and neglect is expressed as abuse being the *presence* of harmful behaviour done to the child, and neglect being the *absence* of fundamentally important care for the child, such as lack of primary care, emotional security, stable living conditions, protection from harm, and appropriate stimulation (Kvello, 2020).

Neglect arises from different sorts of difficulties that parents might experience, such as alcohol and substance abuse, mental illness, immaturity in parenting and lack of parenting skills, cognitive, emotional, and social dysfunctionalities, as well as lack of mentalisation skills and ability to prioritise the child's needs over their own. Some of these issues might also go hand in hand, at times, with abusive behaviour, increasing the risk to the child (Kvello, 2020). How this might be connected to the parent's own trauma history and how it affects their parenting skills will be covered in more depth in Chapter 5.

In Chapter 1, I outlined various essential things that parents need to do to secure an infant's healthy development, and, during these early stages of a child's life, it's crucial for their health, development, and well-being that they receive appropriate care from the parents. Thus, in my terms, safety issues also relate to neglect and deprivation in this critical period as they might endanger the child's development, causing brain impairment and developmental trauma that can be difficult to heal later. In particular, the first 2 months are the most vulnerable of all and can result in severe damage to brain development. According to Bruce Perry, owing to the rapid growth of the brain early in life, if the child receives healthy care, connection, and protection in the first 2 months and then, afterwards, experiences high adversity for 12 years, they will be better off than a child who experiences high adversity and minimal care, connection, and protection in the first 2 months and then spends 12 years in a healthy environment (Perry & Winfrey, 2021). So, early prevention, involving being close to the vulnerable parents before and immediately after the baby's delivery, must be of very high priority if we want to establish a safe environment for the child to secure their healthy development from the beginning.

The parents' issues and traumas may hinder them from having a calm state of mind owing to a lack of basic regulation skills. Having a baby adds extra stress to their high arousal because of the intense demands associated with meeting the infant's fundamental needs. They might find it challenging to put the baby's needs before their own, and they might need to learn about all the critical aspects of caregiving, such as establishing structure, predictability, routines, rhythms, and stability for the baby to develop safely. With insufficient care, the baby or child may be vulnerable, uneasy, and unregulated, and this might make extra demands of the parents, and the situation spirals downwards. In these situations, the parents may need professional help to provide good enough care for the child. However, the safety-oriented, trauma-informed, and solution-focused approach covered in this book has helped many parents to become good enough parents to keep their children in their care, including parents whom many other professionals have given up on.

Case example: Baby Mary

Several years ago, a child protection office asked me to support a pregnant woman who was already the mother of three children in care since their early childhood and was now expecting a baby with her new partner. Because the fourth child had a different father and many things had changed in the mother's life, the child protection office wanted me to assess whether the parents could care sufficiently for the newborn. Through intense safety planning and family therapy from birth, their private network and I were able to support the parents in providing calm, structured, nurturing care, with routines and rhythms and with the right stimuli. In my family therapy, I sometimes showed them specifically what to do, so they could learn from it and adapt my guidance to their care, continuously building on it. Step by step, it became clear that, with the support of their network, they could provide good enough care for the baby to develop healthily with less and less help from me.

There is a greater risk of experiencing abuse and neglect when growing up in a family suffering from mental illnesses and/or substance abuse (Kvello, 2020), and this often relates to unpredictable life conditions and instability coming from uncertainty about how the energy and mood are in the family on a day-to-day basis.

Sometimes, the situation is so critical that it endangers the child's safety, and they must be placed in care immediately. From my experience, many children experience alcohol and other substances accelerating conflicts in families caused by decreased control and heightened levels of aggression as the number of substances consumed rises. For children in such families, they can feel as though they are walking on eggshells, constantly sensing the environment and the emotions that might cause the next outburst or relapse. These children often start to take responsibility for the family situation early and care for their own needs as they can't trust their parents to do so, or at least not the addicted parent. However, this responsibility is too big and comes too early for children to handle and causes numerous challenges for them, both in the short and long term; for example, it can lead to a lack of trust in others, a need for control, and elevated stress levels.

In Denmark, with a population of just around 6 million people, estimates are that 122,000 children grow up in families where there is alcohol abuse (Sundhedssty-relsen, 2019), excluding drug abuse. The number might be much higher, as research from 2015 suggests, because it showed that 19.3 per cent of people aged 18–64 answered that one of their parents was drinking while they were growing up. Over half of the children growing up in these families don't experience problems as adults, but there is a greater risk of suffering from loneliness, low self-esteem, nervousness, and depression than there is for people who didn't grow up in families with alcohol issues (Jensen et al., 2015). In the United States, numbers published in 2015 from National Surveys on Drug Use and Health show that about 1 in 8 children (8.7 million) aged 17 or younger lived in households with at least one parent who had, in the past year, recurrently used alcohol or other drugs (or both) that resulted in significant impairment; about 1 in 10 children (7.5 million) lived in households with at least one parent who had, in the past year, an alcohol use disorder; and 1 in 35 children (2.1 million) lived in households with at least one parent who had, in the past year, an illicit drug use disorder (Lipari & Van Horn, 2015). Regarding the consequences of growing up in a family with alcohol problems, the statistics show that every third child is at risk of having or developing a DSM-IV diagnosis, half of them have emotional issues above the norm, and another third display heightened hyperactivity and more signs of attention deficit than usual. Also, every third child shows social difficulties, but around 50 per cent don't display any symptoms, which is worth noting (Lindgaard, 2012).

When addressing issues of substance abuse in dialogues about the details of the consumption in a parent's life, it's more important to talk about the consequences of the intake than the amounts of substances used. In my conversations with parents about substance abuse, without exception, I emphasise that, if their children and relatives experience their consumption as problematic, then it's a problem. We need not discuss whether a particular quantity of consumption is considered normal or not. Having been trained by some very experienced therapists with many years of experience in working with families affected by alcohol problems, I lean into a definition of a substance abuse problem seen from the children's perspective, when the consumption disrupts essential family tasks and functions as well as undermining emotional bonds and connections between humans owing to someone else's substance use (Hansen, 2009).

If it impairs a person's ability to parent, it's a problem that we need to take seriously and be able to talk about openly in safe ways for both children and parents. From this perspective, there is no difference whether it's alcohol, drugs, hash, or other substances. Therefore, we must be brave enough to talk to parents and ask about their substance use behaviour if we are worried about a child's development and well-being. One of my teachers has taught me to talk to the parents and families using the three Cs – respectively, caring, concretising, and consequences – inspired by the late Birgit Brembacz, a clinical psychologist who specialised in working with families influenced by alcohol abuse. Caring is the ability to talk about it in a respectful way that acknowledges the parents and their good intentions. Concretising is talking about what the substance use looks like when it comes to frequency and quantity, along with the behaviour and the dilemmas that follow. Consequences cover the honest dialogue about the consequences if the use continues and what kind of help the child would need to heal (Trembacz, 2002).

Problems arise if parents can't protect their children from their personal issues, such as behaving in unsafe and unregulated ways with changing boundaries, rules, and strategies to deal with life, or being emotionally unavailable. Issues also arise if the substance is becoming the ruler of the family life to the point that the child never knows if they are being taken care of by a sober or drunk parent, or if they will be cared for or must care for themselves. Growing up in these circumstances might leave the child with a strong need to control and predict their life in order to feel safer. If they don't have any adults with whom they can share their overwhelming thoughts and feelings arising from these life circumstances, they tend to turn the problem inwards and make it about them, believing they are bad, feeling shame and guilt, and taking on a huge responsibility for their family. They might also feel unimportant, not good enough, or not worthy of love when the substance is more important than they are, and there is a general risk of developing co-dependent behaviour, which I will return to in Chapter 5 (Trembacz, 2002). Other aspects might show up as general trust issues because they can't count on their parents and feel helpless, powerless, and lonely, with a strong need to control their life themselves.

What signs do we need to be aware of regarding substance abuse? First, it's difficult to tell whether the signs in the child's health, well-being, and development come from such an issue or other issues, as they look identical to other signs of dissatisfaction and distress. Altogether, the best way to know why the child is showing signs of distress is to ask directly. How to do this in a respectful and caring manner will be investigated after a brief introduction to a family that I have been working with.

Case example: Peter, Michael, and Maria

When Child Protection requested me to help create safety for Peter, Michael, and Maria in light of their parents' substance abuse, the care situation was so unsafe for them that they needed to stay with their wider family network for a short period while the parents got clean and sober again. The children were stressed, angry, and frustrated about experiencing the neglect and unpredictability from their parents again, and the oldest child, Peter, had just had enough and did not necessarily want to return home. The parents periodically relapsed throughout their childhood, but they were good parents in the long clean and sober periods in between.

In the reunification process, I worked intensely with the parents to get the children back but also witnessed them affected by substances a couple of times. I confronted them, but they used different excuses and believed they had fooled me. This led me to have a conversation with them about whom they were trying to fool, making it clear that child protection and I were not the biggest threat. They should be more concerned about potential rejection by, and loss of connection to, their children, now that Peter did not want to come home again.

From this conversation, the parents realised that they had to do something different in caring for their children, but somehow kept believing that the children had never experienced anything, and they had protected their children from their own difficulties. However, as a part of taking responsibility for the neglect they had caused the children throughout their childhood, they agreed to engage in the process of creating a words and pictures story, described later in Chapter 10. Through this process, while talking about signs of being affected by substances and what the children would have noticed, and with me also putting words to my own experiences of seeing them affected, the father suddenly said: "Did you really notice all this?" I confirmed by saying, "I tried to tell you". The mother continued, "We didn't really cheat you?" I replied, "No – it was quite obvious to me and it must have been to your kids too". It took some time for them to digest the realisation that they were living a lie and needed to change, but, from that day, they took on full responsibility for themselves and their children. The mother never touched anything again, and it has been many years now, and the father only had a few slips, protecting the kids by staying away from home when it happened.

How to create safety from violence, abuse, and massive neglect for vulnerable and traumatised children

This first part of the Circle of Safety and Reconnection assesses whether the child is safe or critically at risk and, if at risk, how to work around creating safety and stopping the harm from happening as the most important thing first. Always safety first, and, during my EMDR training for children and adolescents, I learned that it's necessary to be aware of not processing past traumatic events if similar traumatic events are still happening in the present, because children need an activated nervous system to help protect themselves if they experience danger.

In the following, I will explain risk assessment in general terms, but, for clarification of the use of the Circle of Safety and Reconnection, the first step in this model only considers reflection on the initial danger/safety aspect in the risk assessment. All the information needed to do a complete and comprehensive risk assessment of the child's safety, health, development, and well-being will be provided throughout the first six steps of the circle. Then, the following two steps will use the overview of the full risk assessment as a foundation for setting goals for each individual child and young person and to create the action plan, treatment plan, or safety plan from the prioritised goals. Suppose the first step in the circle already shows us danger, and the child needs immediate protection; we know clearly what to prioritise first and go directly to creating safety. If the child is assessed to be safe enough in the current situation, we do a full view of the case to do a comprehensive risk assessment and prioritise what is most urgent, still acting fast on potential safety issues first. This all depends on the character of the danger, the legal aspects, and the position you hold as a professional. Therefore, the use of this model must always be adapted to your circumstances, and it only shows ways to support your work in helping children and young people better according to your specific context.

We have now investigated the major risks that can endanger the child's health, development, and well-being, but, for us to do a balanced risk assessment, we must also look at the signs of safety and the signs of protection that the families are providing for their children (Parker, 2011; Turnell & Edwards, 1999). Assessing each child's safety using a balanced risk assessment means investigating as many detailed descriptions as possible of both the current risk behaviour and the existing safety created by the people involved in the child's life, because creating safety for a child is a collaborative process (Parker, 2011; Turnell & Edwards, 1999). This balanced view of the child's situation will help us keep a balance between being too problem-focused or too solution-focused in a context where children's life can be in danger. If we become too solution-focused, they might suffer tremendous harm to their development and well-being, and, if we become too problem-focused, we might assess the danger as higher than it is and remove them from the care of parents to whom they are safely attached and who provide good enough care for them to keep healthy and well.

There are models developed to be helpful for this: Signs of Safety, developed by Steve Edwards and Andrew Turnell (Turnell & Edwards, 1999), and Partnering for Safety, developed by Sonja Parker (Parker, 2011). I have been trained in both and use a combination of different tools developed within both frameworks. I use the balanced risk assessment after every meeting as a tool to support the ongoing process of assessing the situation for each child, it always being a "here and now" assessment. However, in time, I gather more information to qualify the assessment when I know the child's circumstances and the quality of the collaborative process better.

One question to constantly reflect on concerning the collaborative process is whether we are moving towards the necessary change fast enough for the child. There will be ups and downs throughout life, but there are levels good enough to continue in one direction, whereas other situations might suddenly create a shift in perspective of what's best for the child. Throughout the whole process, it's our job to be very clear about our assessment of this according to the context and to communicate it honestly to the relevant people engaged in the process. In families with more children, there might be different assessments of each child's situation, but, in families with abusive behaviour and neglect, where one child shows signs of well-being and another shows signs of harm, it's crucial to notice the difference. No matter the context, I would still always collaborate with parents on changing their care for all children to prevent abuse and neglect from happening at all. In this way, I am holding the parents accountable for the situation for all children, because a home is supposed to be a safe space for all and not a place for the survival of the fittest.

To have the best possible outcome when working with families in high-risk contexts, we must strive to make "skilful use of authority and leverage" (Turnell & Essex, 2006, p. 45) to engage vulnerable families in a working relationship achieved by meeting them with dignity, respect, honesty, openness, curiosity, and compassion. They are people in crisis and pain, with a high level of protection for themselves and their families, and we need to treat them accordingly and be mindful that their resistance more likely relates to the situation rather than us personally. From my training with Susie Essex on denied child abuse, I have learned that there are many good reasons for people to deny any allegations against them concerning child abuse because the risk of loss when admitting it is incredibly high. There is the risk of losing their children, their spouse, their network, their job, and their financial status, the risk of being put in jail and being expelled from the local community. So, people will protect themselves the best they can, but this doesn't mean we can't work around this, creating safety for the children and families displaying denial and resistance. It's always helpful to collaborate around creating safety instead of discussing the problems and worries by walking around the wall of denial, as Susie Essex calls it, instead of driving into it (Turnell & Essex, 2006). Focusing on safety instead of discussing whether something happened or not or why child protection is worried will move us forward to collaborate around demonstrating safety and showing everyone that the children are safe and well. In these processes, the child protection worker must be very clear about what they need to see the parents do for the situation to be assessed as safe enough (Turnell & Edwards, 1997). This is what I bring to the family. From a solution-focused standpoint, there is no such thing as resistance, and there are no reluctant clients (Ratner et al., 2012); it's still possible for unwilling clients to find a joint project to build a working relationship around. If everything else fails for me, it has always been possible to create a common project that involves demonstrating to all the professionals around the children that there is nothing to worry about.

As described in Chapter 2, we, by default, have blind spots, and, to minimise error, it's important to be mindful that our assessment of things might be wrong and to use our colleagues as part of the risk assessment. The different perspectives on the child's situation are helpful when reflecting on how safe the child is assessed to be and if any critical information is missing to qualify the assessment. To support this process, it's helpful to build a respectful culture at work and within our working relationships, where we can disagree and challenge each other's assessments to ensure a coherent and in-depth analysis of all relevant information as a foundation of the assessment. This also supports seeing the quality of other people's input as an important safety net for us, and it goes for all the different contexts where professionals are working on creating change for children. The following can be adapted to risk assessments at home, at school, in institutions, in foster care, online, or wherever the child might be harmed.

To make a safe, balanced risk assessment for the child requires concrete details about both the risk behaviour and harm the child is exposed to and how it impacted them and also the strength and safety demonstrated by the adults in relation to the risk behaviour. This assessment is based on what the child, parents, and people around the child have said about the child's situation after being asked specific questions during interviews (Turnell & Edwards, 1999). Concerning the harm, there would be questions such as: What harm has the child been exposed to? When did it start? How often does it happen? What was the worst time? What was the last time? What do we know about harm done to other children in the care of these parents? Concerning the impact on the child, we can ask for detailed information on the child's reaction to the harm, how the child experienced it, and if there are any other signs of the child's health, development, and well-being being damaged.

When we are very clear about what harm and danger are involved, we can ask questions about signs of safety and protective behaviour around the child that are directly related to the concern. Questions on safety could be: What actions have the adults around the child taken to protect them against harm? How did they succeed in doing this? How often do they succeed with this? Here, we also start to ask exception questions from the solution-focused approach (Ratner et al., 2012; Turnell & Edwards, 1999) such as: Are there times when these things aren't happening? What are they doing instead in these circumstances? What might the person experience to be helpful in preventing harm during these times? Based on the idea that "it takes a village to raise a child", we also seek information about other people protecting the child, asking who else has helped do this, and what they have done. If the network resources available around the family aren't used as protection yet, we don't consider them to be displaying protective behaviour but, rather, as a protective factor that might be activated in future work to secure the child. We will go into more depth in Chapter 7.

After investigating this in depth, we also look at the impact of the protection of the child on their strength, capabilities, health, and well-being. This involves asking questions about whether the child shows signs of thriving or being age-appropriate in its development and health. What might the child say or do that shows signs of safety and protection? Also, here we can look at expectations such as: Are there times or places where the child is showing more signs of thriving and healthy development? Who and what are present in these situations? And so on.

After eliciting this information in a straightforward and detailed way, with equal consideration of both harm and safety, you can hold the two sets of information up against each other and assess them with the use of a scale of 0–10, where 10 indicates that there is no concern for the child's safety and well-being and you don't have to worry about them at all, and 0 is the opposite, the situation being so harmful that immediate action needs to be taken to protect the child. Ask everybody involved in the assessment where they are on that scale and use the numbers chosen to argue appropriately, taking into consideration your knowledge and experience of the child's health, development, and well-being at the time of the assessment. Throughout this book, I will provide you with a lot more information and knowledge about important aspects of a child's life that will qualify your balanced risk assessment in the future. We will try it the first time with the exercise at the end of this chapter.

At the centre of each risk assessment I make, I always put the child's perspectives on their situation, letting the child's voice become the North Star of my work with everybody around the child. For this, I use different tools developed for having conversations with children and using different toys and materials to support a creative and playful process with the children. Regarding talking about safety issues, I use the Safety House tool developed by Sonja Parker, shown in Illustration 3.1 (Parker, 2009). It can be adapted to any context with concerns about safety issues, and more aspects of engaging children will be described in greater detail in Chapter 8.

When talking to children, it's always important to inform them about the purpose of the conversation, what the information they provide us with is used for,

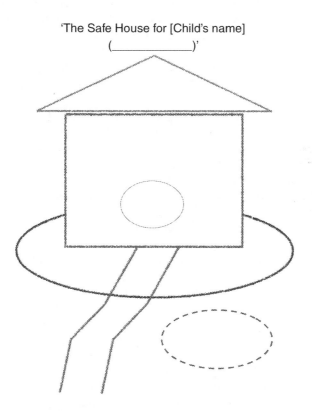

Illustration 3.1 The Safety House

and that it isn't a confidential conversation between you and the child. Instead, the information is used to create safety for them and needs to be shared with their parents, private network, and professionals around the child. The purpose of using the "Safety House" is to have a solution-focused conversation with the child about their perspective on safety in a way that supports the child's sense of safety during the conversation. This also means providing them with as many choices as possible during the conversation – for example, if the house was to be shown to their parents, whether I should do it or we should do it together (Parker, 2009).

To begin with, I start by drawing an empty house, with a circle inside the house and a roof on top. Then, I draw half circles around the house, representing a fence and a pathway to the door, and a red circle outside the fence on one side, while explaining to the child what each part symbolises. The house represents a safe home, and the circle inside shows the child themself and the people in the house when the child feels safe. Some of the questions I ask concerning the centre of the house, after drawing the child in the circle first, are as follows: When you feel safe at home, who is living with you? What are they doing at home that makes you feel safe? What might be the most important things they would do to make you feel safe? What would you mother/father/siblings be doing when you feel safest and happiest at home? What do you need your mother/father/siblings to do differently to feel safer at home? What else? I also get a detailed description of the actions and behaviour of the people mentioned.

As you see, I get information about what the family members are doing and might be doing in the future that feels safe and okay for the child and try to visualise a new and better situation at home during these conversations. They will also often tell us details about what they prefer to move away from. When this happens, it's helpful for the child to convert these details into positive, detailed descriptions of safe actions and behaviour in their hoped-for future, using our solution-focused questions, and putting these in the house too. Nevertheless, we also note what the child has said about worries or harmful experiences and use this in our risk assessment. In this way, it becomes safe for the child to talk about the problematic stuff without being put on the spot and having to deal with the dilemma of what to say or not to say. We must be aware of doing this with care and, afterwards, safely use the information from the child.

The roof of the house represents the child's perspective on day-to-day rules that make the child safe and well cared for, and inside the fence are the people the child feels safe with who can come and visit the family to offer help and support. Here, I talk to the child about which people they would like to visit to make them feel safe at home and what these people might be doing to make them feel safe. But I also ask, who of these people would notice if things were not going well, and what would they do to help when noticing it? The circle outside the fence represents the people the child doesn't feel safe with whom they would like not to be in the house. When talking to children about this, I tell them that I can't promise them that these people won't be in the home because I don't have the authority to decide this. However, it's still important for me to know the child's perspective on this to consider all the details and make the safest plan for the child. If one or both parents are in that circle, I will ask the child what the parents need to be able to do in the care of the child for it to be okay for them to come into the Safety House. Then, I move back to the solution-focused conversation about what safety looks like for the child.

When I have gone through all the different parts of the house with the child, I go to the pathway in front of the house. It represents the scaling question in the solution-focused approach and the measurement of the level of safety the child feels at the time of the conversation. Then I ask them,

> If the door is 10 on a scale where you are the safest you can be and you are ready to enter the house, and 0 is the opposite, you are as far from the house as possible and the most unsafe you have been, where are you now on that path?

Then they show me that, for example, they are on 3, and I ask questions about what is already working in the home that makes it feel as safe as 3 and elicit all the details about what 3 looks like. Next, I ask them what would be a sign that they have moved up the path one step towards the door and elicit more information about this. Finally, I finish by complimenting them on the beautiful house they have created and the strengths, skills, and resources they have illustrated throughout the conversation and highlight how I will use them and reach the final agreement about how to move forward, sharing the details from the conversation in a safe way for the child.

Exercise

To adapt this to your specific context, you can replace or supplement information on the parents with information on other adults' and peers' behaviour of relevance to the child's challenges.

Gather three pieces of paper, take two of them, and label one "Harm" and the other "Safety". Divide both papers into three sections: parents'/adults' behaviour, impact on the child (negative and positive), and risk factors/protective factors. Place them side by side, with harm on the left and safety on the right. On the third paper, create a scale by drawing a line from one side to the other, with 10 being safety, on the right, and 0 being harm, on the left.

Start by writing information about the harm the parents have caused the child and other children on top of the harm paper. Try to focus on detailed descriptions of actions and behaviour that are causing the child not to be safe and stop when there is no more information to share. Use the questions introduced in this chapter.

Underneath, describe the negative, harmful impact on the child's safety, health, development, and well-being in detail, using the questions introduced earlier. If harm is happening in a day-care/school/online/sport setting, do the same while you focus on the people in these arenas instead of the parents.

Repeat the process for the safety paper. First, describe in detail how the parent provides safety for the child or engages their network to help create safety.

Explore exceptions and describe the positive impacts that help the child to thrive and develop healthily. Again, if it's happening outside the home, do the same for the people surrounding the child in this context.

Now assess the scale from 0 to 10, where 10 represents that the child is completely safe, and no help is needed as there are no concerns; 0 is the opposite: it's the most unsafe situation possible, and the child must be secured immediately. Where do you assess this situation to be on this scale?

Also, be aware of questions that arise from this process that you would like to know more about to qualify your risk assessment and make a list of them to ask everyone involved with the child.

Reflect on the need to create immediate safety for the child. If the child's life is endangered, the priority must be to create safety first. This could also be caused by massive neglect and instability in a baby's first month. If you assess the situation as urgent, I advise you to prioritise going through all the exercises immediately to get a comprehensive and balanced risk assessment to qualify work and share with your colleagues to secure the child's safety according to your rules and regulations. Then, read the following chapters to understand the knowledge behind the exercises.

By completing this exercise, you might have realised that the parents have created enough safety for the child to secure their development and well-being enough in the here and now. Then, the child's challenges might be a trauma response caused by past experiences or be something in the child that they are genetically predisposed to, which we will investigate further in the next chapter. It could also be caused by other, less harmful concerns regarding the care situation, covered in Chapter 5.

References

Bengtson, Susanne, Sørensen, Thorkil, & Kristensen, Ellids. (2020). Behandling og diagnostik af pædofile. *Ugeskrift for Laeger, 182*(2).

Børns Vilkår, B. (2021). *Svigt af børn i Danmark – Status 2021.* Børns Vilkår og Trygfonden. https://bornsvilkar.dk/wp-content/uploads/2021/06/Svigtrapport-2021.pdf

Bugge, Anne Birgitte, Dyhre, M. B., Kristensen, Anders Raastrup, Haahr-Pedersen, Ida, Jensen, René Nicolai, & Markman, Maja. (2022). *Systematisk retsmedicinsk screening af børn ved mistanke om vold.* Børnehus Hovedstaden.

Council of Europe. (2007). Council of Europe Convention on the Protection of Children against Sexual Exploitation and Sexual Abuse, Lanzarote Council of Europe Treaty Series No. 201. https://rm.coe.int/1680084822

D'Lima, Tanya, Solotaroff, Jennifer. L., and Pande, Rohini Prabha. (2020). For the sake of family and tradition: honour killings in India and Pakistan. *SAGE Journals, 5*(1).

Finkelhor, D., & Office of Juvenile Justice & Delinquency Prevention. (2009). *Children's exposure to violence: a comprehensive national survey.* U.S. Department of Justice, Office of Justice Programs, Office of Juvenile Justice and Delinquency Prevention.

Friberg, M., & Bjørnset, J. H. (2019). *Migrasjon, foreldreskap og sosial kontroll.* Fafo. www.fafo.no

Hansen, F. (2009). *Metoder i Familieorienteret alkoholbehandling – om at inddrage partner og børn.* Sundhedsstyrelsen.

Henden, J. (2008). *Preventing suicide using a solution focused approach*. Wiley.

Human Rights Watch. (2014). 25th anniversary of the Convention on the Rights of the Child. www.hrw.org/

Januscentret. (2021). *Januscentrets statusrapport 2003–2021*. www.januscentret.dk/wp-content/uploads/2022/04/Statusrapport-JanusCentret-2003-2021.pdf

Jensen, H. A. R., Juel, K., & Ekholm, O. (2015). *Alkohol i Danmark 2015 – vaner, skader og holdninger*. Statens Institut for Folkesundhed & Syddansk Universitet, for Sundhedsstyrelsen.

Kitzmann, K. M., Gaylord, N. K., Holt, A. R., & Kenny, E. D. (2003). Child witnesses to domestic violence: a meta-analytic review. *Journal of Consulting and Clinical Psychology*, *71*(2), 339–352.

Krug, Etienne G., Dahlberg, Linda L., Mercy, James A., Zwi, Anthony B., & Lozano, Rafael. (2002). *World report on violence and health*. WHO.

Kvello, Ø. (2020). *Børn i risiko* (C. Pietsch, Trans.). Samfundslitteratur.

Lev uden vold. (2018). *Socialfaglig definition af psykisk vold i nære relationer*. https://levudenvold.dk/viden-om-vold/lovgivningen/socialfaglig-definition-af-psykisk-vold/

Lindgaard, H. (2012). *Familier med alkoholproblemer: Et litteraturstudium af familieorienteret alkoholbehandling*. Sundhedsstyrelsen.

Lipari, Rachel N., & Van Horn, Struther L. (2015). *Children living with parents who have a substance use disorder*. CBHSQ.

Mary Fonden. (2022). *Partnervold før, under og efter graviditet. En undersøgelse af partnervold i forbindelse med graviditet blandt kvinder på danske krisecentre*. Social Respons.

McLeod, David A., Dunnells, Zackery D. O., & Ozturk, Burcu. (2021). Female offenders in child sexual abuse. In E. Kalfoglou & S. Kalfoglou (Eds.), *Sexual abuse – an interdisciplinary approach*. Intechopen.

Naughton, C. M., O'Donnell, A. T. & Muldoon, O. T. (2017). Exposure to domestic violence and abuse: evidence of distinct physical and psychological dimensions. *Journal of Interpersonal Violence*. doi.org/10.1177/0886260517706763

Oldrup, Helene, Christoffersen, Mogens Nygaard, Kristiansen, Ida Lykke, & Østergaard, Stine Vernstrøm. (2016). *Vold og overgreb mod børn og unge i Danmark i 2016*. Det Nationale Forskningscenter for Velfærd.

Olsen, Rikke Fulgsgang, & Lausten, Mette. (2017). *Anbragte børns udsathed*. Det Nationale Forskningscenter for Velfærd.

Ottosen, May Heide, Frederiksen, S., & Henze-Pedersen, Sofie. (2020). *Psykisk vold mod børn i hjemmet – Et vidensgrundlag*. Det Nationale Forsknings – og analysecenter for Velfærd.

Parker, S. (2009). *The "Safety House" – a child protection tool for involving children in safety planning*. SP Consultancy.

Parker, S. (2011). *Partnering for safety case consultation process: a process for consulting on child protection cases using the Partnering for Safety Risk Assessment and Planning Framework*. SP Consultancy. www.partneringforsafety.com

Pedersen, Hanne Søndergård, Nørh, Katrine, & Kloppenborg, Hans Skov. (2017). *Børn, der krænker andre børn – erfaringsopsamling*. Det Nationale Forsknings- og analysecenter for Velfærd

Perry, B. D., & Winfrey, O. (2021). *What happened to you? Conversations on trauma, resilience, and healing* (1st ed.). Flatiron Books.

Radford, Lorraine, Allnock, Debra, & Hynes, Patricia. (2015). *Preventing and Responding to Child Sexual Abuse and Exploitation: Evidence review*. UNICEF.

Ratner, Harvey, George, Evan, & Iveson, Chris. (2012). *Solution focused brief therapy: 100 key points and techniques*. Routledge.

SafeLives. (2019). *Psychological violence*. www.safelivesresearch.org.uk/Comms/Psychological%20Violence%20-%20Full%20Report.pdf

Schweitzer, J. K. (2019). *Tegn og Reaktioner På Vold*. Social - og boligstyrelsen.

Seldin, Melissa, & Yanez, Christina. (2019). *Student reports of bullying: results from the 2017 School Crime Supplement to the National Crime Victimization Survey*. Institute of Education Sciences.

Stephensen, I., & Møller, S. (2004). *Mobning og selvmordsdfærd*. Faktaserien 13.

Stop It Now! (n.d.). Tip sheet: age-appropriate sexual behavior. www.stopitnow.org/ohc-content/age-appropriate-sexual-behavior

Sudermann, M., & Jaffe, P. G. (1999). Child witnesses of domestic violence. In R. T. Ammerman & M. Hersen (Eds.), *Assessment of family violence: a clinical and legal sourcebook* (pp. 343–366). Wiley

Sundhedsstyrelsen. (2019). *Børn i familie med alkoholproblemer*. Sundhedsstyrelsen.

Tardif, Monique, & Spearson-Goulet, Jo-Annie. (2012). *Sexual assault by women*. Public Health Expertise and Reference Centre.

Trembacz, B. (2002). Rusmiddelproblemer i et familieperspektiv – Alle kan være med til at forebygge alkoholproblemer. trembacz.dk

Turnell, A., & Edwards, S. (1997). Aspiring to partnership – the signs of safety approach to child protection. *Child Abuse Review, 6*, 179–190.

Turnell, A., & Edwards, S. (1999). *Signs of safety: a solution and safety oriented approach to child protection casework*. W. W. Norton.

Turnell, A., & Essex, S. (2006). *Working with "denied" child abuse. The resolutions approach*. Open University Press.

United Nations Children's Fund. (2014). *Hidden in plain sight: a statistical analysis of violence against children*. Author.

United Nations Committee on the Rights of the Child. (2011). The right of the child to freedom from all forms of violence. Convention on the Rights of the Child, General comment No. 13. www.ohchr.com

Wang, K., Chen, Y., Zhang, J., and Oudekerk, B. A. (2020). *Indicators of school crime and safety: 2019*. Institute of Education Sciences.

Wurtele, S. K. (2009). Preventing sexual abuse of children in the twenty-first century: preparing for challenges and opportunities. *Journal of Child Sexual Abuse, 18*(1), 1–18. doi.org/10.1080/10538710802584650

Chapter 4

The Circle of Safety and Reconnection, Step 2

An overview of the child's trauma history, diagnoses, and current state of mind

In every trauma-informed training session I run, I have two main, important messages for professionals supporting children's healing processes. The first is that we should shift our focus from trying to understand what's wrong with them to being curious about what happened to them (Perry & Winfrey, 2022), as these children don't need to be fixed. They need to be loved, healed, and cared for properly, which is the responsibility of adults. The second crucial standpoint involves understanding the connection between their present challenges and past experiences when they misbehave and act out their pain in ways that are challenging for us. This understanding enables adults to relate to the child and their difficulties differently, providing us with new and more manageable solutions to the challenges.

When we approach a situation like this, we must be aware of using gentle, non-blaming language with the parents and other important people around the child to ensure that we aren't creating resistance against taking it in and causing more guilt and shame than are already present. One way to do this is to consider intergenerational trauma, which we'll investigate in the next chapter. If the traumatic events happened in a professional context, we must be aware of the same and acknowledge the difficulty of the task of dealing with this kind of complexity and not being able to prevent the trauma from happening.

Chronic traumatisation and developmental trauma

After assessing the current safety in the child's life, we now move on to Step 2 in the Circle of Safety and Reconnection, which concerns the child's physical, mental, and emotional challenges, symptoms, and trauma history to investigate whether something essential from the past is disturbing the child in the present. Childhood trauma can cause a child to fail to thrive and develop in essential areas, leading to behavioural issues or symptoms of different psychiatric diagnoses such as ADHD, ADD, autism, depression, anxiety, attachment, or personality disorders, and so on (Struik, 2019; Van der Kolk, 2015). Chronically traumatised children most commonly have fewer PTSD symptoms and more behavioural problems and symptoms of the diagnosis (Struik, 2019).

DOI: 10.4324/9781003322672-4

For many years, Bessel van der Kolk and the National Child Traumatic Stress Network have worked hard to get a diagnosis for developmental trauma. This is to acknowledge the impact of childhood trauma on a child's development and to change the diagnosis and treatment of many abused and neglected children who don't meet the criteria for PTSD but instead are accumulating multiple diagnoses over time and receiving treatment they don't benefit from (Van der Kolk, 2015). Developmental trauma is assessed as affecting around 3 million children a year in the United States (Heller & Lapierre, 2014). Recently, ICD-11 has recognised this and included the new diagnosis of complex PTSD. So, let's take a look at the symptoms of PTSD and complex PTSD, but be aware that further criteria concerning the character of the events, duration of symptoms, and such must also be met for an individual to be diagnosed with one or the other (World Health Organization, 2023).

According to the *ICD-11 for Mortality and Morbidity Statistics*, the symptoms of PTSD are characterised by all of the following: (1) re-experiencing the traumatic event or events in the present in the form of vivid intrusive memories, flashbacks, or nightmares; re-experiencing may occur via one or multiple sensory modalities and is typically accompanied by strong or overwhelming emotions, particularly fear or horror, and strong physical sensations; (2) avoidance of thoughts and memories of the event or events, or avoidance of activities, situations, or people reminiscent of the event(s); and (3) persistent perceptions of heightened current threat – for example, as indicated by hypervigilance or an enhanced startle reaction to stimuli such as unexpected noises. The symptoms persist for at least several weeks and cause significant impairment in personal, family, social, educational, occupational, or other important areas of functioning (World Health Organization, 2023).

The diagnosis of complex PTSD, which encompasses developmental trauma, identifies three additional symptoms to PTSD that revolve around these issues: (1) problems in affect regulation; (2) beliefs about oneself as diminished, defeated, or worthless, accompanied by feelings of shame, guilt, or failure related to the traumatic event; and (3) difficulties in sustaining relationships and feeling close to others (World Health Organization, 2023).

Chronic traumatisation refers to the severe trauma that happens early within the family, caused by caregivers who should provide children with protection, safety, and care. It includes various forms of traumatic events covered in the book, such as violence, abuse, neglect, painful medical procedures, discontinuity in the attachment process caused by the loss of a parent, adoption, prolonged hospitalisation, and such (Heller & Lapierre, 2014; Struik, 2019). Chronic traumatisation happens before the child is 8 years old and is assumed to cause more serious consequences than trauma at a later age (Struik, 2019). Though referred to as chronic, this doesn't mean it can't be healed; it's just the clinical definition.

The developmental trauma that arises from this chronic traumatisation causes impairment of the brain, potentially leading to lifelong psychological and physiological challenges (Heller & Lapierre, 2014); these children "demonstrate chronic and severe problems with emotion regulation, impulse control, attention and cognition, dissociation, interpersonal relationships, and self and relational schemas"

(Van der Kolk, 2015, p. 161). Also, the body constantly pumps out stress hormones to deal with real or relived threats and causes many physical problems, such as sleep disturbance, headaches, unexplained pain, and oversensitivity to touch or sounds (Van der Kolk, 2015). Moreover, such children are often delayed in their cognitive, social, linguistic, and motor skills, requiring different treatment than the traditional clinical treatment for PTSD (Heller & Lapierre, 2014).

Case example: Michella

In her 13 years in the psychiatric system, Michella received six diagnoses, from chronic depression at age 10, to dissociative disorder, to her present eating disorder. For all these years, professionals have searched for the correct diagnosis and the proper treatment for her, but, despite this, her condition worsened. At our initial appointment, she was the most suicidal person I have dealt with. The description of symptoms of developmental trauma sounded familiar to her when she heard about it from a professional trained in the Circle of Safety and Reconnection, but she didn't understand why. She didn't consider her upbringing traumatic, but a different story appeared when we started to unfold her trauma timeline.

This was a story of early trauma related to neglect, abuse, and what appeared to be intergenerational trauma, but she didn't consider it to be "that bad" and, owing to dissociation of her feelings, she couldn't feel it as being "that bad". From my understanding of trauma, her symptoms made sense from a developmental trauma perspective, and we started a healing journey together. Slowly putting all the pieces of the puzzle together, we discovered that she had been traumatised as an infant, and she suddenly understood her whole life experience differently. Together, we worked on healing the symptoms by stabilising the nervous system and slowly reconnecting her to her body through breathwork as a start, which helped her feel better instantly. This was the first real difference she had felt in her overall treatment so far. So, where the psychiatric system had told her to accept her condition as her baseline, with no significant chance of recovery, she bravely decided to embark on another journey to find her way home to herself and found hope for recovery.

Recovery

In the tutorial YouTube clip called "How childhood trauma leads to addiction" from 2021, Gabor Maté describes recovery as "to recover something means to find it again, and, as the essence of trauma is a loss of self, when people recover, it means that they find themselves again" (Maté, 2021). Therefore, he claims that the real purpose of addiction treatment, mental health treatment, and other kinds of healing is reconnection. Gabor Maté's talk was mainly on recovery from addiction here, but recovery is also possible for people when it comes to some psychiatric diagnoses, such as schizophrenia and the diagnoses mentioned in Michella's case. With bipolar disorder, autism, and ADHD, recovery is more about someone learning to manage the symptoms in ways that make it possible to live a well-functioning life according to their special needs, called functional recovery (Harvey and Bellack, 2009). This reconnection also aligns with Gabor Maté's notion of rediscovering the true self.

Whether full recovery is possible depends on multiple factors of the disorder's underlying cause and finding the proper treatment and support to create the needed changes for recovery (Anthony, 1993; Siegel, 2020). Concerning psychiatric recovery, the Danish child psychiatrist Søren Hertz's perspective has challenged the dominating views on diagnoses over the years by stating that you only qualify for a diagnosis as long as the symptoms are present (Hertz, 2015). His systemic approach perceives children's symptoms and behaviour in relation to their surroundings and living conditions and works to create change in these as part of a healing modality. This modality opens up the possibility of reconnecting to self through understanding what the children tell us through their behaviour and symptoms, and we can work on changing the surroundings as the most appropriate way forward, because children are too young to take on the responsibility for their recovery.

Full or functional recovery perspectives are very valuable for opening up new possibilities and hope for healing and improvement of children's well-being and development to the extent that biology allows it. Recovery also concerns the ability to cope and build resilience to the best possible extent, but it will most likely happen if we, as professionals, believe in it and our methodologies support it. Particularly here, the trauma-informed mindset makes a difference when focusing on what happened to the child and why they struggle instead of what is wrong with them. One way or another, in all the children with a diagnosis with whom I have worked, the trauma has been intertwined, and my work around the trauma has, with no exceptions, helped lessen the symptoms. In many ways, engaging in the recovery and trauma-healing process is hard for the children and everybody around them, but the fantastic changes and the growth it leads to make it all worthwhile for them.

Case example: Chris

In his mid-teens, Chris underwent a psychiatric assessment and was evaluated to qualify for a personality disorder diagnosis at the age of 18 if nothing radical happened. For this reason and owing to his traumatic upbringing, I was asked to help him with processing his trauma. His motivation for the treatment was to avoid getting a personality disorder diagnosis, and, after 2 years of trauma work and very hard inner work for him, at the age of 18, he no longer qualified for any diagnosis. He was thriving in a new and better way, relating to himself and other people much more healthily and coping with difficulties more easily. There was still more inner work to do in the future, but, overall, we could finish the treatment by celebrating that he had reached his goal. It was such a joy to him, me, and the people around him.

Hopefully, one day, psychiatric systems around the world might follow the Dutch psychiatry example, where, I have been told, they first scan for trauma and treat this before diagnosing children, to ensure that we become better at helping them in the right way from the beginning.

Reflections on trauma versus diagnosis and their correlation

Children born with conditions such as ADHD, autism, and OCD might unintentionally have endured years of not having their special needs for care seen, understood, and met before they were diagnosed. When these special needs aren't met at home, school, and in day care, it disrupts the integration of social connections and may cause trauma for those children (Siegel, 2020). Growing up with both the organically developed condition and trauma can cause symptoms to be more severe than they would otherwise be, and so we need to become better at spotting children with special needs and, hopefully, prevent them from also getting traumatised and ending up more vulnerable than they were to begin with. As it's beyond the scope of this book to cover the topic of children with developmental disorders and other diagnoses, I will only highlight the issues around trauma in relation to their condition and not the conditions as such.

Whether it's diagnosis, trauma, or both can be very difficult to assess, as symptoms are similar (Szalavitz & Perry, 2010), and you won't know this without an in-depth psychiatric assessment by people authorised to do so in your country. So, it's not our job to access this. However, professionals in various contexts working with vulnerable and traumatised children can benefit from using the knowledge and awareness of the impact of trauma to reflect on what the children are showing signs of and what support they might need to get the best possible help to deal with the symptoms. In many ways, whether it's one or the other, the children concerned need the same care and support to deal with their difficulties (Szalavitz & Perry, 2010), which will be covered in more detail in Chapter 8. Still, there will be a huge difference in how you assess the child's care situation and the interventions needed, whether the situation is caused by external factors or a genetically predisposed disorder. Depending on this assessment, there are also different healing perspectives and estimates of their prognosis.

Parents have sometimes been unjustly blamed for their children's diagnoses with the accusation that they provided bad parenting (Szalavitz & Perry, 2010). Several times, I have seen parents hide neglect behind the diagnosis and avoid taking responsibility for their child's well-being, wanting someone to fix their child when what is most needed is a change in the caregiving for the child. Similar things happen in schools and institutions where children might show signs of ADHD or autism as a nervous system reaction to the context. Owing to limited resources, the teacher or carer may focus on fixing the child so that they can deal with the classroom or group setting better, whereas it would be more appropriate to work on the context so that the child becomes calmer and more regulated. These issues and dilemmas appear in many forms, with each person having a story to tell without there being an exact fact sheet to guide us as professionals, except for the knowledge, understanding, mindset, and skills we carry with us. For us to help the individual child in the best possible way requires being aware of the different possibilities – that the child's challenges arise from a genetically predisposed disorder, external factors, or a combination – and being open to all the nuances through reflective practice.

Recently, there has been an increasing emergence of children who refuse to go to school owing to what I assess as stress and burnout in children. Many of them have gone unnoticed, have been diagnosed late, and are traumatised as a result of not being seen, heard, and understood in relation to their special needs for many years. School is filled with demands, and they have undoubtedly worked hard to meet the demands, leading to a high stress level. Many of them refuse to go to school and are isolated at home, in their room, to such an extent that it increasingly damages their well-being over time. It often ends with complete withdrawal from school, causing parents, teachers, and social services enormous difficulties in handling it. According to my understanding, it's important to consider these severe symptoms from a nervous system perspective, as most likely being caused by an overwhelming feeling of fear and shame activating the stress responses into a hyper- or hypo-aroused condition when met with demands. Part of the plan for the children I am working with who refuse to go to school is to help them stabilise their nervous system and build emotion regulation skills. We will come back to this later.

Case examples: Louise and Anna

Louise was in second grade when she started to struggle at school with difficulty attending classes and engaging socially with classmates owing to her frequent, violent tantrums during and between classes. Her parents were supportive and provided good care, but she had siblings with severe special needs. Therefore, her vulnerabilities had previously been explained as a nervous system reaction to problematic experiences followed by a stressful situation at home caused by the siblings. As her situation at school worsened, and she was isolated more and more at home, she was also assessed by a child psychiatrist and diagnosed with infantile autism. This helped her get into a new school for children with special needs. The process has helped her get back to school slowly, one step at a time, at the pace her nervous system has allowed.

During her late teens, Anna faced significant challenges attending school and struggled with isolation at home. Despite her efforts, she often failed to leave the house, causing frustration for herself and her parents. While she could easily socialise and party with friends, she seemed sensitive to demands that would trigger a shutdown response in her nervous system. Recognising trauma as a potential cause, I explored the underlying factors behind her hypo-aroused state. During our sessions, we discovered that Anna held a negative belief – "I can't do it" – and experienced overwhelming powerlessness when faced with demands. We focused on stabilising her and developing emotion regulation skills. However, I sensed there was more at play beneath her response than trauma. With a child psychiatrist's assessment, Anna received a diagnosis of Asperger's, allowing for psychoeducation and understanding of her unique needs at school and home. Understanding the reasons behind her difficulties in a traditional school setting relieved Anna immensely. It helped release the shame she had carried for years, feeling like a failure. With this new-found knowledge, her journey towards recovery could finally begin.

Creating a view of the child's trauma

Being trauma-informed in our practice with vulnerable children aims to reconnect them with their true, authentic selves, obtaining the ability to bounce back from the challenging experiences in their lives and to heal the wounds arising from them. Therefore, clarity about what happened to the child is crucial for understanding of the child's symptoms and difficulties in the present. For this reason, I always create a trauma timeline to outline the child's behavioural, emotional, mental, and physical challenges and the symptoms of diagnosis that the child experiences at a given moment. This information is based on detailed descriptions from conversations with parents, children, and other professionals and from case files.

Combining the actual trauma incidents and traumatic periods in the child's life with their present challenges and symptoms helps me understand the child's condition in depth. It also helps me understand their behavioural and emotional patterns, reactions, and triggers. If important information needed to make the best possible treatment plan for the child is missing, this timeline also makes me aware of what information I need and what questions to ask. If it is impossible to access this information, I use the situation to be mindful that other trauma might appear during our work together that must be dealt with. In most cases, enough information is available to understand the child. I have yet to encounter a trauma timeline overview for any person – child, adolescent, or adult – that didn't show a direct correlation between their present difficulties and trauma history, always making perfect sense to me. When I get clarity and understanding of this, I can help the children and adults around them to understand the same and make sense of it in the same way. This alone is very healing for the child because it releases much shame and guilt and provides new hope for healing.

Professionals engaged with the child must cultivate curiosity about this understanding, regardless of their work context, as it provides the gentlest and most caring way to help the child, leaving them with a better prospect for progress than if they are dealt with in the traditional way. How this is applied to our work will differ from context to context, as teachers can provide different support than a foster parent, a family therapist, or a trauma therapist, but, one way or another, it will be helpful for all to use this to meet and support the children differently and create sustainable change for them.

At first, working in a trauma-informed way might look like a slow process, with no quick fixes and easy answers, that leaves the professionals impatient. Still, most professionals I have trained in trauma-informed work have realised that the fastest way is to go slow and align with the child's nervous system. Thus, forming an overview of the child's traumatic events is an essential yet simple task with a strong possibility of creating a more sustainable impact faster.

My usual process is as follows:

1 On the top of a piece of paper, I draw a straight line from one side to the other.
2 At the right-hand end of the line, I briefly note current physical, behavioural, mental, and emotional challenges, diagnosis symptoms, and triggers.

3 Moving back along the line from the right, I write every traumatic event in chronological order until I reach conception. If the child experienced one or more traumatic periods, I draw smaller lines underneath, from the start to the end of the period, and write a label for the period, such as bullying or domestic violence.
4 If traumatic periods appear, I investigate them in more depth by drawing squares underneath the lines and give details of particularly the first event, the last event, and the worst event within all the various types of trauma that might have happened in this period. To go into every single event is too much, and so I narrow it down to these three incidents within each category of trauma. This helps me get a clear overview of the overall trauma history and its connection to the present symptoms.

As part of the trauma treatment, this helps me plan the treatment and find out where to start, how to proceed, and what psychoeducation to do with the child, and so it's crucial for me in this setting. Also, as a consultant working in the family setting, it helps me to develop a treatment plan in collaboration with parents and other professionals around the child, with a clear focus on the most beneficial elements to work with in the various contexts, supporting the child's healing in the best possible way. For example, it helps me dig deeper into finding out more about what experiences trigger the child and choose the relevant psychoeducation for the child and all the people involved. Being aware of this helps us deal with triggers better and be curious about, and listen carefully for, the negative cognitions the child has about themself and what kinds of suppressed feelings might be located in the body that cause the dysregulation of the nervous system. To understand how we can use this in the process of helping the child, I will explain a little about what I have learned from my EMDR training about what causes a traumatic event to become a trauma.

According to the understanding of trauma that forms the foundation of EMDR protocols and procedures, trauma consists of four elements: (1) the worst part of the traumatic event, (2) the negative cognition about the self that it has left the person with, (3) the disturbing feeling associated with the worst part of the event and the negative cognition, and (4) where the feeling is placed in the body. Also, the trauma processing protocol isn't completed until (5) a new positive cognition that feels completely true inside the body is integrated, which is done after the trauma processing phase (Shapiro, 2001). For example, if one negative cognition is "I am in danger", the new positive cognition should be "I am safe", as the positive cognition should be the direct opposite of the negative one. From this understanding, you can see the connection between memory, thought, emotion, and the sensations of the body and why it's essential to work on thoughts, feelings, and body when stabilising the child's nervous system and supporting the child in reconnecting with themself. There are many ways to do this, some of which will be shared throughout the book.

As previously mentioned, traumatic events can play a part in a child's current dysregulated behaviour in several ways. Sometimes, without even knowing it, the child can unconsciously be triggered by overwhelming dissociated feelings or suppressed memories (Knipe, 2018). The overwhelming experience of triggers will activate the stress response and shut down the neocortex, which is crucial for regulation. This activation can be triggered by experiencing a physical event that reminds the person about the trauma; this could be a smell connected to the memory or a feeling similar to the overwhelming dissociated one, or a negative cognition such as "I am stupid" can be activated. When we know their trauma history, their reactions will make more sense to us, and the situation will begin to become more manageable for everybody involved, including the child, because we can then actively do something to help them deal with the situation better, helping them see that they don't have to be afraid anymore, putting words to a positive cognition instead of the negative one that might get triggered, or just helping them breathe through it.

In contrast, if we don't know a child's trauma history, their behaviour will often not make sense, and we will most likely misinterpret their behaviour and deal with it in ways that make it more unsafe for them. The reaction in these trigger situations can be unconscious for the child, and sometimes they might also dissociate in such situations owing to the overwhelming sensation in the present. Then, they won't remember how they dealt with a situation, what they said or did that could have been harmful to other people, for example, in relation to a fight response (Knipe, 2018). So, when children say they don't remember what happened, it's always worth being curious about whether they really don't remember rather than automatically assuming they refuse to take responsibility for their actions.

The best way for me to describe the disconnection of trauma is as a condition where the body and head are disconnected from each other and where the body hijacks the consciousness, so that the response to events can become uncontrollable and illogical for the mind to comprehend. When a child has experienced overwhelming feelings that have been dissociated from the body because of the overwhelming sensation, they might not feel their body and emotions at all. So, they can't feel any pain, hunger, or thirst, whether they are cold or warm, or when they need to go to the toilet (Struik, 2019). That's when they are entirely disconnected. To find out whether this is the case, you can investigate how much they can eat without feeling full or test them with warm and cold water on the skin or strong tastes that the body would typically respond to, such as chilli. Another sign could be if they pee or soil their pants at an age where that wouldn't normally happen and with no medical reason to do so.

Others might be less disconnected and sense their body better, but not the suppressed emotions causing stomach pain, headaches, or other psychosomatic symptoms. These forms of disconnection and dissociation appear in many different individual states (Knipe, 2018). Every child has a level of connectedness to themself. If they are completely disconnected from their body, professionals collaborating around them must do something different and have different expectations of the child's capability to deal with things than if they are only not sensing some of their emotions. So, we must plan accordingly, knowing the importance of investigating all these aspects of the trauma's impact on the body, feelings, and mind. Not being safe in their body, they experience a constant stress response that keeps them dysregulated, with consequences for their ability to connect with others, sense and regulate themselves, and develop new skills and learn everything a child needs to know throughout childhood (Struik, 2019). Trauma healing helps reconnect the body, mind, and spirit so that the child becomes one whole integrated entity again, and most adults around the child can play an essential role in this process.

Also, to understand more about the impact of trauma on a child, we can listen carefully to what negative beliefs the child has about themselves – for example, "I am bad", "I am stupid", "It's all my fault", "I am not in control", "I am powerless", "I am unworthy of love". Most of the time, you can hear these negative beliefs showing up in different ways in the child's communication and can understand what kind of unhealthy soundtrack of thoughts is playing in the child's mind. However, if you can't hear it in the child's communication, you can look at the trauma timeline and see what would be most likely. For example, if there was violence, it could be "I am in danger"; in cases of neglect, "I am not worthy of love" or "I am not important". You can try to test with the child whether they recognise having thoughts like this. If they do, you can explain to them how they are linked to their traumatic experiences and start a slow process of teaching the child that this isn't the truth about them but how they perceive themselves as a consequence of the traumatic events.

For any child, the truth is "I am worthy of love" or "I am okay as I am", and, whatever your context, you can work consciously on slowly challenging the old negative cognition by integrating the positive instead and slowly building new neural networks in their brain. This will help them rewire their brain, support better emotion regulation, and improve their self-esteem, among other things. This shift can't be brought about in everyday life as quickly as in trauma therapy sessions; instead, it needs countless repetitions of these new thoughts to make a difference and must be supported by caring adults with the patience to keep doing this slow and vital task, creating an important impact over time.

The most important focus when assisting the child in managing triggers, being more present in the body, and thinking new, better thoughts, besides physiological regulation, is emotion regulation skills. When we improve these skills, step by step, we secure better well-being, better and safer emotional development, a more robust nervous system, and healthier brain development for the child (Struik, 2019).

The importance of emotions and emotion regulation

Understanding the nature of emotions and why they are such an essential building block for human health, development, and well-being is pivotal. I have learned from trauma therapist Arianne Struik to explain the importance of emotions to traumatised children and young people in a straightforward way, comparing feelings to road signs. These emotional road signs are here to help us navigate through life in a safe and protected way and to help us make good choices about where to go, what to do, and whom to be with, based on how they make us feel and what we like or dislike (Struik, 2019). Being connected to our gut feeling helps us use our whole sensory system to protect us from danger and know when something isn't right, inside and outside ourselves. Therefore, emotions are strongly connected to bodily feelings; if, for example, you sense danger, your body will be alarmed and will respond to the danger adequately if you are connected to yourself and feel it correctly (Struik, 2019).

Very clearly, feelings aren't dangerous but are here to help and protect us. However, many young and older people are afraid of feeling emotions and suppress them the best they can. Often, overwhelming feelings, disconnection from emotions, lack of emotion regulation skills, and disturbance can result in not having any, or the right, road signs to use (Struik, 2019).

Regulating our emotions will help us navigate life and get where we want to be by communicating and expressing our feelings, reaching out for comfort when needed, and setting our boundaries safely for ourselves and others. This is why it's so important for adults to soothe, comfort, and teach children emotion regulation skills and show them how to deal appropriately with emotion in ways that will help them be familiar with and understand the nature of feelings (Maté, 2019; Van der Kolk, 2015). It is also crucial to acknowledge, validate, and put words to children's emotions, both to soothe them and so that children know the different emotions, know the differences between them, and, over time, express them healthily (Struik, 2019). A part of this is also to be aware of the importance of not dismissing, devaluing, or reacting negatively in other ways to children's emotions. This helps children feel themselves simultaneously as they learn some fundamental things about emotion regulation. Through these processes, emotions become natural, and we learn that we can feel better if we share these things with others.

Arianne Struik also uses a very helpful metaphor to explain the nature of feeling that I have adopted in my practice. She describes feelings as waves that build up, peak, and then break and roll on to the beach, until they become one with the ocean again. She explains to a child that, like waves, feelings can become very strong, but, if you surf them, they will carry you safely to the beach. However, blocking the feelings will be like falling off the surfboard in the middle of the wave, and you will tumble and feel as though you are drowning (Struik, 2019). In my practice working with families and adults in trauma therapy, I have found that adults also benefit from hearing this explanation, which helps them regulate their own emotions better and helps them understand the importance of emotion regulation for their children.

When caregivers help children regulate their emotions, they learn to comfort themselves when they are sad and calm themselves down when angry or afraid, and this helps them cope with challenges later in life. This happens when adults contain the emotional outbursts of children and help them feel better again without using food, sweets, toys, or whatever they can think of as comfort, bribery, or reward, but simply by using words, body language, and their own calm, regulated nervous system to co-regulate the child. Through these processes, children learn that feelings come and go and that they can feel better by sharing with others without feeling shame and guilt, and, if they dare to share, they can get the support they need to help them cope with life.

Sharing emotions and our vulnerability can achieve cohesion, closeness, intimacy, community, connectedness, and much more. On the other hand, not sharing will often lead to a feeling of disconnection from others, leaving people with the sense of being on their own and feeling alone, causing more overwhelm, pain, and disconnection from ourselves (Maté, 2019). This is the vicious spiral many traumatised children and adults are caught in that we need to help transform by being present with them in their pain and helping them find another way of dealing with the suffering and pain from the past that they are carrying.

Case example: Chris – continued

In our early work together, Chris couldn't and wouldn't bring up anything related to feelings in our sessions. Even though he wanted to heal the pain caused by an upbringing with massive abuse and neglect and no safe adults or communities around him to connect to, whenever he briefly touched on the feelings inside, his whole body would shut down. Then, he would sleep and sleep for hours, almost passing out so that no one could wake him up. It was his way of unconsciously shutting down the overwhelming feelings and protecting himself, but it hugely disturbed his everyday life and how he lived it, leaving him vulnerable and disconnected from himself, others, and the world. He mainly used food and alcohol to numb himself when not sleeping. He told me he didn't feel safe anywhere else but with me in our sessions together. Therefore, it was critical for me to establish a sense of safety, both externally and internally, and make his trauma processing a very slow process, ensuring that he would never be too overwhelmed and scared by his feelings to return to me again.

Over time, he learned to deal with the emotions by starting from scratch, where he would only feel something briefly each time, just like dipping a toe in the water, lifting it up again, and moving away from it again. Slowly, he was able to stay longer with his ordinary emotions and dip his toe in the water a bit longer, and so he gradually got more accustomed to dealing with feelings in general. After a year or so, he was stable enough to start working on processing the overwhelming feelings from the past trauma. At the end of a 2-year process, he could deal with things without numbing or shutting down, and his everyday life and relationships had become more stable and healthier to such an extent that we could end the process. In the last session, he looked back and laughed about how much resistance he initially had but was also proud of what he had accomplished, and so was I.

Many children and young people would be as successful in turning their situation around as Chris if they had a calm and collected adult to help them connect to and regulate their emotions at a gentle pace, making them feel safe rather than overwhelmed. So, no matter what context you are working in, remember that "dipping the toe in the water" can lead to significant changes faster than you can imagine. Two years is no time if we compare it with a long adult life dealing with problematic relationships with self, others, food, and alcohol. Family and community can help children heal using "therapeutic dosing", as Bruce Perry calls it, which refers to the process where meaningful relational interactions help children regulate their experiences, making them less stressful and frustrated, by "dipping the toe in the water" (Perry, 2022).

Human nature encompasses four basic feelings – sadness, anger, fear, and happiness – and more complex feelings such as jealousy, shame, pride, hate, love, and so on (Struik, 2019). As described in Chapter 1, newborns don't know these feelings or the differences between them but will learn this through their adult caretakers mirroring them, putting words to them, and acknowledging them. So, levels of emotional maturity will differ from person to person, depending on how emotionally mature their caretakers are (Maté, 2019; Siegel, 2020).

From my experience, in many families, certain emotions aren't allowed. Still, the less you deal with them, the more they will show up in disturbing ways for yourself and others. Let's take anger, as many people are afraid of anger and see it as an enemy instead of befriending it, as reacting with anger is healthy in many ways. Often, it shows up when something important is at stake, and you must be clear with your boundaries and protect either yourself, others, values, or belief systems of importance to you, or if you experience injustice, to name a few situations. In such situations, it helps you communicate your boundaries, and your job is to regulate yourself to share this appropriately with others and avoid attacking others while protecting yourself. The problem isn't the anger but how it's often expressed in unhealthy and unregulated ways when old, suppressed feelings stored inside and accumulated year after year are being triggered and make you lose control over it when you come into contact with it. The same goes for other feelings. In general, many traumatised children have difficulty recognising different emotions and differentiating them from each other, with little chance of being able to regulate them appropriately, leading to severe dysregulation and disturbances in their relationships with themselves and others. Therefore, it's helpful to stabilise traumatised children and make management plans for whatever feeling is involved to build children's emotion regulation skills (Struik, 2019).

Emotions and thoughts are closely intertwined and influence each other. Our thoughts and interpretations of events can cause an emotional response, and our feelings can also affect our thoughts about an event. Daniel Siegel describes "the central features of emotion – are interwoven with the representational processes of 'thinking'" (Siegel, 2020, p. 271). It is crucial to know our entire emotional register and monitor, accommodate, and modulate it, but I have experienced many vulnerable and traumatised children who only had one primary emotional response to everything, such as anger, sadness, or fear. So, whatever is happening, they respond with this emotion instead of the appropriate emotional response for a certain kind of event. For example, they react with anger when sad and anxious or with anxiety when feeling anger. This is an unhealthy development, as every feeling has its own purpose and expression that help us deal with life and each other and connect us. When this is impaired, it leaves the child vulnerable in many ways, and it calls for long-term work to return to the process of building the foundation of the brain with the building blocks that are required in early childhood, explained in Chapter 1, in order to repair what has been broken.

I always try to assess the child's emotional age to find out how far back we need to go to restore the development. For us to heal the damage of people's development and carry them on in healthy development, we need to meet them with an initiative matching their emotional age at any given time – in many ways, similar to Bruce Perry's neurosequential model assessment of what areas of the brain to stimulate first to heal the early impairment of the brain. Often, traumatised children must be taken back to infancy, starting with physiological regulation, followed by emotional regulation, and then moving forwards with the neocortex. It's never too late, and always possible, to do this work, even as an adult. As I wrote earlier, our brain is plastic all our life, and it's never too late to start picking up the things that have been lost. The extent of the ability to heal will differ, depending on how early and in what area of the brain the damage was done, but, in this matter, a little is always better than nothing. To learn more about working with this reconstruction of the brain, I recommend Bruce Perry's neurosequential model of therapeutics.

Case example: Louise – continued

One emotion regulation skill I helped Louise develop was to install a visual impression of a "never mind button" that she could push when she got worked up. Pressing the button in her mind reminded her to say, "Never mind", and to calm down and relax, which helped her in conflicts with her classmates. To help her understand and manage her tantrums, I also used "the volcano", developed by Arianne Struik to help children understand their anger (Struik, 2019).

"The volcano" is a simple and handy tool to support children in their anger management, helping them understand that the eruption of anger in the present is based on all the anger they have suppressed during the traumatic event(s). So, when the memories trigger them now, they experience uncontrollable anger with the intensity of a volcano; when they understand the link, it releases a lot of shame and guilt. Then, we can start to talk about how to deal with it in a healing way that helps them manage it much better for themselves and their surroundings. By externalising it in this way, Louise could explain it to her teachers, which helped them to make an anger management plan for what to do and how to help her when the volcano erupted. This led to fewer and fewer episodes of outbursts, which made her better at socialising with her peers as they became less and less frightened of her.

Through my work with trauma processing, I have come to understand that self-harm is often closely connected to deep, unresolved, dissociated anger turned inward instead of being expressed outwardly. As a result, the anger is directed towards oneself as a massive self-destructive force. Therefore, focusing on and working on anger regulation and management with individuals who engage in self-harm and suicidal thoughts would be highly beneficial. However, before they can address their anger, they may need to learn to regulate other emotions first so that, later, anger can be processed in a safe and secure manner for them.

In general, the experience of being alone in overwhelming and scary situations, with no control and not enough capability to manage the situation, leads to an overwhelming feeling of helplessness and trauma. Somehow, I have come to understand that a traumatised mind has more fragmented parts than normal and, in many ways, is a scattered mind (Knipe, 2018). What happens when the trauma timeline is created is that it helps the brain to make connections and links between fragmented parts and creates much-needed coherence, and talking to people about it in the here and now means they are no longer alone; therefore, it's a very powerful tool to use with children and the adults around them.

Exercise

To adapt this to your specific context, you can replace or supplement information on the parents with information on other adults' and peers' behaviour of relevance to the child's challenges.

Use the same child from the exercise in Chapter 3.

1 Draw a straight line from one side to the other at the top of a new piece of paper.
2 On the right-hand side, write a brief overview of behavioural, mental, and emotional issues, triggers, and present symptoms of diagnoses.
3 Move back along the line and note all the single traumatic events in the child's life since conception. If there are one or more traumatic periods in the child's life, draw smaller lines underneath the line, from the start to the end of the period, and label it.
4 For each traumatic period, draw three squares and write as much detail as you know about what happened in the first event, the last event, and the worst event, with all the different types of traumatic event that happened in this period.

Then, take out the piece of paper from your exercise in Chapter 3 concerning harm and the harmful impact on the child and add a summary of the detailed information about what kind of trauma the child has experienced, how severe it has been, and how it has impacted on the child's health, development, and well-being.

Now, with the additional information, assess the scale from 0 to 10, where 10 indicates the child is completely safe and well, you don't need to worry about them, and no help is needed. 0 is the opposite: it's the most unsafe possible, and the child must be secured immediately.

Where do you now assess this situation to be on this scale? Compare this assessment with the one you conducted in the last exercise and assess whether this potential difference requires action.

Also, be aware of questions that arise from going through this that you would like to know more about and make a list of them to ask everyone involved with the child.

References

Anthony, W. A. (1993). Recovery from mental illness: the guiding vision of the mental health service system in the 1990s. *Psychosocial Rehabilitation Journal*, *16*, 11–23.

Harvey, Philip D., & Bellack, Alan S. (2009). Toward a terminology for functional recovery in schizophrenia: is functional remission a viable concept? *Schizophrenia Bulletin, 35*, 300–306.

Heller, Laurence, & Lapierre, Aline. (2014). *Udviklingstraumer* (Healing developmental trauma) (M. Chack, Trans.). Hans Reitzels Forlag.

Hertz, S. (2015). De Uærbødiges Klub. *Magasinet vinter 2015*, Vejlederforum.

Knipe, J. (2018). *EMDR Toolbox. Theory and treatment of complex PTSD and dissociation* (2nd ed.). Springer.

Maté, G. (2019). *When the body says no – the cost of hidden stress*. Vermilion, Penguin Random House.

Maté, G. (2021). How childhood trauma leads to addiction [video]. YouTube.

Perry, B. D., & Winfrey, Oprah. (2022). *What happened to you? Conversations on trauma, resilience and healing*. Bluebird

Shapiro, F. (2001). *Eye movement desensitization and reprocessing: basic principles, protocols, and procedures* (2nd ed.). Guilford Press.

Siegel, D. J. (2020). *The developing mind* (3rd ed.). Guilford Press.

Struik, A. (2019). *Treating chronically traumatized children: the sleeping dogs method* (2nd ed.). Routledge.

Szalavitz, M., & Perry, B. D. (2010). *Born for love: why empathy is essential – and endangered* (1st ed.). William Morrow. Contributor biographical information www.loc.gov/catdir/enhancements/fy1011/2010280500-b.html; publisher description www.loc.gov/catdir/enhancements/fy1011/2010280500-d.html

Van der Kolk, B. A. (2015). *The body keeps the score: mind, brain and body in the transformation of trauma*. Wellbeing Collection, Penguin Books.

World Health Organization. (2023). *ICD-11 for Mortality and Morbidity Statistics*. World Health Organization.

Chapter 5

The Circle of Safety and Reconnection, Step 3

Parents' trauma, diagnosis, intergenerational trauma, and their impact on parenting skills

Different factors influencing on the healthy development of a child

A child's healthy development is intricately linked to family dynamics, environment, and genetic inheritance from their biological family. Numerous biological and environmental factors influence human development and have been extensively researched so that their impact is understood. The ongoing quest is to determine the relative importance of genes compared with the environment and their interaction, shaping individuals from conception throughout life and across generations.

For a child's well-being and healthy development, the role of parents and the biological family can't be understated, whether the child lives with them or not. This influence must be examined within a larger framework to ensure that children receive optimal conditions for growth, development, and potential healing if they have already encountered traumatic experiences. From my perspective, it's crucial to explore various aspects of a child's life, such as epigenetics, intergenerational and collective trauma, attachment and prenatal attachment, mental health, family patterns, and parenting skills. These elements significantly impact a child's healthy development and must all be considered.

The nature of epigenetics

When the research into DNA first revolutionised our understanding of biology and answered many questions about human existence, a deterministic view of genetics emerged, considering our blueprint to be set in stone. In the last 15 years, the new body of research into epigenetics has shown a different picture, revealing many new answers about the level of impact humans have on inherited genes, turning them on or off (Moraes & Ferreira, 2020, p. 255).

Epi is Greek and means "above", and epigenetics means "on top of" or "in addition" to genetics and answers *how* genes are expressed throughout life and between generations. The British embryologist Conrad H. Waddington (1905–1975) coined this term and defined it as "the interaction of a gene with the environment that defines a phenotype" (Moraes & Ferrerira, 2020, p. 14). Genetics gives answers to *what*

DOI: 10.4324/9781003322672-5

genes consist of and the heredity passed on from parents to children, and the building block of the genes is our DNA, which is the "molecule responsible for transmitting genetic information from parents to children" (Moraes & Ferrerira, 2020, p. 3). Gene expression is the information running from the DNA to the protein of which each gene consists, and it shows that the gene is being "stimulated", "activated", or "switched on". This happens when the protein is produced through the process of the gene being accessed, read, copied, and translated (Moraes & Ferrerira, 2020).

Epigenetics doesn't change the DNA but creates changes around it, influencing gene expression. This has helped us understand that environmental influences can send information to the DNA to either support the gene to be activated and switched on or to be repressed and turned off (Morares and Ferrerira, 2020). This means we can influence our biology to a more considerable extent than we ever thought possible, through our experiences, habits, and states of mind, and this also impacts future generations as it leaves an imprint on genetic expression. Depending on whether experiences, habits, and states of mind are good or bad, we can either activate the gene, leaving us more vulnerable, or repress it, leaving us healthier and more resilient.

Individually, we can support our health and well-being through our diet, exercise, sleep, relationships, location, our emotional and nervous system regulation, and such. Our actions, thoughts, and emotions shape our health and well-being. Wise choices now leave much hope for healing in individuals and families. For each child, it also means that, through conception, pregnancy, and upbringing, parents can do many things to actively turn the genetic material on or off. This is why it's crucial to help parents create the needed changes in their lives if they struggle and have difficulties. Most of a child's healing relies on parents' taking responsibility and actions to improve living conditions and family patterns, rather than fixing the child's difficulties.

With regard to intergenerational trauma, several important studies have provided valuable insights into the transmission of biological changes resulting from trauma across generations. Research on mice and humans demonstrates that parental trauma can manifest in altered gene expression and health outcomes in their offspring. According to researchers, mice and humans have very similar genetic expressions, which means we can learn much about humans from experiments with mice (National Human Genome Research Institute, 2010).

An experiment with male mice involved applying mild electric shocks during exposure to cherry blossom, leading to fear of this smell. The results showed that the mice developed receptors to detect this smell at lower concentration rates, and their sperm was packaged differently to control mice around the gene that could detect this scent. After 2 weeks, they bred with healthy female mice. Without meeting the fathers, their pups turned out to have more receptors to detect this smell and were more agitated when the smell appeared than the control pups (Dias & Ressler, 2014).

A Dutch study was undertaken of people from a region in the Netherlands that experienced a shortage in supplies and severe hunger owing to occupation by the

Germans towards the end of the Second World War. The children of women who were pregnant during the period of hunger were examined later in life and compared with their siblings born at different times. The results showed that the children born in this period weighed more and displayed more obesity, diabetes, and neurological conditions such as schizophrenia as adults. A study on the same topic, in 2018, later confirmed the result (Tobi et al., 2018).

Another recent study on women from Kosovo with PTSD from sexual violence and torture during the war in Kosovo in the late 1990s demonstrated that children born to mothers who experienced symptoms of PTSD during pregnancy exhibited higher cortisol levels than those of mothers without PTSD symptoms during pregnancy. Additionally, the study revealed that children of mothers with PTSD during pregnancy displayed epigenetic modifications in several genes, particularly those involved in regulating the stress hormone cortisol, compared with children whose mothers did not have PTSD. Those genes that are, in particular, important for regulating the stress hormone cortisol were found to have these alterations in gene inheritance, which signify changes in epigenetic patterns (Line Hjort et al., 2021).

Additionally, new research indicates that women's eggs are formed during their fetal development (Serpeloni et al., 2017). This means that the egg you were conceived from lay in your grandmother's womb during her pregnancy with your mother, and, therefore, a grandmother's experiences, nervous system, and biology can potentially influence the genetic material inherited by her grandchildren. These findings also highlight the intergenerational nature of trauma and its impact on the vulnerability of future generations (Serpeloni et al., 2017).

While further research is still required, the current understanding of intergenerational trauma can be utilised to prevent and address its negative effects and to reverse the harmful impact of parents' trauma on a child's vulnerability. It is not irreversible, as epigenetics creates a window of opportunity to reverse this damage to our biology through the dynamic and changeable gene expressions in protein that "change all the time depending on what kind of stimuli the cell receives" (Moraes & Ferrerira, 2020). Supporting parents in addressing their own traumatic experiences is crucial to break the cycle and promote healing within individuals and families. Rather than solely addressing the child's difficulties, parents must create positive changes in their own lives, providing better living conditions and fostering healthier family patterns.

Case examples: Peter, Michael, and Maria – continued

While working with Peter, Michael, and Maria, from Chapter 3, my focus was on preventing future relapses in the parents' substance abuse to help them in the long term. Therefore, I suggested that social services support the parents in addressing their trauma. When not using drugs, they were good parents, and I couldn't teach them much about parenting they didn't already do when clean and sober. Their problem was staying clean and sober over time owing to their traumatic past.

To support long-term, sustainable recovery, trauma therapy was assessed as more beneficial for them than family therapy. Until then, their substance abuse treatment offered them mainly substitution treatment, not therapy. With the children temporarily placed elsewhere, the parents could use their resources to start therapy and get stable enough to both care for the children and continue their therapy. The following year, both parents embarked on their healing journey, divorced, but stayed best friends and co-parented their children, and the children started to bloom again. Now, many years later, they are still clean and sober, and the children have healed their trauma and are feeling better than ever before through experiencing the parents' stability and better emotion regulation and nervous system regulation.

The transformation for the children also happened through the parents' dialogues with the children about all the bad experiences in their past and how they arose from intergenerational trauma in their family, and not because the children were not loved or were bad. From the beginning of the parents' recovery, the children knew their parents had chosen to finally become clean and sober because of their love for them so that they could stay home together as a family. This demonstration of love and the knowledge that this effort and hardship were all because of them has been more healing to them than any therapy. I often see this in the recovery from intergenerational trauma, when the parents both are the ones who have harmed the children but also become the ones healing them, leaving them prouder, stronger, and more empowered.

Intergenerational and collective trauma influencing children's well-being

We have now investigated the footprint trauma in one generation leaves biologically on future generations, if not reversed by supportive actions towards health and healing. Still, intergenerational trauma also contains other dimensions concerning individuals' emotional, mental, and social development and influences family patterns, attachment styles, and broader community dynamics. Understanding these aspects is crucial to comprehend the full scope of intergenerational trauma. Now it's time to look further into these aspects and the influence of collective trauma that also impacts intergenerational trauma in families and communities.

Inspired by Thomas Hübl's impactful work on collective trauma, I use this term to describe the traumatic events that affect not only individuals and families but communities and cultures at large (Hübl, 2020). These events encompass global crises such as the COVID-19 pandemic that, worldwide, caused a significant rise in numbers of people with stress, anxiety, depression, and suicidal thoughts and also increasing safety issues for both children and adults (WHO, 2022; UN Women, 2020). In a critical situation unlike any other we have experienced, many parents were also affected by the overwhelming collective situation of uncertainty, instability, and lack of meaning, but also lack of possibilities to communicate and provide reassurance to children about what was happening.

Additional examples of collective trauma include discrimination against black people in the United States, the oppression and colonisation of various indigenous peoples worldwide, ethnic cleansing, civil wars, and world wars. It must be acknowledged that, in current and historical settings, these issues have influenced different societies, cultures, and groups of people over a generational span and, thereby, also influence many of the vulnerable and traumatised children we are working with in one way or another. Dr Maria Yellow Horse Brave Heart, PhD, defines historical trauma as "cumulative emotional and psychological wounding over the life span and across generations emanating from massive group trauma experiences" (Hûbl, 2020, p. 74). Responses to historical trauma can manifest as collective PTSD, with depression, anxiety, aggression, low self-esteem, self-destructive behaviour, and self-sabotage, such as addiction, suicidal ideation, physical symptoms, and more emotional and mental health difficulties. Unresolved grief associated with historical trauma affects people both individually and collectively, and the children and grandchildren of mass trauma survivors experience higher rates of PTSD and are more vulnerable to psychological health than their peers (Hûbl, 2020). Traumatised communities around the world also often show lower socioeconomic conditions, poorer health, and higher stress rates, which become risk factors in children's life, which we will dive deeper into in Chapter 6 (Hûbl, 2020).

In Chapter 2, we explored the concept of secondary traumatisation and its impact on professionals working with trauma-affected individuals. However, it's equally vital to recognise the significant risk faced by children living with parents who have PTSD resulting from experiences such as warfare, torture, sexual violence, and other traumatic events. When parents can't protect their children from their own pain and suffering, the children become directly exposed to the traumatic effects, which can create an environment of chronic stress and emotional dysregulation. Witnessing a parent's distress can be deeply distressing and confusing for a child and, potentially, can lead to the activation of the child's own trauma responses and impairment of their healthy development and well-being (Howard, 2021). These children may exhibit similar symptoms to their parents, including flashbacks, nightmares, avoidance behaviours, and heightened arousal within their own nervous system (Howard, 2021). Thus, professionals working with trauma-affected families must recognise the unique challenges faced by children living with parents with PTSD and provide trauma-informed interventions and support to create a safe and healing environment for both the parent and child.

Another significant consequence of parents' trauma is an increased risk of self-harm and suicide attempts, which can further perpetuate trauma within the family. Bessel van der Kolk's research revealed strong links between histories of childhood sexual abuse and physical abuse and repeated suicide attempts and self-cutting (Van der Kolk, 2015). Another study focused on self-destructive and suicidal behaviour, where two-thirds of the patients showed significant improvement after treatment, but further examination revealed that those who did not respond to treatment often reported a lack of feeling safe with anyone during their childhood (Van der Kolk, 2015).

Research also highlights a heightened risk of suicide attempts among teenagers within 2 years of a parent's mental illness, suicide attempt, or completed suicide (Mittendorfer-Rutz et al., 2012). This alarming risk can be transmitted across generations, emphasising the importance of addressing it effectively. Understanding the relationship between parental trauma, self-harm, and suicide attempts is crucial for developing comprehensive interventions and support systems. By providing trauma-informed care, creating safe environments, and promoting mental health and resilience, we can help break the cycle of intergenerational trauma and mitigate the risk of self-harm and suicide. Along with various other aspects covered in this chapter, suicidal behaviour is among the adverse childhood experiences (ACEs), and, therefore, we will examine this deeper in the following chapter.

There is a risk of perpetuating cycles of neglect and abuse within families, as parents who were harmed as children may unintentionally harm their own children owing to a lack of alternative models. Research shows that the more severe neglect and abuse are, the bigger the transfer from generation to generation (Schickedanz et al., 2018; Kvello, 2020). For instance, mothers exposed to violence tend to exhibit more hostility towards their children, and mothers whose attachment and mentalisation abilities were compromised in their own childhoods may pass on similar internal working models to their children, making it challenging for them to provide the sensitive care they themselves did not receive (Kvello, 2020; Van der Kolk, 2015). Thus, neglect and abuse tend to be passed down from generation to generation, although the degree and form may vary based on the child's developmental stage and the family's circumstances.

The damaging impact of neglect and abuse on a child's development depends on various factors, such as the child's personality, resilience, protective factors, and available support networks. While it's an individual assessment, it can generally be stated that the earlier it happens and the more severe the neglect and abuse, the more damage is caused (Kvello, 2020; Perry & Winfrey, 2022; Struik, 2019). However, many parents have also turned these intergenerational traumas around through their determination to provide their children with everything they didn't get themselves and are succeeding in doing so, and we must always be aware of this and acknowledge it. These aspects will be investigated in more depth later.

Neglect

Collective and intergenerational trauma is particularly relevant in terms of parenting skills and the potential related threats to a child's healthy development and well-being. When family patterns are shaped by dysfunctional bonds or abusive dynamics resulting from unresolved past traumas, neglect and abuse can occur (Hübl, 2020; Kvello, 2020). The experience of neglect and abuse significantly influences the inherited family patterns parents carry from their own childhood. This might cause mental health issues, nervous system reactions, abusive behaviour, or a lack of parenting skills such as attunement and mentalising abilities not learned from their parents (Kvello, 2020; Siegel, 2020; Van der Kolk, 2015).

Chapter 3 described various aspects of abuse and high-risk neglect during infancy, and now neglect will be explored in more detail. Neglect relates to the emotional and physical attention and actions that children don't receive from their parents and that are essential to their health, development, and well-being. Neglect is divided into three main types: inadequate care, inadequate protection from danger, and inadequate, inappropriate, or damaging stimulation of the child (Kvello, 2020, p. 255). The main reasons for neglect include parents' own childhood experiences, a lack of social support networks, and parents' personality traits, including their coping strategies and mental health issues. Research has shown that many neglectful parents have psychiatric diagnoses, with personality disorders being the most common (Kvello, 2020). Interestingly, personality disorders were frequently diagnosed among individuals who were victims of childhood trauma before the recognition of complex PTSD. The introduction of this new diagnosis holds the potential to facilitate proper treatment for parents and children caught in the painful patterns of intergenerational trauma, allowing healing instead of repetition of these patterns.

Recognising the impact of the parents' trauma and diagnosis on their parenting abilities is crucial when assessing the balanced risk for children's safety, development, and well-being. This is not to suggest that parents with their own challenges will automatically neglect their children, but the risk is heightened, especially if they aren't consciously aware of the effects of their upbringing and its subsequent consequences for their development. If parents aren't ready to break the cycle of the family pattern resulting from their own experiences, the risk to children's well-being may increase.

Conversely, parents who are aware of their own traumas and who have received appropriate help and support to process and address them can approach parenting with a nuanced understanding and sensitivity towards children's needs. In such cases, this awareness can be considered a protective factor (Kvello, 2020). Assessing whether parents fall into either category for each child we work with enables us to provide appropriate assistance if needed or alleviates excessive concerns if everything is well.

By acknowledging the influence of parents' trauma and diagnosis on their parenting abilities, we can better support families in need and ensure the well-being of children within these contexts. This may involve providing accessible resources for parents to address their own trauma and the root causes of their problems and provide appropriate parenting education and support.

Case example: Victor

When Victor was 5 years old, he often attacked his mother violently, and in response – out of powerlessness – she would beat him, and so, for safety, they moved in with the grandparents.

This led to an intense safety planning and family therapy process lasting for 1 year owing to the severe trauma in the family. His mother had the best intentions and wanted to become a good and caring mother for Victor. Still, it turned out that Victor and his mother came close to dying during his birth, and his mother had postpartum depression afterwards, making the first months of their life together very difficult and traumatic. Through the years, ongoing difficulties in their relationship appeared, with aggression on the one side and clinginess and fear of separation in Victor's attachment to his mother on the other side. In their contact with each other, Victor became aggressive in his attempts to connect with his mother, and his mother shut down in her contact with Victor, overwhelmed by his aggression. It was like a vicious spiral, affecting each other's trauma and causing unintentional ongoing pain and harm.

Working around their trauma histories made it clear that the shutdown survival pattern the mother was experiencing came from her childhood trauma, caused by a violent father and other traumatic experiences within the family. First, when we went way back to the root of her own trauma history, this pattern started to change. She got agency to create the necessary lasting changes in Victor's care and her own empowerment, making her a safe adult for herself and her son. Step by step, she took back the power and healed her trauma through trauma therapy with one of my colleagues. Through her healing, things started to fall into place for Victor too. He also got trauma therapy to process his preverbal trauma from birth and the early life experiences of his mother's postpartum depression. This process made him more regulated and happier again, ending the circle of violence in the family from this generation onwards.

Attachment and authenticity

It's widely recognised that attachment styles and inner working models for relationships play a significant role in the transmission of intergenerational trauma. Our attachment to our parents and the quality of care we receive from them greatly influence the development of our attachment style, which in turn shapes how we interact with others and care for our own children (Perry & Szalavitz, 2007; Siegel, 2020; Van der Kolk, 2015). As most trauma happens in relationships between humans, and our biological family members are the ones closest to us and form our inner working model for relationships, there is this correlation between attachment and intergenerational trauma.

Attachment is considered a fundamental and non-negotiable need, along with basic physical needs and the need for authenticity (Maté, 2021). It involves the connection and bonding between a child and their caregivers, which are crucial for the child's survival in a world where they are dependent on the care and protection provided by adults. Infants have a built-in attachment system that prompts them to seek and maintain contact with their caregivers to ensure their safety (Struik, 2019). This attachment behaviour can be observed in cues such as smiles, cries, reaching out, and seeking eye contact.

Bonding between parent and child, facilitated by the production of endorphins in infants and the release of oxytocin and vasopressin hormones in parents, supports the establishment of a secure attachment (Szalavitz & Perry, 2010). This secure attachment is the foundation for the child's further development and overall well-being, and the quality of care provided by parents is a primary determinant of the child's attachment style. Bowlby's attachment theory was further expanded upon by Mary Ainsworth, who identified the three attachment styles: secure, avoidant, and resistant/ambivalent. Main and Solomon later added a fourth one called disorganised attachment (Siegel, 2020; Van der Kolk, 2015).

Mary Ainsworth's research highlighted the importance of sensitive caregiving behaviour in promoting secure attachment. Mothers who displayed sensitivity by attuning to their infants' signals, appropriately interpreting them, responding to them, and reacting promptly without causing excessive frustration were likelier to have infants with secure attachment styles. The caregiving a child receives forms their expectations and internal working models of human interaction, which can persist throughout life (Brandon et al., 2009).

Early years, particularly infancy, are critical for establishing a secure attachment and a safe representation of relationships. However, the work of creating a safe attachment continues to be important throughout a child's life, benefiting their resilience, mental health, and ability to provide appropriate care to their own children when they become parents (Perry & Szalavitz, 2007; Siegel, 2020; Van der Kolk, 2015). It's important to note that, while attachment styles and intergenerational trauma are closely related, they aren't deterministic. With self-awareness, healing, support, and therapeutic interventions, individuals can work to overcome the effects of intergenerational trauma and develop secure attachment styles. The different attachment styles and prenatal attachment are described in more depth briefly.

Attachment versus authenticity

Authenticity "means to be connected to ourselves and to know what we feel and act on it. In other words, it means our gut feelings" (Maté, 2021). The recognition of this paramount survival need, alongside the critical need for attachment, sheds light on the complex interplay between a child's innate instincts and its relational experiences. While, in the past, trusting our gut feelings was vital for survival in the natural world, in modern society, expressing our authentic selves can sometimes jeopardise our attachment relationships and become a source of stress (Maté, 2019). For children, this occurs when they reveal emotions or aspects of their identity that are met with rejection or criticism from the parents, who may themselves struggle with emotional difficulties. When this happens, the child will learn to suppress or hide certain aspects of themselves to stay attached to their parents, because they won't be able to survive without them, and this adaptive strategy allows them to maintain a sense of control and agency within the attachment relationship.

Thus, attachment wins over authenticity every time, which is very beneficial for the child's survival but comes at the cost of loss of essential parts of their self and damages their personal development (Maté, 2021). It leads to disconnection from essential parts of their authentic self, causing them to lose contact with their core being and making it difficult for them to show up in the world as their authentic self, which then leaves them more disconnected from others and the world.

This process also gives rise to a deep-rooted, core belief within the child that something is inherently wrong with them, fuelling a pervasive sense of toxic shame coming from the negative cognitions "I am wrong" or "I am bad". Toxic shame is at the core of developmental trauma (Heller and Lapierre, 2014), but, paradoxically, from a protective standpoint, it's less threatening for children to internalise the belief that they are wrong instead of their parents being wrong. This is because they depend on their parents for survival, and it would be too scary to realise they are cared for by adults who can't provide the appropriate care and safety. Also, it's out of the child's control to change the parents; instead, they can try to fix the situation by adapting their behaviour and changing themself, which helps them stay attached and maintain self-agency and control around the situation. Seen from this perspective, it makes perfect sense. However, it still leaves the child with a disrupted image of reality and harmful negative cognitions about themself that cultivate toxic shame inside. As we saw in Chapter 4, this distorted self-perception and toxic shame form the foundation of developmental trauma and leave children with a disturbed view of the world, their sense of self, and their ability to form healthy relationships.

These are some of the dynamics that cause intergenerational trauma to be transferred from one generation to another, and it's imperative that professionals working with children and parents be aware of these dynamics to address this effectively.

Case example: Michella – continued

During one of Michella's trauma release sessions after a long time with minimal progression, I asked her what was holding her back from healing. Investigating this question curiously, it became apparent that she still didn't acknowledge how severe the neglect, physical abuse, and other traumatic incidents in her upbringing were. What blocked her was her fear of letting go of the belief that she was bad and something serious was wrong with her. She couldn't make that cognitive shift to say, "It was not my fault" or "I am okay as I am", because it would be putting the responsibility back on her parents instead of on her shoulders. Her need for attachment was critical as a child, and dismissing her authenticity helped her survive, but now it was almost killing her through her suicidal and self-harming behaviour. Her resistance to acknowledging the cause of her suffering and trauma turned out to be the block that wouldn't allow her to move forward towards healing. It helped to look at it through the lens of intergenerational trauma, acknowledging that her parents didn't mean to harm her and they did the best they could with what they knew. Slowly, she started to take in the new perception of things moving towards ending a vicious circle running in their family of family members not being allowed to feel, show, and express emotion at all, leaving them depressed and suicidal instead. This is one aspect of intergenerational trauma many families know.

Prenatal attachment and attachment styles

Prenatal attachment encompasses the emotional connection and relationship between the pregnant woman and her unborn child and between the co-parent and the fetus (Brandon et al., 2009), a relatively new concept that has gained attention in the fields of psychology, health, and neuroscience. Research in neuroscience suggests that the mother's nervous system can influence the developing fetus's nervous system during pregnancy (Coussons-Read, 2013). So, if the mother experiences unprocessed trauma, stress, or mental health issues, this can impact the fetus's nervous system, potentially producing stress hormones such as cortisol during a very vulnerable period of brain development.

The development of prenatal attachment evolves through different phases, with the level of attachment typically increasing during pregnancy and peaking towards the end. It involves cognitive, emotional, and behavioural components, particularly empathy, and the mental imagination of the unborn child is significant for the quality of prenatal attachment. It relates to the experience of love that will enhance the development of lasting emotional bonds between the mother and child during pregnancy and involves positive emotions towards the fetus such as warmth and happiness and behaviours such as talking or singing to the fetus or cuddling the stomach as if one was touching the baby (Brandon et al., 2009).

Prenatal attachment varies in intensity, ranging in a continuum from low to high. Low levels are linked to women with minimal or no awareness of their pregnancy until they give birth, and higher levels of prenatal attachment are associated with better child development outcomes. The higher the level of prenatal attachment, the better the child's development (Stenstrup & Højland, 2017). To prevent attachment issues and trauma, Bruce Perry advocates investment in community programmes with nurses, as one piece of research revealed a 50 per cent drop in substantiated reports of child abuse or neglect among families receiving nurse visits. Another study showed that, for every $1 spent on nurse visits, $6 could be saved in future welfare, health, and juvenile costs. One study found a 59 per cent reduction in arrests of teenagers whose mothers had home visits from nurses, compared with those who didn't (Szalavitz & Perry, 2010).

After birth, the attachment process progresses into an attachment style shaped by the child's quality of care in early childhood, as the child's early interactions and experiences with caregivers shape their internal working models of relationships. Attunement with the child and the ability to repair any ruptures in the caregiver–child relationship are crucial factors in the development of a secure attachment (Siegel, 2020; Van der Kolk, 2015). Professionals working with infants play a critical role in observing and assessing children's healthy development, looking for signs of secure or insecure attachment, because it's a critical time in children's development, and damage arising from a lack of care and inadequate attunement is serious.

Therefore, risk assessment for an infant includes observation of the baby smiling, connecting with its parents and you, reaching out for contact, crying for help, being comforted when getting the needed help, and similar healthy signs. The signs of risk are when babies withdraw into their own world and don't expect any contact with their surroundings, maybe even sleeping too much for an infant. They also include signs of being passive and lack of connection with or affection for the parents, such as not smiling, not interacting with others, not reaching out or crying for help, or not allowing comfort when upset. When these signs are observed and the child doesn't suffer from any physical issues, you should be extremely worried and act according to your rules and regulations for high-risk cases or contact child protection for it to do so.

Attachment styles evolve through childhood and adolescence, shaped by various relationships and contexts. If a child's caregiving environment undergoes significant changes from, for example, family therapy or other therapeutic interventions, it's possible to shift from an insecure attachment style to a secure one (Siegel, 2020). The quality of attachment and attachment style becomes more apparent in moderately stressful situations, where the child's responses, expectations, and beliefs about others are observable. A child's attachment is assessed through observation and descriptions of the responses in situations where the child is stressed; this is only done by specialists qualified to determine it. In one study of 2,000 infants in middle-class environments, 62 per cent were securely attached, 15 per cent were avoidant, 9 per cent were anxious, and 15 per cent were disorganised (Van der Kolk, 2015, p. 119).

Securely attached children are open and explorative, seek and provide support, and know the difference between situations they can control and where they need help. They learn to regulate their emotions, tolerate high-intensity emotional states, demonstrate resilience and good mentalisation skills, and learn what is good and bad for them. They are good at balancing closeness and distance and demonstrate independence, getting sad when their parents leave but engaging in other relationships and play shortly after. They function well in a community and will also provide support for others in need (Kvello, 2020; Siegel, 2020; Van der Kolk, 2015).

Avoidant children hide their distress and avoid seeking comfort or support; they self-manage their care as they don't rely on getting care from adults. They experience a high level of disconnection from themselves and others and are passive and withdrawn in relation to their parents. They learn to minimise their emotional expression by suppressing their emotions and not dealing with them, because they are too overwhelming to cope with. These children don't cry when their mother leaves and will not react when she returns. In general, they appear to be better off than they are, but research shows that they have chronically increased heart rates, showing a constant hyperaroused state (Kvello, 2020; Siegel, 2020; Van der Kolk, 2015).

Ambivalent children fear not receiving sufficient attention and care, leading them to display attention-seeking behaviours such as clinging, crying, yelling, and screaming, and their level of arousal can fluctuate uncontrollably. They fear separation, become highly distressed when their mothers leave them, and are difficult to comfort when they return. They seek closeness and intimacy and are open in their contact with other people, even to the point of being uncritical. Guilt might be used to maintain relationships and fulfil their needs because expressing their needs proves difficult. Being anxious about rejection might lead them to reject the other person first, or they might appear attention-demanding, dominant, and self-centred, trying to enforce the care and attention they need (Kvello, 2020; Siegel, 2020; Van der Kolk, 2015).

Disorganised attachment is prevalent among children exposed to substance abuse, violence, abuse, and mental illness in their households and accounts for up to 50–80 per cent of the children in contact with social services and child psychiatry. Their attachment is rooted in terror, and they exhibit disorganised behaviour owing to a conflictual nervous system response, applying the accelerator and brake at the same time, followed by elevated stress levels and the development of a range of psychiatric problems. In their contact with others, they might show emotion and cry but, owing to fear, avoid seeking help or even reject comfort. Instead, they might go off to cry alone and comfort themselves. They can freeze, send mixed signals, and show fearful, provoking, violent, or abusive behaviour, and sometimes they might intentionally provoke a violent response to their behaviour to have a sense of control over and predictability of when harm will happen to them (Kvello, 2020; Siegel, 2020; Van der Kolk, 2015).

Clear boundaries and safe communication within the child's environment are essential for children's healthy development, and I return to this topic in Chapter 8. However, in relation to attachment, it's worth noting that parents who have not learned healthy boundary-setting and emotional regulation from their upbringing may struggle in these areas. Boundaries may be too weak or too rigid, and emotional reactions can be excessive or inadequate, leading to unpredictability and a sense of insecurity in the child about what to expect from their parents on a day-to-day basis. Mentalisation, the ability to understand one's own and others' mental states, is a critical component of both prenatal attachment and attachment after birth. Parents who can engage in mentalisation provide a solid foundation for their attachment to and care of their child.

Parenting and mentalisation

Mentalisation is crucial to parenting and the foundation of good and sufficient care for a child as it helps create a secure and nurturing environment for the child's development. The parent's ability to mentalise correlates with understanding and interpreting the child's inner world, including their thoughts, emotions, and mental states, creating "a map of the mind of the other", as Daniel Siegel describes it (Siegel, 2020, p. 317). This aligns with the concept of mirroring the child's experiences and becoming attuned to their emotional and psychological needs. Also, it fosters authentic intimacy and healthy interactions based on understanding the child's true self and recognising and acknowledging their strengths, weaknesses, and needs, separate from the parent's own needs (Kvello, 2020).

According to Kvello, mentalisation involves three key elements. First, it recognises one's own psychological experiences from an introspective perspective, being attentive to and mindful of what is happening on the inside. Second, it involves adopting an observer's standpoint to gain a meta-perspective and understand one's own experiences from an outside perspective. Lastly, mentalisation encompasses the ability to see others through a similar introspective lens, trying to understand their experiences from an empathic and internal perspective, and to see oneself "from the outside" and others "from the inside" (Kvello, 2020, p. 87). It's a curious exploration and reflection of one's own intentions and actions and those of others, promoting self-insight, respect, and understanding for others (Kvello, 2020; Struik, 2019).

Parents skilled in mentalisation can see and understand their children for who they truly are rather than projecting their desires and ideas on to them. They recognise their children as unique, with individual needs, and can describe them holistically, open-mindedly, and positively, displaying warmth, coherence, and genuine interest. They can articulate and validate their children's internal experiences and support their children in reflecting on others' perspectives (Kvello, 2020). For children to be good at mentalisation, they must learn from people who have strong mentalisation skills, and parents with such skills are often associated with secure attachment styles in both parents and children, profoundly influencing the intergenerational heritage (Struik, 2019).

Various factors can influence a person's capacity for mentalisation, including their attachment style, personality traits such as IQ and language skills, mental health conditions, substance abuse, and the quality of care they have received (Kvello, 2020). It's important to consider these factors when assessing an individual's mentalisation capabilities. Additionally, individuals with good mentalisation skills may experience limitations during times of high stress, which can impact their ability to engage in mentalising. Stressful situations can temporarily reduce mentalisation capacities, as the neocortex shuts down, and being outside their "windows of tolerance" hinders a person's ability to mentalise. This should also be considered when assessing parents' mentalisation capabilities.

Often, I have seen people described as having difficulties in mentalisation, but, when they feel safe with professionals and become more relaxed, they show more skills because their nervous system is better regulated. As professionals working with individuals and families, when we bring the parent's abilities to the centre of attention to create change, it's important to create a safe and supportive context that allows an individual to show their true self and accurately assess their mentalisation abilities, other parenting skills, and their ability to learn new skills, rather than evaluating them solely on their survival state. One aspect of this is remembering to acknowledge that they do the best they can, to the best of their abilities, and, inside them, there might also be histories of traumatised children who need to be seen, heard, and understood for who they truly are. With the right help and the trauma-informed and solution-focused mindset, I have seen countless people rise to the occasion and do what it takes to learn and develop the skills needed to become good enough parents for their own children.

Co-dependency runs over generations

Parents bear the responsibility of establishing a nurturing family environment where all members can thrive and develop healthily. However, in many families, children are assigned specific roles within family patterns and dynamics, placing a significant responsibility on their shoulders for the family's overall well-being. This burden is far too great for a child to bear, as they lack the understanding and capacity to address and resolve complex family issues. This is particularly evident in families affected by alcohol and drug abuse, high levels of conflict, mental illness, and trauma. Intergenerationally, one such pattern is the interplay between dependency and co-dependency, which manifests in different behaviour and roles that enable the problematic behaviour and issues to continue over time.

Co-dependency manifests in various ways, but the core consists of performing tasks for a loved one that they can and should do for themselves (Hazelden Betty Ford Foundation, 2021), such as when one parent is overly dependent on the other or is dependent on the child to care for them and make them happy. Despite the intention behind co-dependent behaviour being to keep a balance in the family system, it leads to an imbalance in the family dynamics with some main characteristics such as self-sacrifice, a primary focus on others, a need for control that might fuel conflicts, and difficulties in recognising and expressing emotions (Bacon et al., 2020; Trembacz, 2002).

This can result in the child growing up with a sense of responsibility for the family's well-being, and they may struggle to prioritise their own needs, feelings, and boundaries. They may suppress their emotions and desires while constantly attending to the dysfunctional parent's needs to maintain control over their lives and strive for harmony within the family, often sacrificing their own well-being. They may struggle to express themselves, set boundaries, or assert their own needs and feelings. Feelings of worthlessness, shame, guilt, and anger may arise, and trust in others and self-trust can be significantly compromised. These children may become skilled at hiding the true nature of their family situation and engage in cover-up behaviours to protect the family's image (Bacon et al., 2020; Lindgaard, 2008; Trembacz, 2002). Consequently, they may be challenging to identify as they keep up appearances while internally suffering the consequences of a dysfunctional environment.

Co-dependent behaviours and dynamics experienced in childhood are most likely developed as an adapted child response to a life imprinted by uncertainty, unpredictability, neglect, and maybe even violent and abusive relationships and can have long-lasting effects continuing into adulthood (Berne, 1961). The patterns can potentially be passed down to the next generation when adults continuously use actions and behaviours developed as a child to survive a traumatic childhood. Healing and breaking these patterns require a comprehensive understanding of the underlying factors contributing to co-dependency, and interventions and support systems must address these underlying traumas, providing opportunities for healing and promoting healthy parenting skills and mental well-being.

Including different information in the balanced risk assessment

In conclusion, a child's healthy development is shaped by a wide range of factors, including genetic and environmental elements such as epigenetics, intergenerational and collective trauma, attachment and prenatal attachment, mental health, family patterns, and parenting skills. By understanding and addressing these factors, we can ensure that children have the best conditions to grow, develop, and heal if needed.

Now that we have covered various aspects of intergenerational trauma, collective trauma, and family patterns and their potential impact on children, applying this knowledge in the risk assessment of a particular child you are working with becomes crucial. This is done by being curious and open to investigating how a parent's own issues might impact children, or not, and whether it's risk behaviour or more a risk factor, a topic we will move on to in Chapter 6. These aspects must always be considered against how the child is functioning and thriving and what protective behaviours support the parents and children to prevent these influences from impacting the child.

The next step to assess all this, in a fully comprehensive risk assessment, is to concretise the parents' difficulties in detailed descriptions of actions and behaviours and how they impact the child, with definite signs showing that the child isn't thriving and developing in healthy ways.

Exercise

To adapt this to your specific context, you can replace or supplement information on the parents with information on other adults' and peers' behaviour of relevance to the child's challenges.

With the same child in mind from the exercises in Chapters 3 and 4,

1   Draw a straight line from one side to the other at the top of a separate piece of paper.
2   At the right-hand side of the paper, write a brief overview of the present symptoms of diagnosis/substance abuse the parents are suffering from.
3   Moving back along the line, list all the traumatic events and periods in the parents' life.
4   Describe in detail how these might have been influencing their parenting skills today and in the past, and how this might have impacted the child now and previously that you haven't already noted in the last exercise.

Look at the papers from your exercises in Chapters 3 and 4 and add more detailed descriptions of how the family patterns and parenting skills have been influenced by intergenerational trauma in this family. Lastly, note how the child has been influenced by this, in their health, development, and well-being, now and earlier.

With the additional information, assess the scale from 0 to 10, where 10 means the child is completely safe, you don't need to worry about them, and no help is needed; 0 is the opposite: the child is the most unsafe possible and must be secured immediately.

Where do you now assess this situation to be on this scale? Compare this assessment with the one you conducted in the last exercise and assess whether this potential difference requires action.

Also, be aware of questions that arise from going through this that you would like to know more about and make a list of them to ask everyone engaged with the child.

References

Bacon, Ingrid, McKay, Elizabeth, Reynolds, Frances, & McIntyre, Anne. (2020). The lived experience of codependency: an interpretative phenomenological analysis. *International Journal of Mental Health and Addiction, 18*, 754–771.

Berne, E. (1961). *Transactional Analysis in Psychotherapy.* Grove Press.

Brandon, Anna R., Wayne, S. P., Denton, H., Stringer, Allen, & Evans, H. M. (2009). A history of the theory of prenatal attachment. *Journal of Prenatal and Perinatal Psychology and Health, 23*(4).

Coussons-Read, M. E. (2013). Effects of prenatal stress on pregnancy and human development: mechanisms and pathways. *Obstetric Medicine, 6*(2), 52–57.

Dias, Brian G., & Ressler, Kerry J. (2014). Parental olfactory experience influences behavior and neural structure in subsequent generations. *Nature Neuroscience 17*, 89–96.

Mittendorfer-Rutz, Ellenor, Rasmussen, Finn, & Lange, Theis. (2012). A life-course study on effects of parental markers of morbidity and mortality on offspring's suicide attempt. *PLoS One, 7*(12).

Serpeloni, F., Radtke, K., de Assis, S. G., Henning, F., Nätt, D., & Elbert, T. (2017). Grandmaternal stress during pregnancy and DNA methylation of the third generation: an epigenome-wide association study. *Translational Psychiatry, 7*(8).

Hazelden Betty Ford Foundation. (2021). *The five most common trademarks of codependent and enabling relationships.* Hazelden Betty Ford Foundation. www.hazeldenbettyford.org

Heller, L., & Lapierre, A. (2014). *Udviklingstraumer* (Healing developmental trauma). (M. Chack, Trans.). Hans Reitzels Forlag.

Howard, S. (2021). A causal model of children's vicarious traumatization. *Journal of Child and Adolescent Trauma., 14*(4).

Hûbl, T. (2020). *Healing collective trauma.* Sounds True.

National Human Genome Research Institute. (2010). Why mouse matters. Author.

Kvello, Ø. (2020). *Børn i risiko* (C. Pietsch, Trans.). Samfundslitteratur.

Lindgaard, H. (2008). *Afhængighed og relationer – de pårørendes perspektiv.* J. & R. Frydenberg.

Hjort, Line, Rushiti, Feride, Wang, Shr-Jie, Fransquet, Peter, Krasniqi, Sebahate P., Çarkaxhiu, Selvi I., Arifaj, Dafina, Xhemaili, Vjosa Devaja, Salihu, Mimoza, Leku, Nazmie A., & Ryan, Joanne. (2021). Intergenerational effects of maternal post-traumatic stress disorder on offspring epigenetic patterns and cortisol levels. *Epigenomics, 13*(12), 967–980.

Maté, G. (2019). *When the body says no – the cost of hidden stress.* Vermillion, Penguin Random House.

Maté, G. (2021). How childhood trauma leads to addiction [video]. YouTube.

Moraes, Emanuela, & Ferreira, Anna Beatriz E. (2020). *Your destiny isn't your genes: learn basic concepts of epigenetics and their impact on your health and well-being* [e-book]. Self-published by Emanuela Moraes and Anna Beatriz E. Ferreira.

Perry, B. D., & Szalavitz, M. (2007). *The boy who was raised as a dog and other stories from a child psychiatrist's notebook: what traumatized children can teach us about loss, love, and healing.* Basic Books.

Perry, B. D., & Winfrey, Oprah. (2022). *What happened to you? Conversations on trauma, resilience and healing.* Bluebird.

Schickedanz, Adam, Halfon, Neal, Chung, Paul, & Sastry, Narayan. (2018). Parents' adverse childhood experiences and their children's behavioral health problems. *Pediatrics, 142*(2), 1–9. PMCID:PMC6317990

Siegel, D. J. (2020). *The developing mind* (3rd ed.). Guilford Press.

Stenstrup, Christina, & Højland, Anna-Katherine. (2017). Tilknytning, prænatal tilknytning og familiedannelse – en relationel proces. *Tidsskrift for jordemødre, 9.*

Struik, A. (2019). *Treating chronically traumatized children: the sleeping dogs method* (2nd ed.). Routledge.

Szalavitz, M., & Perry, B. D. (2010). *Born for love: why empathy is essential – and endangered* (1st ed.). William Morrow. Contributor biographical information www.loc.gov/catdir/enhancements/fy1011/2010280500-b.html: publisher description www.loc.gov/catdir/enhancements/fy1011/2010280500-d.html

Tobi, Elmar W., Slieker, Roderick C., Luijk, René, Dekkers, Koen F., Stein, Aryeh D., Xu, Kate M. Biobank-based Integrative Omics Studies Consortium, Slagboom, P. Eline, van Zwet, Erik W., Lumey, L. H., & Heijmans, Bastiaan T. (2018). DNA methylation as a mediator of the association between prenatal adversity and risk factors for metabolic disease in adulthood. *Science Advances, 4*(1).

Trembacz, B. (2002). Rusmiddelproblemer i et familieperspektiv – Alle kan være med til at forebygge alkoholproblemer. Copenhagen. trembacz.dk

UN Women. (2020). The shadow pandemic: violence against women during COVID-19. UN Women. www.unwomen.org/en/news/in-focus/in-focus-gender-equality-in-covid-19-response/violence-against-women-during-covid-19

Van der Kolk, B. A. (2015). *The body keeps the score: mind, brain and body in the transformation of trauma.* Wellbeing Collection, Penguin Books.

World Health Organization. (2022). COVID-19 pandemic triggers 25% increase in prevalence of anxiety and depression worldwide. www.who.int/news/item/02-03-2022-covid-19-pandemic-triggers-25-increase-in-prevalence-of-anxiety-and-depression-worldwide

Chapter 6

The Circle of Safety and Reconnection, Step 4

Assessing the ACEs and other
important risk factors in
the child's life

Understanding the nature of risk factors

Conducting a comprehensive risk assessment to find appropriate solutions for vulnerable and traumatised children involves considering both present risks and risk factors from a future perspective. Professionals must carefully balance acknowledging the potential long-term risks and not jumping to conclusions or misinterpreting facts and numbers. Research emphasises that assessing the long-term influence of risk factors is a complex process, highlighting the necessity to recognise that multiple factors influence children's lives. The presence of risk factors doesn't guarantee a specific outcome, making it impossible to predict precisely who will be influenced by these factors. However, it's possible to identify individuals who are at a higher risk of being impacted (Kvello, 2020; Perry & Winfrey, 2022).

Professionals working with children may become overly concerned about future risks through misinterpreting facts and numbers. For instance, assuming children of addicts will inevitably become addicts themselves is a false conclusion. Morten Ejrnæs's research illuminates this misconception by indicating that, if parents face problems, there is an 8 per cent chance the child will experience at least one problem. However, there is a significant – 92 per cent – chance that the child won't be affected by those problems (Ejrnæs et al., 2004).

In comparison, a child of parents with no problems whatsoever will have a 4 per cent risk of experiencing a minimum of one problem and a 96 per cent chance of not experiencing it. So, while children with struggling parents might face a 50 per cent higher risk than those without issues, it's essential to note that the overall percentages are minimal (Ejrnæs et al., 2004). Understanding statistics this way helps us not to overlook the impact of the resilience of children and adolescents and the importance of protective factors in a child's life, the topic of Chapter 7.

Protective factors in a child's life can mitigate the impact of risk factors, which makes assessing the interplay between the two pivotal in risk assessments. Recognising their complex interaction, an assessment shouldn't seek definitive answers but rather should reflect on protective factors and supports that may outweigh the short- and long-term risk factors. This assessment aims to inform interventions and

DOI: 10.4324/9781003322672-6

support for vulnerable children in the present while acknowledging the limitations of predicting long-term outcomes with certainty.

Rather than considering a 1:1 ratio, research has shown that we need to investigate the cumulation of risk factors to predict a significantly higher risk situation. The 1997 ACE study undertaken by Kaiser Permanente on adverse childhood experiences (ACEs) and their impact on adult health showed that each ACE heightened the risk of experiencing more problems. However, a significantly higher risk compared with others was more pronounced when individuals experienced four or more ACEs (Felitti et al., 1998). Øjvind Kvello, in his book *Børn i Risiko* from 2010 (Kvello, 2020), also highlights the importance of considering cumulative risk over individual risk factors. He stresses the importance of taking into consideration that the more severe they are and the earlier in a child's life they occur, the more damaging the impact on the child's health, development, and well-being.

The complexity of determining a child's risk extends beyond the accumulation of risk owing to all the information needed to be addressed and assessed. Three types of risk factors within a child's life must be considered: (1) the child's own condition, including developmental issues and illnesses requiring hospitalisation; (2) risk factors within the family and parental care; and (3) risk factors present in the child's communities, such as low-quality day care or schools and neighbourhoods with high levels of crime, substance abuse, or unemployment (Kvello, 2020). Moreover, societal challenges, such as unequal chances for social class mobility, education, and employment, have been identified as significant risk factors. Studies by Morten Ejrnæs and others, conducted in the United States, have highlighted the impact of societal factors on children's outcomes (Ejrnæs et al., 2004). This is to the extent that the premise for the American dream, "being born poor and making it to the top", no longer exists, making it obvious that changing social mobility can't be done solely on an individual level but needs to be supported by societal and systemic changes (Graham, 2017). Although beyond this book's scope, it's crucial to acknowledge this topic's relevance.

Generally, we possess much knowledge about factors potentially negatively influencing children's long-term health, development, and well-being. By using this knowledge wisely, professionals can assess the best possible ways to support children in the present moment based on their unique situations. This chapter will cover the risk factors that are the most important to highlight but can't offer a complete list of risk factors.

The ACE study and the impact of adverse childhood experiences

In the context of trauma-informed work with vulnerable children, it's crucial to highlight the concept of adverse childhood experiences and the groundbreaking 1997 ACE study in the United States. The study involved 17,000 middle-aged, middle-class, mainly white American citizens from Southern California with education and health insurance. Its primary objective was examining the long-term effects of traumatic childhood experiences on health, well-being, and behaviour (Felitti et al., 1998).

At Kaiser Permanente's San Diego Health Appraisal Clinic, the ACE study employed physical exams and confidential surveys to gather data. After completing the physical exams, informants completed surveys sharing childhood experiences, health status, and behaviours. The researchers focused on ten categories of severe traumatic experiences within areas of: (1) abuse, (2) neglect, and (3) dysfunctional living conditions. These categories encompassed various forms of abuse, neglect, and adverse family circumstances, including physical abuse, psychological abuse, sexual abuse, emotional neglect, lack of care for basic needs, parental divorce, violence against mothers, substance abuse, mental illness, and parental incarceration (Felitti et al., 1998).

Comparing this data with ten US risk factors contributing to morbidity and mortality (such as smoking, obesity, and alcoholism) and fatal diseases (such as ischaemic heart disease and cancer), the ACE study revealed a significant correlation between ACE occurrence and increased risks of behavioural, mental, emotional, and physical health challenges. Furthermore, it tied ACEs to shortened life expectancy. Kaiser Permanente's report concluded there was a strong graded relationship "between the breadth of exposure to abuse or household dysfunction during childhood and multiple risk factors associated with leading causes of death in adults" (Felitti et al., 1998, p. 245), underscoring childhood trauma's profound impact on long-term health.

The ACE study has gained significant recognition and is cited in over 1,500 subsequent studies. It's used as an assessment tool by the WHO and numerous US states to improve public health. Additionally, 36 US states have conducted their own studies on ACEs, further validating the original findings (Nakazawa, 2016).

Almost two-thirds of the respondents reported at least one ACE, and 87 per cent of those experienced multiple ACEs. Interestingly, while all ten ACEs were found to have a similar negative impact, the ACE related to parental humiliation had a slightly stronger impact on adult health and depression, and specific ACEs were found to correlate with different diseases (Nakazawa, 2016). For instance, parental divorce doubled the likelihood of suffering a stroke, losing a parent tripled the chance of depression in adulthood, and childhood emotional abuse was the strongest predictor of adult depression (Felitti et al., 1998; Nakazawa, 2016).

The study also demonstrated a direct relationship between the number of ACEs and risk, indicating increased risk for various health and social outcomes with each additional ACE. With four or more ACEs, individuals faced a significant risk of several conditions and behaviours, including smoking, obesity, substance abuse, depression, suicide attempts, lack of physical activity, unemployment, chronic lung disease, cancer, broken bones, heart attacks, and heart disease.

This highlights the interrelated nature of ACEs and their association with multiple health risks. In the original ACE study, approximately 12.5 per cent of the participants had an ACE score of four or more (Felitti et al., 1998; Nakazawa, 2016).

While this book can't encompass all ACE study findings, I encourage readers to explore the full online report for more information. However, it's crucial to recognise that these statistics underscore the significant challenges and vulnerabilities faced by those with multiple ACEs – for example, statistically, individuals with four or more ACEs were 1,220 per cent more likely to attempt suicide than those without ACEs (Nakazawa, 2016). Before going into more detail about the study, I want to share the questions the informants were asked about childhood experiences as a representation of risk factors. These ten closed, yes/no questions will allow you to calculate your ACE score by counting the "yes" responses. Maybe you are up to counting your own ACE score while going through it?

ACEs questions

Prior to your eighteenth birthday:

1   Did a parent or another adult in your household often or very often swear at you, insult you, put you down, humiliate you, or act in a way that made you afraid that you might be physically hurt?

Yes _____ No _____

2   Did a parent or another adult in your household often or very often push, grab, slap, or throw something at you, or ever hit you so hard that you had marks or were injured?

Yes _____ No _____

3   Did an adult or person at least 5 years older than you *ever* touch or fondle you, have you touch their body in a sexual way, or attempt to touch you or touched you inappropriately or sexually abuse you?

Yes _____ No _____

4   Did you *often* or *very often* feel that no one in your family loved you or thought you were important or special? Or did you feel that your family members didn't look out for one other, feel close to one another, or support one another?

Yes _____ No _____

5   Did you *often* or *very often* feel that you didn't have enough to eat, had to wear dirty clothes, or had no one to protect you, or that your parents were too drunk or high to take care of you or take you to the doctor if you needed it?

Yes _____ No _____

6   Was a biological parent *ever* lost to you through a divorce, abandonment, or another reason?

Yes _____ No _____

7   Was your mother or stepmother *often* or *very often* pushed, grabbed, or slapped or did she have something thrown at her? Or was she *sometimes, often,* or *very often* kicked, bitten, hit with a fist, or hit with something hard? Or was she *ever* repeatedly hit over the course of at least a few minutes or threatened with a gun or a knife?

Yes ____   No ____

8   Did you live with anyone who was a problem drinker or alcoholic or who used street drugs?

Yes ____   No ____

9   Was a household member depressed or mentally ill, or did a household member attempt suicide?

Yes ____   No ____

10 Did a household member go to prison?

Yes ____   No ____

Add up your "yes" scores: _____; this is your ACE score.

(The questionnaires aren't copyrighted, and there are no fees for their use. They are available at www.cdc.gov)

Since the original 1997 ACE study, researchers have conducted additional studies to expand our understanding of ACEs and their impact on individuals. One such study, conducted by Finkelhor, Shattuck, Turner, and Hamby in 2015, included four additional categories: bullying/peer victimisation, isolation/peer rejection, exposure to community violence, and low socioeconomic status. These additional categories aimed to capture evolving societal changes since the 1950s and 1960s, when the original ACE study participants were children. By incorporating these new categories, researchers hoped to gain a more comprehensive understanding of contemporary ACEs (Finkelhor et al., 2015; Nakazawa, 2016).

Recently, increasing interest in understanding the impact of childhood trauma on health has emerged. Researchers recognise the importance of exploring various forms of trauma and their influence on individuals' well-being and long-term outcomes. This growing body of research aims to deepen our knowledge and inform efforts to address and mitigate the effects of childhood trauma on individuals' health and overall quality of life. Similar studies to the above-mentioned have incorporated additional factors such as poverty, discrimination, and witnessing abuse of not only mothers but also siblings and fathers. These studies emphasise the significance of embracing a broader range of traumatic experiences in childhood (Nixon et al., 2017). Also, a childhood trauma questionnaire has been developed that demonstrates the strong scientific relationship between family dysfunction, brain development impairment, and the negative impact on health, including medical trauma.

This questionnaire also addresses the impact of bullying and exposure to violent communities (Liebschutz et al., 2018).

Returning to intergenerational trauma, discussed in Chapter 5, the ACE study provides insights into various related aspects such as epigenetics and collective and intergenerational trauma persisting across multiple generations. The single common denominator of all ACEs is that they are unpredictable and, rather than being ordinary, small challenges in childhood, they are scary, chronic, unpredictable stressors for children with no adult support to navigate safely through them (Nakazawa, 2016). Studies conducted on rats have demonstrated that unpredictable stressors have the most damaging impacts on brains. Rats tolerate more severe stressful events if they are predictable, whereas unpredictability induces traumatic experiences that alter the brain's architecture.

Chronic stress states release high levels of stress hormones, which influence genes and trigger an overactive inflammatory stress response. Consequently, children exposed to such conditions are predisposed to diseases as inflammation eventually manifests as symptoms and illnesses. For each ACE individual's experience, there is a 20 per cent increase in the risk of being hospitalised with an autoimmune disease in adulthood, and the higher the number of ACEs, the higher the number of doctor visits and unexplained symptoms, showing that the number of ACEs correlates with the number of doctor visits and the presence of unexplained symptoms. Individuals with an ACE score of 6 or higher have their lifespan shortened by almost 20 years (Nakazawa, 2016).

Scientists term this correlation between childhood trauma, brain architecture, and adult well-being the new psychobiological "theory of everything" (Nakazawa, 2016, p. 24). The theory's underlying principle is that "your emotional biography becomes your physical biology" (Nakazawa, 2016, p. 25), echoing the message conveyed by Bessel van der Kolk in his book *The Body Keeps the Score* (Van der Kolk, 2015). This theory recognises that diseases are multifunctional and result from various factors, not solely ACEs. Still, the ACE study reveals that even individuals who lead healthy lives, have good habits, aren't overweight or diabetic, and don't have high cholesterol, but have an ACE score of 7, still face a 360 per cent higher risk of heart disease compared with those without ACEs (Felitti et al., 1998; Nakazawa, 2016).

When investigating the numbers and implications of ACEs, it's essential to remember that the damage caused to health by these adverse experiences is reversible, as discussed in Chapter 5 concerning epigenetics. The brain's plasticity allows adaption and change, offering potential healing and recovery from the consequences of ACEs for vulnerable and traumatised children's brains and bodies. However, often these adverse conditions are concealed, which further isolates the child and intensifies feelings of shame and guilt because they don't have a safe space in which to express themselves, regulate their emotions, and correct any false assumptions or beliefs they may hold, such as feeling responsible or inherently bad.

Working with children's ACEs has significant pitfalls, and professionals working with these children must utilise this knowledge with caution and act in ways that prioritise their physical and emotional safety. Having direct conversations with children about ACEs might leave them vulnerable and caught in a loyalty bind about the risk of harming their parents or individuals close to them, particularly if disclosures of sexual abuse or violence are made. Hence, I never ask children and young people under 18 these sensitive questions directly, but I use the knowledge of ACEs to inform and enhance risk assessments, building on existing information in their files. Engaging parents in conversations about their own ACEs can provide insights into potential neurobiological inheritance within the family. The key is to use the knowledge of ACEs to inform and guide interventions that promote healing and well-being while minimising the risk of re-traumatisation or further harm.

Case examples: Victor and Michella

At the beginning of my safety planning process with Victor, I used my knowledge about ACEs to determine the best intervention for him after safety had been established. I counted Victor's ACEs score to be 5 (questions 1, 2, 4, 6, and 9), with severe preverbal trauma, including the loss of his father, being a continuous stressor to him. From this, I assessed a need to work more directly with processing his trauma with EMDR trauma therapy to ensure that he wasn't carrying these pre-language traumatic events forward, unprocessed, in his nervous system. So, after the safety plan had been developed, tested, and adjusted, and his mother's trauma treatment had been completed, he also had his trauma processed with the help of an EMDR therapist colleague.

Another way to use an ACEs score was to help Michella (23 years old) understand why she had developmental trauma symptoms. You might recall from Chapter 5 her struggle to acknowledge her traumatic upbringing. As she counted 5 ACEs, it helped her understand that her upbringing wasn't as good and normal as she recalled it, and she also got an understanding of why she didn't remember much at all.

Consideration of other risk factors present in a child's life

Additional significant risk factors within a child's family and local community beyond those already discussed can profoundly affect children's well-being and development. These factors relate to the individual child and their respective country's structural conditions. Societal factors such as discrimination, poverty, increasing inequality gaps in various countries, and others significantly influence children's lives and opportunities.

According to Bruce Perry, marginalised individuals, including those discriminated against because of gender, race, sexual orientation, and so on, experience trauma owing to their exclusion from society. This leads to prolonged and uncontrollable stress, gradually sensitising individuals and evolving into a significant risk factor to be considered when we work with vulnerable and traumatised children, youth, and their families (Perry & Winfrey, 2022).

While a transformation of the overall living conditions of these children might be beyond reach, it's crucial to recognise and address systemic issues and their impact on the well-being of children and their families and reflect on how we can mitigate the negative effects of these risks. By understanding and acknowledging these broader societal factors, professionals can work towards creating supportive environments, advocating for change, and providing resources and interventions that help mitigate the impact of these risks on children's lives. Even small actions might make a difference for each individual child.

Inequality in wealth and possibilities

The inequality gap is rising within and between countries, where some get wealthier while many get poorer, with unequal possibilities of moving between social classes and climbing the social economic ladder, also known as social mobility (OECD, 2022). Social mobility refers to individuals' ability to move between different social classes based on their hard work, skills, and resources (OECD, 2022). It's linked to equality of opportunity and is often associated with the "American dream". Historically, social mobility implied that anyone could achieve success and prosperity through personal endeavours, regardless of their starting point, and everyone should have a fair start in life and then create the best possible outcome for themselves. Some succeeded, while others didn't, and this was up to the individual (Rank & Eppard, 2021).

However, research shows that social mobility and equality are decreasing in some of the world's most developed countries. This means that individuals are more likely to remain in the social class they were born into, and the opportunities for upward mobility are diminishing (OECD, 2022). Inequality levels and their consequences vary significantly across countries. In welfare countries such as Denmark, there is a strong emphasis on equality and equal opportunities, whereas, in countries such as India, inequality in both wealth and opportunities is more prevalent. As a result, the extent of the risk that children will face poverty and inequality consequences differs widely from country to country, but, generally, the impact of poverty and inequality on children's health, development, and well-being is substantial (Christiansen et al., 2021).

Recent analysis, such as the one conducted by Egmont Fonden in Denmark, highlights the negative impact of low-income households on children's well-being, education, and social participation. This research investigated "relative poverty", defined as having a disposable income of less than half of the median income of the overall population (Christiansen et al., 2021). Children from low-income families often face poorer conditions in terms of well-being, education, social activities, and access to essential resources such as digital devices for online socialisation. These challenges can lead to isolation, deprivation, and hindered learning abilities, ultimately affecting their future prospects. Financial poverty independently influences children's outcomes, as they may achieve lower test scores, reduced educational attainment, and limited advancement to higher education levels. Despite parents' attempts to protect their children from concerns, the burden of financial worries about the family situation and the limitations it imposes on the family can profoundly impact children's well-being and academic performance (Christiansen et al., 2021).

Numerous global studies have consistently demonstrated that living in poverty poses a risk to children's well-being and development. Professor Robert Putnam, a renowned expert in this field, carried out research for his book *Our Kids* and found similar outcomes, demonstrating that even academically talented children from lower-income backgrounds have fewer opportunities to graduate from college compared with wealthier peers. His research also shows that, as mentioned above, the American dream is becoming increasingly out of reach for children from lower-income households (Putnam, 2016).

Children raised in poverty often encounter isolation and deprivation in various aspects of their lives, including limited community connections and participation in extracurricular activities and social institutions. Regardless of race or ethnicity, isolation from family, school, church, neighbours, peers, and other social interactions has become common for children from low-income backgrounds (Christiansen et al., 2021; Putnam, 2016).

The Danish poverty report's findings echo my personal experiences with vulnerable families I have worked with. It's crucial for professionals engaging with such families to be aware of these challenges and consider how we can support them in breaking the isolation cycle. We can encourage their striving to succeed in school, foster positive relationships, and help them identify and pursue opportunities that may not be immediately visible to them or their parents. While we can't provide financial resources directly, we can still empower children and families by teaching them skills, building their resilience, and guiding them towards avenues that enhance their chances and possibilities in life.

Inequality in communities, schools, and day care

In addition to violence in communities now being considered an ACE, other aspects of the community can also be considered risk factors for children and young people. Communities characterised by low income, high crime rates, and substance abuse pose risks to children's well-being and development (Kvello, 2020). Such areas often suffer from limited resources in day-care centres and schools, adding another identified risk factor to a child's life. High rates of sick leave, staff turnover, lack of structure, and limited teacher–student interaction within these educational settings can further contribute to challenges faced by children (Kvello, 2020).

Quality contact and interactions in day-care centres and schools are crucial for the healthy development of children in modern society. Reduced opportunities for meaningful relational interactions beyond these settings, such as decreased time with extended family and friends and increased screen time, have caused children and young people to rely more on structured environments for social engagement (Perry & Winfrey, 2022). Bruce Perry addresses the issue of relational poverty in modern society. Several societal trends contribute to this relational poverty, including a decrease in the number of people living together in the same household, fewer adults available to care for children in day care and schools, a decline in the number of trusted confidants, an increase in screen time to about 11 hours daily across home, school and work, and a decrease in outdoor play and unstructured playtime (Perry & Winfrey, 2022; Szalavitz & Perry, 2010).

According to Bruce Perry, in ancient hunting/gathering clans, four adults were dedicated to shaping, nurturing, nourishing, and guiding each child under the age of 6. In today's world, a ratio of one adult to four children is considered a decent standard, but it falls significantly short of providing the level of social interaction our developing brains require. For children growing up in single-parent households, with multiple children and the parent working long hours, the adults in daycare centres and schools often become the primary caregivers and are influential figures during the day.

The reliance on adult figures in these settings leaves them extra vulnerable to inadequate-quality day care and schooling, adding to their experience of relational poverty, and thus becomes a significant risk factor. In contrast, good-quality daycare centres and schools serve as protective factors for children, fostering their healthy development and well-being. This will be covered in the next chapter.

The consequences of this relational poverty are significant, particularly in terms of brain development, because "belonging is biology" (Perry & Winfrey, 2022, p. 137), and "Poverty of relationship can disrupt normal development, influence how the brain works, put you at risk for physical and mental health problems and it's absolutely not good for you" (Perry & Winfrey, 2022, p. 266). Studies have shown that college-age adults today exhibit 30 per cent less empathy and increased self-absorption compared with those from two decades ago. Additionally, there has been a documented 40 per cent increase in psychopathology among American college students over the last 30 years (Perry & Winfrey, 2022, p. 260). These trends aren't limited to a specific country or region. In Denmark too, an alarming increase in the number of children entering the psychiatric system has been registered, leading to long waiting lists and system breakdowns owing to high demand. These findings highlight the urgent need to take research seriously and address our interactions with each other relationally and culturally in modern society.

These risk factors can significantly impact traumatised and vulnerable children, as their trauma symptoms or diagnoses potentially affect their behaviour at school, leading to the possibility of rejection and punishment by peers and teachers. This can create a vicious cycle of further traumatisation and vulnerability (Van der Kolk, 2015). For instance, 10-year-old children with ADHD are likely to hear 20,000 more negative messages than their peers in school (Jellinek, 2010), and research suggests that they are more sensitive to criticism, which can have a greater impact on their health, development, and well-being (Furukawa et al., 2017).

Professor Bo Vinnerljung's research at Stockholm University, based on numerous international studies of children in foster care and their education, reveals that these children generally face more difficulties in school compared with other children. They frequently exhibit weaker academic performance, lower grades relative to equally intelligent peers, and an elevated likelihood of not pursuing higher education, getting unskilled work instead. If they pursue higher education, premature dropouts are common. These challenges are attributed to the instability in their upbringing, lack of expectations from teachers and caregivers, and a higher prevalence of additional problems such as poor working memory (Vinnerljung, 2010). Consequently, these factors pose a highly significant risk for outcomes such as suicide, suicide attempts, mental illness, substance abuse, alcohol abuse, involvement in serious crime, teenage parenthood, and unemployment. Vinnerljung emphasises that school failure consistently correlates with negative outcomes, while the absence of school failure correlates with positive outcomes. Thus, children who struggle academically become a high-risk group, irrespective of their socioeconomic background (Vinnerljung et al., 2010).

Children in care doing well at school have 0 per cent of all of the risks mentioned above, but only 39 per cent of the boys and 44 per cent of the girls did well compared with the standard group, where 81–83 per cent did well. Still, this factor can be influenced. Bo Vinnerljung advocates that it's crucial to identify and support children in foster care at the start of their educational journey, providing appropriate guidance and interventions based on assessments to reduce the number of children experiencing academic difficulties in their early years of education. Addressing school failure can mitigate future risks and improve outcomes for these vulnerable children and also for other children (Vinnerljung et al., 2010; Vinnerljung, 2010).

Risks arising from climate change and war

The increasing risks from climate change and conflicts around the world have resulted in a rising number of forcibly displaced people worldwide, including refugees, asylum-seekers, and internally displaced people. The figures have been steadily increasing, with an estimated 103 million forcibly displaced people in mid 2022, of which 36.5 million were children (UCHR, 2023).

In November 2011, I attended a social workers' conference where renowned social work author and academic Malcolm Payne presented his work. He prophesied that climate change and the growing refugee population would significantly impact future social work, prompting a shift towards crisis management and mitigation in times of emergencies and catastrophes (Nørum, 2011). Since the European refugee crisis began in 2015, this prediction has become a reality. Professionals in various contexts now increasingly support refugees, including children and adolescents, who face immediate danger during their flight and subsequently require assistance settling and starting a new life in a foreign country. These individuals carry the burden of hardship, loss, and potentially traumatic experiences.

Some children arrive with family members or kin, while others come alone. All are vulnerable, with no or only a few safe connections, no access to a network, little or no ability to communicate in the native language of their new country, and a lack of understanding of its culture, norms, and daily life. All of these expose them to inequality compared with the children surrounding them. Yet, they are also resilient beings who have conquered great challenges. We must never underestimate the strength, resources, skills, and willpower it takes to survive such an extreme and dangerous situation as refugees have mastered.

Since 2015, there has been an increasing demand for knowledge on how to work in a trauma-informed way with refugees in different professional contexts. In several cases, I have facilitated other professionals' creating a words and pictures process, as described in Chapter 10, with the parents of refugee children and adolescents. The words and pictures explanations I have heard presented to these children by their parents or relatives are some of the most empowering and healing stories I have ever heard and seen. One story literally made my eyes tear up when one of the other professionals read it to me for the first time.

The stories are different variations of what their life back home looked like and their experiences throughout the flight, but also powerful stories about how the adults have protected them all the way, making them feel loved and protected in this unsafe situation. The stories also explain things that happened in Denmark after they arrived here and finish with a hopeful perspective on their lives in Denmark. This has instantly helped the children's well-being, but it has also changed the parents' and relatives' perspective on themselves, as they have become empowered by the feelings of pride and strength with which they have connected during the process of making the words and pictures for the children. Also, it has helped them to really understand that the flight is over, and they survived it, enabling them to transform some of the stress energy in their nervous system and become calmer and more regulated, which is one of the intentions behind facilitating such processes.

Individual risk factors

Individual risk factors relating to a child can vary greatly and significantly impact their overall well-being. One such risk factor is the disease or death of a parent, which can have profound emotional and psychological effects, and recent research has shown that it leaves them at a higher risk of suicidal behaviour (Guldin et al., 2015). Other individual factors are broken relationships with close individuals, being taken into care, being born premature, being exposed to severe and prolonged bullying for at least 1 year, and having a diagnosis of a physical or mental health condition (Kvello, 2020).

Personal traits such as shyness or introversion can also be considered risk factors. Intelligence can play a role as either a risk or a protection in a child's life. Research suggests an inequality created by differences in intelligence, where people with low IQ live shorter lives, while a high childhood IQ can indicate potential academic success and greater educational opportunities, positively influencing future outcomes (Lund, 2023). However, high intelligence can also become a risk factor, leading to mental challenges (Franck, 2021). Sometimes, a child's intellect exceeds their emotional maturity, causing difficulties in understanding and navigating their emotions. Their social life might also be challenging because, compared with other children, they don't have many peers to be mirrored by. This mismatch can result in the child feeling unseen, misunderstood, and lacking appropriate emotional support and can cause a great disturbance, as turned out to be the case for Michella. During Michella's trauma treatment, her high intelligence became evident. Unfortunately, it left her – as a child and adolescent – with no sense of meaning and a feeling of disconnection from others, a feeling that she was always wrong as she couldn't make sense of the world as others did. This caused disturbance within herself and others. With understanding and acknowledgement of this, we worked on reconnecting her to a sense of meaning in life to see if it could lead to another way of being in the world.

Assessing and predicting the cumulative risk for a child and understanding how these factors may interact and impact the child's development over time form a complex task. It requires careful consideration of various risk and protective factors and recognition of their potential interplay and the extent to which the protective factors in a child's life can counterbalance the risks they may face. Thus, a comprehensive assessment should encompass both risk and protective factors and a mindful and reflective awareness of potential actions that can be taken in the present moment to positively impact the child's long-term well-being and prevent the development of further issues. The next chapter will investigate the protective factors and positive childhood experiences in more depth to qualify these reflections.

Worry statements and trauma-informed worry statements

After risk behaviour, risk factors, and their potential impact on the child's health, development, and well-being have been investigated, the overall information on the worries part of the risk assessment is now clear and precise. Thus, you are now able to formulate precisely what describes the parents' difficulties, how they impact the child, and what the risk might be for the child in the long run if nothing changes. From my training in signs of safety by Andrew Turnell, I learned a helpful tool to clarify this, called danger statements (Turnell, 2010). Sonja Parker calls them worry statements, and, as I like the term worry statement better than danger statement, I will continue using this throughout the rest of the book (Parker, 2015).

This tool was designed to communicate transparently child protection concerns to all stakeholders involved with the child. Worry statements comprise precise and detailed descriptions of the information available for child protection offices to assess the current situation and use professional expertise to predict what future harm it might cause to a child if nothing happened (Turnell & Parker, 2009). This is written in simple language that children and adults can understand, leaving out all professional vocabulary and terms. This little task is complicated because professionals often use professional terms without considering whether children, parents, and private networks need help to understand them. Also, we need to be very clear about the actual risk for a child, keeping close to the factual situation and the knowledge we have about these particular risk factors. The statements are formed from answers to four essential questions (Turnell & Parker, 2009): (1) Which people are worried? (2) What are the parents doing or not doing in the care of the child that they are worried about? (3) What is the impact on the child's health, development, and well-being? And (4) what are they worried might happen in the future, if nothing else changed?

In 2014, Sonja Parker and Arianne Struik introduced the concept of "trauma-informed safety planning" during a training session in Copenhagen. Through this, Sonja introduced me to what she called trauma-informed worry statements. They are based on actual safety issues and worry statements based on previous traumatic events the child has been exposed to that might impact the child's health, development, and well-being in the long term if they don't have their trauma processed (Parker & Struik, 2017). Thus, the trauma-informed worry statements describe the actual worries of children and, using a trauma lens, also explain how they could impact them neurobiologically and psychologically, now and in the future, if they can't process the traumatic events.

In a trauma-informed manner, Sonja Parker not only describes the worries arising from the parents' current care, but also considers harm that happened to the child in the past that might disturb them in the future if they don't have the chance to heal it. She also takes into consideration the child's risk of being re-traumatised and of being traumatised by the child protection services and their interventions, which sometimes – unintentionally – end up being a risk to the child instead of the help they are supposed to be, which we will investigate a bit further in the following chapter (Parker & Struik, 2017).

Case example: Alma's worry statement and trauma-informed worry statement

To illustrate how it works, I will show one worry statement and one trauma-informed worry statement concerning a girl named Alma, with whom I was working some years ago. I was working with her at her mother's and father's places to see if I could create a full-circle safety plan for her in both her parents' homes. Since Alma was her parents' only child together, and her mother had her siblings with her former partner, I made separate ones for Alma and for her siblings, because their situations were different. I have chosen to show one worry statement for worries concerning her father's home and one trauma-informed worry statement for worries relating to her mother's home, and the connected safety goals are in Chapter 9. There were a couple more done, forming the basis of the safety plan.

Worry statement: Alma

Child protection is worried that her father and stepmother can't protect Alma and her stepbrothers from dangerous, violent conflicts and harmful fights between the children where they slap, tear, kick, and threaten each other, and it's almost impossible for her father and stepmother to separate them. In these situations, Alma gets so angry with her father that she also hits him, and he must use physical force to stop her. As these conflicts often happen when Alma is home, she gets blamed for them and becomes the scapegoat. Alma reacts by isolating herself from her family, rejecting contact with them and almost every adult around her except her uncle and aunt, and it seems as if she has almost given up on adults. If nothing changes, there is a significant risk that she will end up harming herself and others. There is also a risk that she will grow up feeling wrong and guilty, losing trust in adults, and continuing to think that adults are stupid and not to be counted on, leaving her feeling lonely and unworthy and with a negative view of herself, others, and the world.

Trauma-informed worry statement

Child protection is worried Alma's mother has been unable to protect Alma and her siblings from witnessing her being exposed to massive violence from her former partner. Alma has witnessed her mother being threatened with a knife and continuously beaten violently, also with a baseball bat in the stomach while pregnant with her younger sister. Often, Alma tried to protect her siblings from experiencing the sounds of it and, when it got too much for her to handle, she reached out for help to her uncle and aunt. When children experience such things, there is a significant risk that they will become so overwhelmed by fear that they will become frozen in the state of fear and might not get out of this state of anxiety and stress again, so their brains can't develop properly, and this will harm their well-being and development both in the short term and long term. There is a particular risk of this harm impacting their experience of value, their handling of stress and aggression, and their relationships with others, all of which are considered difficult for Alma already today.

The words about adults being stupid and not being counted on were her way of telling me that she was at a concerning level of giving up on adults, and, if nothing changed, this would leave her in a very vulnerable place in relation to others, also when becoming an adult herself. This is just one side of the story, and this can never stand alone. We need to clearly formulate a safety goal to show the parents what they need to do for the child to be safe and well in their care, in order to bring clarity, perspective, and hope, which is covered in more depth in Chapter 9. We also need to constantly investigate in depth what the parents are doing well in the care and parenting to keep the risk assessment balanced, as described in Chapter 3. In Chapter 8, we will be looking into the in-depth detail about the good, protective care of a child, but, first, a little about protective factors and PCEs in the next chapter.

Exercise

With the child in mind with whom you are working throughout the exercises, go through the ten ACE questions and count the ACEs in the child's life.

On the same paper used in the exercises in Chapters 3, 4 and 5, write on the lower part of the paper, underneath the other information on the risk side, any other individual, family, community, or structural risk factor you know of in the child's and family's life that you have not yet written down. Also, write down additional information on how it has impacted the child's health, development, and well-being.

Look at the paper and consider the cumulative risk of ACEs and other risk factors present in the child's life and add this reflection to your overall balanced risk assessment.

Now, with the additional information, assess the scale from 0 to 10, where 10 is the child is completely safe, you don't need to worry about them, and no help is needed, and 0 is the opposite: the child is the most unsafe possible and must be secured immediately.

Where do you now assess this situation to be on this scale? Compare this assessment with the one you conducted in the last exercise and assess whether this potential difference requires action.

Also, be aware of questions that arise from going through this that you would like to know more about and make a list of them to ask everyone involved with the child.

Then, from all the information on the paper, try to formulate a worry statement and a trauma-informed worry statement from the questions (1) Which people are worried? (2) What are the parents doing or not doing in the care of the child that they are worried about/what traumatic experience has the child experienced? (3) What is the impact on the child's health, development, and well-being? And (4) what are they worried might happen in the future if nothing else changes?

To adapt the worry statements to your specific context, you can replace or supplement information on the parents with information on other adults' and peers' behaviour of relevance to the child's challenges.

References

Christiansen, Henriette, Bohm, Signe, & Elkjær, Jane. (2021). *Små kår – børn og unges opvækst i økonomisk fattigdom*. Copenhagen, Egmont Fonden.

Ejrnæs, Morten, Gabrielsen, G., & Nørrung, Per. (2004). *Social opdrift – social arv*. Akademisk Forlag.

Felitti, V. J., Anda, R. F., Nordenberg, D., Williamson, D. F., Spitz, A. M., Edwards, V., Koss, M. P., & Marks, J. S. (1998). Relationship of childhood abuse and household dysfunction to many of the leading causes of death in adults. The Adverse Childhood Experiences (ACE) Study. *American Journal of Preventive Medicine*, *14*(4), 245–258. www.ncbi.nlm.nih.gov/pubmed/9635069

Finkelhor, D., Shattuck, A., Turner, H., & Hamby, S. (2015). A revised inventory of Adverse Childhood Experiences. *Child Abuse and Neglect, 48*, 13–21. https://doi.org/10.1016/j.chiabu.2015.07.011

Franck, D. (2021). Flere psykiske udfordringer? www.deafranck.dk/flere-psykiske-udfordringer/

Furukawa, Emi, Alsop, Brent, Sowerby, Paula, Jensen, Stephanie, & Tripp, Gail. (2017). Evidence for increased behavioral control by punishment in children with attention-deficit hyperactivity disorder. *Journal of Child Psychology and Psychiatry, 58*(3), 248–257.

Graham, C. (2017). Is the American dream really dead? *The Guardian.* www.theguardian.com/inequality/2017/jun/20/is-the-american-dream-really-dead

Guldin, Mai-Britt, Li, Jiong, Søndergaard Pedersen, Henrik, Obel, Carsten, Agerbo, Esben, Gissler, Mika, Cnattingius, Sven, Olsen, Jørn, & Vestergard, Mogens. (2015). Incidence of suicide among persons who had a parent who died during their childhood: a population-based cohort study. *Journal of the American Medical Association, 72*(12), 1227–1234.

Jellinek, S. M. (2010). Don't let ADHD crush children's self-esteem. *Clinical Psychiatry News*, May, 12.

Kvello, Ø. (2020). *Børn i risiko* (C. Pietsch, Trans.). Samfundslitteratur.

Liebschutz, Jane M., Buchanan-Howland, Kathryn, Chen, Clara A., Frank, Deborah A., Richardson, Mark A., Heeren, Timothy C., Cabral, Howard J., & Rose-Jacobs, Ruth. (2018). Childhood Trauma Questionnaire (CTQ) correlations with prospective violence assessment in a longitudinal cohort. *Psychological Assessment, 30*(6), 841–845.

Lund, J. S. (2023). Ét tal har enorm betydning for, hvordan du klarer dig i livet. Og det er ikke din skostørrelse. Zetland, www.zetland.dk

Nakazawa, D. J. (2016). *Childhood disrupted: how your biography becomes your biology, and how you can heal.* Atria Books.

Nixon, Laura, Rodriguez, Allison, Han, Sarah, Mejia, Pamela, & Dorfman, Lori. (2017). Adverse childhood experiences in the news: Successes and opportunities in coverage of childhood trauma. *Issue 24.*

Nørum, B. (2011). Klimaforandringer i det sociale arbejde. *Socialrådgiveren* (13).

OECD. (2022). *Understanding social mobility.* Organisation for Economic Co-operation and Development.

Parker, S. (2015). *Partnering for Safety Collaborative Assessment and Planning (CAP) Framework.* SP Consultancy.

Parker, S., & Struik, A. (2017). *Trauma informed safety planning.* SP Consultancy.

Perry, B. D., & Winfrey, Oprah. (2022). *What happened to you? Conversations on trauma, resilience and healing.* Bluebird.

Putnam, R. (2016). *Our kids – the American dream in crisis.* Simon & Schuster.

Rank, Mark R., & Eppard, Lawrence M. (2021). The "American Dream" of upward mobility is broken. Look at the numbers. *The Guardian.* www.theguardian.com/commentisfree/2021/mar/13/american-dream-broken-upward-mobility-us

Szalavitz, M., & Perry, B. D. (2010). *Born for love: why empathy is essential – and endangered* (1st ed.). William Morrow. Contributor biographical information www.loc.gov/catdir/enhancements/fy1011/2010280500-b.html; publisher description www.loc.gov/catdir/enhancements/fy1011/2010280500-d.html

Turnell, A. (2010). *Effective safety planning in child protection casework DVD workbook.* Resolutions Consultancy.

Turnell, A., & Parker, S. (2009). *Signs of Safety DVD workbook. Case examples and questioning skills.* Resolutions Consultancy.

UNHCR. (2023). *Refugee data finder.* UN Refugee Agency.

Van der Kolk, B. A. (2015). *The body keeps the score: mind, brain and body in the transformation of trauma.* Wellbeing Collection, Penguin Books.

Vinnerljung, B. (2010). *Dåliga skolresultat – en tung riskfaktor för fosterbarns utveckling.* Stockholm, Socialtstyrelsen.

Vinnerljung, B., Berlinm Marie, & Hjern, Anders. (2010). Skolbetyg, utbildning och risker för ogynnsam utveckling hos barn i. *Social Report*, 227–266.

Chapter 7

The Circle of Safety and Reconnection, Step 5

Assessing positive childhood experiences and other important protective factors in the child's life

Positive childhood experiences and protection factors

Just as several studies on adverse childhood experiences (ACEs) have been conducted, positive childhood experiences (PCEs) have also been investigated in depth (Bethell et al., 2019, p. 2). PCEs and other protective factors play a crucial role in promoting long-term health, development, and well-being in individuals, particularly in the presence of ACEs. These protective factors encompass both external resources requiring activation or reinforcement within children's lives and internal resources, skills, and competencies that need to be cultivated and taught to foster resilience and mental robustness and secure possibilities for children to create a good life for themselves and their families as adults. Similar to the accumulation of risk factors, it's important to note that these protective factors interact, and their significance may vary depending on individual circumstances.

The impact of positive childhood experiences

In 2015, a study of 8,188 adults in Wisconsin was conducted by a group of researchers led by Dr Christina Bethell, investigating positive childhood experiences identified as buffers against the impact of ACEs on a person's health. The findings emphasised the importance of promoting and assessing PCEs to mitigate the negative effects of ACEs, as "assessing and proactively promoting PCEs may reduce adult mental and relational health problems, even in the concurrent presence of ACEs" (Bethell et al., 2019).

The study identified seven key PCEs that had a protective influence on individuals' well-being. These PCEs are:

1 Feeling able to talk to their family about feelings.
2 Feeling their family stood by them during difficult times.
3 Enjoying participating in community traditions.
4 Feeling a sense of belonging in high school.
5 Feeling supported by friends.
6 Having at least two non-parent adults who took a genuine interest in them.
7 Feeling safe and protected by an adult in their home (Bethell et al., 2019, p. 2).

DOI: 10.4324/9781003322672-7

Not surprisingly, these factors highlight the significance of connection, emotional support, love, and a sense of belonging in fostering healthy brain development and promoting positive outcomes for individuals. They underline the power of supportive networks, within and outside the family, and the role of secure attachment and nurturing relationships during early childhood, as briefly touched upon previously.

While explicitly stating we need to aim for two significant adults alongside the parents, the study's findings align with the understanding that even a single trustworthy, stable, and safe adult in a vulnerable child's life can significantly impact their ability to overcome adversity and thrive as an adult. I was taught this while doing my social work degree many years ago. Throughout my many years in child protection, I have looked for these stories everywhere, and I have heard many different versions of them as testimonials of the importance of "the significant other" being the element that makes the difference (Guillen, 2022). These stories are also testimony of the power of human connection and have become my reason for dedicating my work life to creating safety networks of people around vulnerable and traumatised children in whatever way possible.

The study of PCEs sheds light on the intricate impact of relationships, support, and their long-term effects on health in adulthood. I have categorised the PCEs into three overall subjects: emotions, personal relationships, and social connections/community. I have already addressed emotions in Chapter 4 and will now delve into personal relationships, focusing particularly on bonding.

The quality of personal relationships and social connections accounts for most of the external protective factors in a person's life and constitutes the bedrock of their social capital. While community and personal relationships share a foundation in human connections, their distinction in this context lies in the concepts of bonding and bridging. As human beings, we need close, secure relationships in which we bond with people, as well as connection to a larger community with opportunities and support to bridge to (Gilligan, 2013; Perry & Winfrey, 2022). These insights, influenced by experts such as Bruce Perry, Robert Putnam, and Robbie Gilligan, underline the importance of intimate bonds and active engagement within wider communities. By nurturing positive personal relationships and facilitating connections within supportive communities, we can enhance individuals' social capital and cultivate their overall well-being and resilience over their lifetimes.

Personal relationships and family

The first PCE mentioned above relates to the ability to share your feelings with family and leads back to the importance of being connected to close relations and not feeling alone and disconnected from people. Previous chapters and discussions emphasised the importance of emotional (co-)regulation and quality human contact in securing a child's health, well-being, development, and safe attachment. This is particularly crucial in preventing ACEs from having long-term impacts, as it directly influences the neurobiological development of a child's brain, specifically the limbic system. Healthy brain development and a well-functioning limbic system play a vital role in stabilising and regulating a child's emotions, preventing them from being overwhelmed by stressors and strong feelings. By fostering healthy brain development and providing a stable and supportive environment, we can mitigate the long-term negative consequences of chronic stress and trauma for a child's body, development, and overall well-being.

Bonding

Bonding represents a form of social capital associated with personal relationships, characterising close connections within a group or a community with similar backgrounds and interests, such as family, friends, and neighbours. Bonding occurs between people who are like each other, have strong, close relationships, are "in it together", and provide material and emotional support to each other to get by (Gilligan, 2004; Putnam, 2000). It differs from attachment as it encompasses a greater diversity and quantity of connections (Booker-Drew, 2014; Gilligan, 2013). Bonding is crucial because humans require both attachment and bonding to a wider group to lead fulfilling lives for themselves and their families.

PCEs related to bonding include feeling supported by family during difficult times, feeling supported by friends, having at least two non-parent adults who genuinely care, and feeling safe and protected by an adult in their home. These experiences encapsulate pivotal aspects of safety, incorporating both physical protection over time and emotional safety in terms of love and belonging. Therefore, when working with vulnerable and traumatised children, addressing both safety aspects is imperative. This entails providing short-term protection and safety planning processes to address immediate concerns and focusing on the long-term prevention of adverse consequences by cultivating an environment of emotional safety and support.

A TED talk given by Robert Waldinger, the director of the Harvard Adult Development Study, underscores the significance of connectedness and its profound impact on health (Waldinger, 2015b). The study conducted by Waldinger and his team is one of the longest studies of adult life and reveals that individuals with more social connections tend to be happier, experience better physical health, and live longer compared with those who are less well-connected or more isolated from others than desired. Conversely, loneliness was found to have toxic effects, leading to decreased happiness, earlier health declines in midlife, compromised brain function, and shorter lifespans (Waldinger, 2015a, 2015b).

One key finding from the study is the importance of good, warm relationships, enabling individuals to maintain happiness even when experiencing physical pain. This suggests that quality of relationships continues to matter in later stages of life, not just in childhood. Strong relationships also protect the brain in adulthood, as individuals in securely attached relationships tend to retain sharper memories for longer. The study also highlights that the satisfaction individuals experience in their relationships at age 50 significantly predicts their health at age 80.

Those who were the most satisfied in their relationships at mid-life exhibited better health outcomes in later years (Waldinger, 2015b). This finding aligns with the work of Bruce Perry and his teams, who found that an individual's mental health is strongly predicted by their current "relational health" or connectedness (Perry & Winfrey, 2022, p. 262).

Bruce Perry's perspective on relational health highlights that a strong bond with the community is just as important now as it was before. Being connected and having a sense of home act as a protective shield against stress, frustration, and depression, particularly if relational interactions can give a person a sense of control concerning how much they share difficult aspects of their life and with whom until they are regulated again and their situation is no longer stressful and frustrating. Having a strong support system consisting of dedicated and compassionate individuals is crucial for a positive recovery after experiencing trauma. While therapy can be beneficial, it's greatly enhanced when combined with a sense of community. For children, an ideal situation involves being connected to their family, local community, and cultural background and receiving professional treatment (Perry & Winfrey, 2022).

The evidence presented by Waldinger and Perry, among others, supports the consensus among experts and researchers that connectedness with other people is crucial for thriving, maintaining good health, and fostering healthy development throughout our lives and emphasises the need to prioritise and nurture social connections for overall well-being.

Engaging network

Over the past 15 years of my professional journey, one of the most significant and rewarding lessons I have learned is the paramount importance of involving private networks and relationships in working with vulnerable individuals. As a trainer and supervisor in the child protection field, I have shared this learning journey with numerous social workers and family therapists, witnessing firsthand the transformative power of relationships and networks in supporting individuals in terms of protection and prevention, and recovery.

Building and nurturing relationships within a supportive network have a profound healing effect, particularly when children go through difficult times. These relationships provide a safe space for children to talk about and navigate challenging situations, offering what Bruce Perry refers to as "therapeutic dosing" (Perry & Winfrey, 2022). These small interactions occur in everyday life, when issues arise and need to be addressed at a pace the child can handle. It may involve "dipping the toe into the water" of difficult topics and then returning to other activities, allowing the child to take their time and adjusting the pace according to their needs and the situation.

Such consistent and supportive interactions, over time, can be as essential and healing as formal therapy. In situations where therapy may not be available, recognising that you can provide valuable support to the child in a highly skilled and qualified manner becomes crucial. By being present, engaging in meaningful conversations, and offering a nurturing environment, you can contribute to their healing and well-being. This understanding reinforces the notion that relationships and networks play a central role in supporting individuals' recovery and fostering their overall resilience and mental well-being (Gilligan, 2004). By harnessing the power of human connections, professionals in our field can have a positive and lasting impact on the lives of those they serve.

Case examples: Olivia and Dan

When Dan (15) and Olivia (18) tragically lost their father in a work accident, and their mother couldn't care appropriately for them afterwards owing to her mental health, their family and the parents' closest friends showed up. They gathered around them to support them in every possible way, from practical help in everyday life, to emotional support, to managing financial matters they needed to figure out that their mother couldn't manage. During the first months after the death, with the help of these committed people, Dan and Olivia processed the shock and stabilised the crisis in the healthiest way possible considering the situation. By the time I met them for trauma treatment, the potentially traumatic event had already been dealt with in a way that helped them digest the shock and process the overwhelming experience to the extent that they were able to start the natural grieving process following the loss of a parent.

Their grief was still immense, and the support people couldn't fix that or take it away from them. Still, they stood with them in their pain and dealt with the overwhelming feelings when they occurred, allowing them to process them naturally and helping reorient them in a new and more challenging life situation. This was an ongoing process, but Dan and Olivia did start smiling again and engaging with their peers and ordinary activities. Through the power of the network, they were prevented from being traumatised in a potentially traumatic situation and are instead more likely to gain emotional strength and resilience from this experience.

Several successful models provide systematic and comprehensive approaches when engaging networks in creating safety and facilitating recovery for children and adults. One notable model is safety planning, which significantly reduces the risk of re-abuse and promotes collaboration between parents and professionals. Susie Essex, the developer of the Resolutions Approach addressing denied child abuse, has documented her work over 20 years, revealing a remarkable reduction in the risk of re-abuse to as low as 4–7 per cent, compared with the typical re-abuse rates of 27–33 per cent. This approach has proven highly effective in ensuring the safety and well-being of children who have experienced abuse (Turnell & Essex, 2006). A review of the safety planning work in Copenhagen in 2011 showed that 67 per cent of children could safely stay with their families. For the remaining 33 per cent, who required placement in care, improved collaboration was reported by parents and professionals, leading to enhanced stability in placements (Sørensen, 2012). I return to safety planning in Chapter 10.

In the context of mental health problems within the psychiatric system, the Open Dialogue approach has shown promising results in facilitating recovery (Seikkula, 2008). Developed by Finnish psychologist Jaakko Seikkula, his colleague Markku Sutela, and their team, the Open Dialogue approach involves the participation of private networks in the treatment of psychiatric patients facing acute psychiatric crises. A 5-year study demonstrated remarkable outcomes, including a significantly reduced duration of untreated psychosis, a decrease in antipsychotic drug usage to 33 per cent, high employment rates among participants rising to 83 per cent, and a decline in new schizophrenia cases. Annual incidence dropped from 33 (1985) to 2–3 per 100,000 (2005) (Seikkula et al., 2006).

These examples highlight the importance and effectiveness of engaging support networks and using collaborative approaches in enhancing safety, recovery, and well-being, in various contexts, as a comprehensive and enduring strategy to address complex issues. Various methodologies and approaches that engage private networks in preventing social challenges and aiding recovery from mental health problems are valuable in establishing strong bonds between individuals and their close relations. By harnessing social connections, individuals can create opportunities and use the power of mutual support, aiding each other in navigating life's challenges through reciprocity. This forms the foundation for sustaining life in general, but children at risk often face greater vulnerability concerning social capital. They might possess smaller private networks, inconsistent support, and a greater reliance on professional help (Gilligan, 2013). Limited access to positive role models and the risk of social exclusion from ordinary communities can lead them to form connections that may get them into trouble.

During a conference in Copenhagen years ago, Norwegian psychologist and researcher Tore Andreasen presented evidence suggesting that placing an at-risk child in an environment with well-functioning children positively influences the at-risk child and benefits all involved. Conversely, if these children are placed in environments with other at-risk peers, the negative influence between them increases the risk of unfavourable outcomes, resulting in losses for everyone involved. Keeping this in mind, there might be an advantage in retaining children in their communities, just as Robbie Gilligan claims that professionals must focus on helping at-risk children connect with their existing network, form a broader network, and access the available resources within it, while the professionals play a more background role. This represents a new and broader way of doing social work (Gilligan, 2004, 2013).

Connecting them to their organic networks also helps bridge them to broader communities and networks, providing better opportunities and building more social capital for a brighter future.

According to Robert Putnam, the difference between bridging and bonding is that bonding is good for "getting by", and bridging is crucial for "getting ahead" (Putnam, 2000). Incorporating this into our work aligns with the broader paradigm shift in social work happening at the moment towards creating more meaningful connections and leveraging existing resources to support individuals in creating sustainable change during challenging times.

Social connections and community

Bridging

Bridging, in contrast to bonding, encompasses the social capital between people, communities, and social groups different from ourselves, with different skills, knowledge, and information and different friends (Putnam, 2000). This refers to looser or weaker connections that, nevertheless, help us navigate life and provide access to resources beyond our immediate network (Booker-Drew, 2014; Gilligan, 2013).

These connections may not be as strong as the ones associated with bonding but are crucial in creating opportunities for vulnerable children to bridge into networks and connections they may not typically have access to. For instance, a child's close relationship with a friend's parent who regularly takes them to sports activities can serve as both a bonding and bridging connection.

The significance of weak connections is underscored in a classic study on job searches and contacts called "The Strength of Weak Ties" by Mark S. Granovetter (Granovetter, 1973). The findings showed that 16.7 per cent of people found employment through frequent contact with their connections – at least twice a week. In contrast, 55.6 per cent had occasional contact with their connections – more than once a year but less than twice a week – while 27.8 per cent had rare contact – once a year or less. Surprisingly, weak ties accounted for 85 per cent of job opportunities because they tend to be part of different networks and social circles, providing access to a broader range of information and job prospects (Granovetter, 1973).

In addition to the opportunities arising from connecting with a more diverse range of people, the community itself offers a sense of love and belonging to something greater than individual close connections, fostering an individual's sense of worthiness and value that is vital for building self-esteem and self-worth. PCEs related to community involvement, such as "enjoying participation in community traditions" and "feeling a sense of belonging in high school", contribute significantly to a child's overall well-being and development (Bethell et al., 2019). Enhancing bonding, bridging connections, and fostering a sense of community can give vulnerable children access to more opportunities and a stronger support system, ultimately promoting their healthy development and resilience.

Humans are inherently designed to live in communities and share the responsibility of childcare among many adults in a local community. No single person can fully meet a child's physical, emotional, social, and cognitive needs for optimal development, and to place such expectations solely on parents, especially single parents, is unreasonable (Perry & Winfrey, 2022).

Maintaining strong connections to the local community remains just as crucial now as in ancient days. A sense of belonging and a place to call home are buffers against stress and frustration. Children in families with a strong foundation of relational well-being have ample opportunities for secure and stable interactions. These positive experiences help them build secure attachments and resilience. However, it's not enough for them to be solely reliant on their immediate family. Access to a network of dedicated and caring individuals significantly improves the likelihood of positive outcomes following traumatic experiences. While therapy can be helpful, it's not as effective without connection to a supportive community (Perry & Winfrey, 2022). Ideally, children should experience a sense of connection to their family, local community, and culture and receive professional treatment when needed. The presence of friends, family, and other healthy relationships creates a natural healing environment.

When predicting adults' current mental health, their present relational health and their history of relational well-being during childhood stand out as two primary factors. For individuals with a trauma history, the best indicator of their current level of mental health functioning is the strength of their current sense of connection (Perry & Winfrey, 2022). Chapter 6 mentioned the importance of good-quality schools and day care as protective factors for children and young people. When these educational settings provide a safe space, with positive relationships between adults and children and inclusive practices involving professionals and parents within a clear structure, they can significantly contribute to children's well-being and development (Kvello, 2020).

Bessel van der Kolk and Bruce Perry guide schools towards becoming more trauma-informed in their approach to supporting traumatised children, with the aims of preventing further traumatisation and stigmatisation of vulnerable children and promoting recovery (Szalavitz & Perry, 2010; Van der Kolk, 2015). This involves providing educators with knowledge about the underlying causes of children's behaviours and how to regulate them better.

The relational competencies of adults within the school or day-care setting play a critical role in creating a safe environment and acting as protective factors. Emotional and cognitive support from these adults stimulates children's ability to learn, develop, and establish secure relationships (Guillen, 2022; Kvello, 2020). Being mindful of the potential to be "the significant other", prioritising the development of strong relationships, creating trauma-informed environments, and nurturing these relational competencies are essential to ensure that educational settings foster positive experiences, promote resilience, and enable children to reach their full potential (Guillen, 2022; Detlevsen, 2022). Through gradual implementation of changes, children can become accepted, integrated, and valued members of their peer group and be able to take in new information and teaching, which is simply impossible when in a survival state all the time (Kvello, 2020).

Engaging the private network and community in children's lives

I access the quantity and quality of a child's network using Sonja Parker's Circle of Safety and Support (Parker, 2015), which helps obtain a general overview

"Circles of Safety & Support" Tool

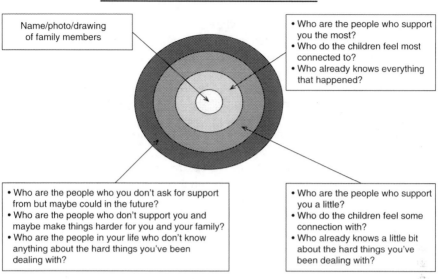

| Name/photo/drawing of family members | • Who are the people who support you the most?
• Who do the children feel most connected to?
• Who already knows everything that happened? |

• Who are the people who you don't ask for support from but maybe could in the future?
• Who are the people who don't support you and maybe make things harder for you and your family?
• Who are the people in your life who don't know anything about the hard things you've been dealing with?

• Who are the people who support you a little?
• Who do the children feel some connection with?
• Who already knows a little bit about the hard things you've been dealing with?

Illustration 7.1 The Safety and Support Circle by Sonja Parker

of a child's and family's network on three different levels of connectedness, respectively:

1   The inner circle of people who are closely connected and engaged in the child's and family's life know all about what happened to the child.
2   The middle circle of people supports the child and family and knows a little about what happened to the child.
3   The outer circle of people aren't supporting them yet or don't know anything about what happened to the child (Parker, 2015).

Simple yet meaningful questions effortlessly elicit information about family networks when we use the tool illustrated here. Through qualified dialogues about the family's support network, we can have conversations about how the network can be helpful in difficult times and identify underutilised resources that benefit the child and family. The goal is to move individuals from the outer and middle circles into the inner circle, actively involving them as protective resources for the child.

Using this model has proven effective in shifting the narrative from "I don't have a network" to a more expansive understanding of the potential resources available. As the questions don't evoke this, I no longer hear this answer. Initially, the parents may not immediately recognise the names that come up as valuable resources, but, from our dialogue, they will do. They need to understand why engaging these individuals is necessary and how to do it in a way that feels acceptable for themselves, their children, and the people they reach out to. Engaging external support during challenging times is a vulnerable experience for most people, and so it must be approached with care and sensitivity and must make sense for them to move people from the outer circle to the inner circle.

As professionals, we are responsible for guiding and supporting individuals to reach out and connect with people within their network, and this process requires grace and understanding.

It can be helpful to put ourselves in their shoes and imagine how it would feel to share intimate details with people who know nothing about our most painful struggles. Resistance may arise, and we must approach it kindly, yet firmly, acknowledging that it's difficult and still continuing to emphasise the importance and necessity of engaging a broader support system around the children in the short and long term. Support throughout the process is crucial to help individuals overcome their apprehensions, integrate additional support into their lives, and empower them to utilise the resources available to create better outcomes for their children.

Case example: Victor – continued

When I started the safety planning process with Victor's mother and the safety network, only the aunt and uncle were engaged initially. They knew everything and massively supported Victor's mother in creating immediate safety for him, but it was assessed to be too small and too fragile a network to rely on to create safety for Victor in the long term. Therefore, I used the Safety and Support Circle with Victor's mother, talking about which people were in the three circles, how they were now or previously had been supporting her and Victor, and how they might not have been supportive before but could be in the current situation. Finally, we ended with a reflection on which of those she would consider engaging in the processes. Some of them turned out to be people from the past that she once felt safe with, such as a couple of mothers of children in Victor's old kindergarten and their old neighbour in their apartment, who had been an ear-witness to all the difficult times and the violence that the mother had exposed Victor to when she felt powerless.

In this way, the neighbour knew everything about what had happened because she had heard it and used to be concerned about both Victor and his mother. Other people in the circles were a young woman from their new neighbourhood, whom they got to know well from talking when walking their dogs, and some of the mothers of children in Victor's school and the playground nearby, all of them being kind and supportive by nature.

Victor's mother found it very challenging to reach out and engage them by talking directly to them, and so I helped her write a letter to inform them about Victor's and her situation. The letter described enough details for them to know the seriousness of the problem without giving all the details. She also informed them about the safety planning process and why she was reaching out to them, so that they could decide whether they could engage in it. Some letters were sent by post, and others were handed over personally when she met people face to face, and Victor's mother was left waiting anxiously for the responses. During a brief response time, I needed to support and acknowledge her in taking this brave but vulnerable action.

After the first response, she called me immediately to share her relief, how happy the network person had been to be asked, and how she could confidently say yes. All the following responses told the mother how grateful and glad the people had been to be asked and how it mattered to them to be considered such a trustworthy person by her. Some agreed to join, and others had to turn her request down. The ones doing so were kind, making it clear it had nothing to do with Victor and his mother but concerned their own situation and that they couldn't deal with more themselves. From this, I learned a big lesson about the reciprocity of using a network and that it matters not only to the people who need help but also to those who provide help or have been asked as a sign of trust and worthiness. Afterwards, the old neighbour, one of the old mothers from kindergarten, and several people engaged in their life in the present joined the inner circle and created a safety plan, providing Victor with a strong safety net.

Building resilience

Resilience is a term describing a person's ability to bounce back from adversity and it involves a complex developmental process of gradually building strength to handle more challenging and complex problems through exposure to an adequate amount of adversity (Gilligan, 2004). Through lived experiences, a child learns to overcome adversity using the internal and external resources available to them. By being exposed to hardships and successfully overcoming them, they acquire valuable lessons and develop stronger coping skills, ultimately becoming wiser and more resilient.

The key to enhancing resilience is ensuring that protective experiences and coping strategies outweigh a child's significant adversity. In contrast, if the adversity is too big for the child to handle, they become vulnerable instead, owing to the overwhelming sensation and stress followed by not coping, which can lead to sensitisation in the nervous system (Perry & Szalavitz, 2007).

Research has shown that the level of security established with the primary caregiver during the first 2 years of life plays a crucial role in enhancing resilience. As mentioned by Bessel van der Kolk, Sroufe found in his work that the ability to cope with life's disappointments when older was strongly predicted by the level of security with the primary caregiver during early childhood.

Van der Kolk writes, "Srofe informally told me that he thought that resilience in adulthood could be predicted by how lovable mothers rated their kids at age two" (Van der Kolk, 2015, p. 163).

Like other things regarding humans, there is no one-size-fits-all formula for building resilience, but, nowadays, we have knowledge about what supports healthy processes and what to be aware of to help a child best. Øjvind Kvello has gathered a considerable body of work on this topic by many of the world's best researchers in his book *Børn i risiko* (Children at Risk), trying to capture the essence of it. As you can see here, we have already covered some of them, and some will follow below. He highlights that contributors to resilience are genetically determined factors such as innate robustness, environmental factors such as parents' sensitivity, warm and stimulating care for the child, and social support from the social network. The care and support from parents and networks contribute to the child developing a secure attachment pattern, a sense of being worth loving, and a positive self-image with the belief that they can master things. These elements also contribute to the child gaining good competence to develop appropriate coping strategies, become independent, and have an optimistic attitude towards the future (Kvello, 2020).

The Center on the Developing Child at Harvard University (Barger et al., 2017) presents another valuable perspective on essential aspects of building resilience in children, called the 7 Cs:

1 Competence: it's important for children to build competence and develop a sense of their own skills and abilities, helping them gain confidence in their capabilities and navigate challenges with a belief in their capacity to succeed.

2 Confidence: supporting children to develop true confidence involves fostering a positive self-image and belief in their abilities. This confidence is a foundation for resilience and enables children to face adversity with resilience and determination.

3 Connection: building strong connections is crucial for resilience. Connecting children to supportive individuals, schools, and communities creates a network of relationships that can provide emotional support, guidance, and resources during difficult times.

4 Character: helping children develop a clear understanding of right and wrong and teaching moral values are essential. This enables them to make ethical decisions, engage in socially accepted behaviours, and stay out of trouble, enhancing their resilience in various situations.

5 Contribution: providing opportunities for children to contribute to the well-being of others is important. By helping others, children learn the value of empathy, experience the satisfaction of making a positive impact, and develop the ability to reach out for help without feeling ashamed or weak.

6 Coping: it's crucial for children to experience a range of healthy coping skills. By learning effective strategies to manage stress and adversity, children can avoid resorting to harmful "quick fixes" or maladaptive behaviours and develop resilience in handling life's challenges.

7 Control: teaching children to make independent decisions and exercise control over their lives is vital for resilience. Developing a sense of control helps prevent fear and excessive stress, allowing children to navigate everyday life with greater confidence and stability (Barger et al., 2017).

By incorporating these 7 Cs into children's lives, caregivers and professionals can enhance their resilience, empower them to overcome adversity, and promote their overall well-being.

A study on high-risk children from the island of Kauai highlighted several protective factors contributing to building resilience and becoming a caring, competent, and confident adult; it also identified strong connections to community groups and churches and a strong bond with a non-parent caretaker as key factors (Werner & Smith, 1992). However, the study also emphasised the role of certain personality traits, such as intelligence and extroversion, as contributors to a child's ability to connect with others and seek support when needed (Werner & Smith, 1992).

More expressive children often receive more attention and support, as negative attention may still be preferable to no attention, while those who don't outwardly show their pain may go unnoticed and won't be given the care, attention, and connection needed to build resilience to the adversity they are facing. This highlights the need for professionals to be aware of and attentive to children who may be silently struggling, and for professionals in various roles, such as social workers, teachers, caregivers, therapists, and psychologists, to recognise the potential harm of children "going under the radar". These children may be affected by adverse conditions but aren't openly displaying their distress and would need professionals who pay attention, connect with them, and provide the necessary support and care, especially when no one else is available.

This leads me to the professionals' roles in children's lives and the dilemmas faced by professionals who play a crucial role in a child's life but may only be present temporarily and without guarantees of long-term involvement. While professionals can be vital resources and preventive factors in a child's life, they must navigate the challenges of limited time and resources. Despite these limitations, it's crucial that professionals strive to create a difference with whatever time they have available for a particular child.

Dilemmas concerning professionals' role in children's lives

Professionals must continually reflect on their roles and professional boundaries when working with children. This reflection is necessary because various dilemmas arise when children see us as confidants and trusted adults outside their families.

While we understand the importance of building relationships with children, it's essential to recognise that our professional relationship with them has limits. Determining how much to engage with a child can be complex, often with no definitive right or wrong answers. Instead, careful consideration of ethical and moral aspects is required to strike a balance and navigate the realm of dilemmas. The closer you come to children in their everyday life as a teacher, day carer, foster carer, other primary carer, family therapist, or similar, the more consideration is demanded. Enhancing our understanding of professional boundaries and ethical considerations helps us maintain a healthy and effective professional relationship with the children we work with. It ensures that we provide them with the necessary support and care while respecting the boundaries of our roles.

One crucial aspect to be mindful of is never making promises to children that we can't keep. Vulnerable children don't need additional disappointment and pain, as they often carry their fair share already. Unfortunately, with the best intentions, many professionals have made promises to children that they would never let them down, only to later disappear from their lives without warning owing to personal circumstances or work situations. Such actions can leave children devastated, feeling betrayed, and with a loss of trust in adults. Therefore, it's essential to exercise caution and avoid making promises that we may be unable to fulfil.

Confidentiality is another critical consideration. Professionals often face legal and regulatory obligations that may compromise the confidentiality between them and the child. For example, in Denmark, professionals have a strict obligation to notify the authorities if they are concerned about a child's well-being. This hinders children from freely sharing information about their life, as they run the risk of having this information reported, and their trust broken, unintentionally causing them to feel let down – again, this is unintentional.

Laws and regulations regarding reporting and intervention differ from country to country. Regardless of the legal requirements, professionals should always inform children about the limitations of confidentiality and explain what will happen if concerns arise regarding their safety and well-being. Through discussion of these matters at the beginning of a working relationship, children experience a sense of control over how much information they share, depending on their situation. This approach enables them to disclose information at a safe pace. In case of disclosure, be mindful of empowering the child, allowing them to maintain a sense of control throughout the process to minimise trauma and anxiety. It's crucial to have open and honest conversations with the child, clearly articulating the purpose of reporting as a means to help them. Discuss the possibilities for getting support and involve the child in the decision-making process and any necessary steps that need to be taken. When faced with such situations, remember to provide thorough explanations for your actions, ensuring the child understands the reasons behind them and can find meaning in the process.

Another important aspect to consider is the extent to which you communicate to the child that they matter to you personally. Many children we work with seek validation and a sense of importance in their relationships with professionals. To find the right balance in conveying to them that they are valued and significant, without crossing boundaries suggesting an inappropriate personal attachment, is crucial. While it's natural to care deeply for the children we work with, it's important to maintain a professional distance.

If you become emotionally invested beyond the boundaries of your role as a professional, open and honest communication with the child is demanded. Clearly explain to them what to expect from you and your family, both in the present and in the future. Setting clear expectations helps prevent potential disappointment and pain that may arise if you are unable to fulfil the child's hopes, longings, needs, and expectations. Transparency in your intentions and limitations is crucial in maintaining a healthy professional relationship.

There are definitely stories of professionals who have gone above and beyond for a child, continuing to support them after the professional relationship has ended and into adulthood. While these stories can be inspiring and heartwarming, it's important to recognise that such outcomes likely result from careful consideration, ethical decision-making, and navigation of the complexities of boundaries while providing meaningful support to the child.

Ultimately, finding the right balance involves being mindful of the child's need for validation and importance while ensuring that their expectations align with what can be realistically provided within the professional context.

Case example: Chris – continued

Working with Chris, who had difficulty feeling safe with anyone other than me, required careful consideration of how to establish a nurturing and secure adult role while maintaining professional boundaries. Given his lack of a supportive adult figure, Chris strongly needed affirmation and validation from me, desiring a sense of uniqueness and importance. Aware of the impact I could have on his life, I constantly reflected on ways to make him feel valued without overstepping professional boundaries. As the trauma treatment concluded, I sought supervision from my supervisor to ensure a smooth transition and bridging to other professionals and to help Chris feel safe and valued. As he lacked other sources of support, I communicated clearly to him that he could reach out to me and specified the steps I would take to assist him, whom I would involve, and how. This approach aimed to shift his reliance from me to other professionals, fostering a sense of safety and continuity. While he reached out a few times within the first year, as agreed, it has been over 3 years since I last heard from him, indicating that the bridge was successfully built. Chris no longer requires my presence to feel secure and protected during challenging times.

From the example with Chris and the discussion on this topic, what ethical and moral areas would you consider important to reflect on with you and your colleagues?

Exercise

Get your papers from your exercise in Chapter 3 with the information on safety and positive impact on the child. Go through the seven PCEs again and write all the details you have on this topic under safety; you are also looking to document other protective factors from the information given to you.

To support this process, you can take another piece of paper and draw four circles; leave the inner circle to be the child and family and put names of the people you already know about in the child's life in the other circles using the Circle of Safety and Support. This helps get a clearer picture of the network resources available to the child. Add this to the bottom of the page as protective factors and also list how these people might have created safety for the child or impacted their health, development, and well-being.

Also, add to the positive impacts on the child and all the signs of resilience the child is showing by going through the 7 Cs again to add information about the details you have about the child's skills, strength, resources, well-being, and development that could be seen as a sign of resilience.

With the additional information, assess the scale from 0 to 10, where 10 indicates the child is completely safe, you don't need to worry about them, and no help is needed; 0 is the opposite: the child is the most unsafe possible and must be secured immediately.

Where do you now assess this situation to be on this scale? Compare this assessment with the one you conducted in the last exercise and assess whether this potential difference requires action.

Also, be aware of questions that arise from going through this that you would like to know more about and make a list of them to ask everyone involved with the child.

References

Barger, J., Vitale, P., Gaughan, J. P., & Feldman-Winter, L. (2017). Measuring resilience in the adolescent population: a succinct tool for outpatient adolescent health. *Journal of Pediatrics, 189*, 201–206.

Bethell, C., Jones, J., Gombojav, N., Linkenbach, J., & Sege, R. (2019). Positive childhood experiences and adult mental and relational health in a statewide sample: associations across adverse childhood experiences levels. *JAMA Pediatrics, 173*(11), e193007. doi. org/10.1001/jamapediatrics.2019.3007

Booker-Drew, F. (2014). From bonding to bridging: using the immunity to change (ITC) process to build social capital and create change. *Dissertations & Theses, 144*.

Detlevsen, L. (2022). Pædagogisk relationskompetence påvirker børns livsmuligheder. EVA. www.eva.dk/dagtilbud-boern/paedagogisk-relationskompetence-paavirker-boerns-livsmuligheder

Gilligan, R. (2004). Promoting resilience in child and family social work: issues for social work practice, education and policy. *Social Work Education, 23*(1), 99–104.

Gilligan, R. (2013). "Bridging" and "bonding" connections for at-risk children. SFI conference, Nyborg.

Granovetter, M. S. (1973). The strength of weak ties. *American Journal of Sociology, 78*(6), 1360–1380.

Guillen, L. (2022). The importance of a significant adult in the life of a child. Behaviours Matters.

Kvello, Ø. (2020). *Børn i risiko* (C. Pietsch, Trans.). Samfundslitteratur.

Parker, S. (2015). *Circles of Safety & Support – a tool to help parents identify people for their family's safety & support network*. SP Consultancy.

Perry, B. D., & Szalavitz, M. (2007). *The boy who was raised as a dog and other stories from a child psychiatrist's notebook: What traumatized children can teach us about loss, love, and healing*. Basic Books.

Perry, B. D., & Winfrey, Oprah. (2022). *What happened to you? Conversations on trauma, resilience and healing.* Bluebird.

Putnam, R. (2000). *Bowling alone: the collapse and revival of American community.* Simon & Schuster.

Seikkula, J. (2008). *Åben dialog og netværksarbejde.* Gyldendal.

Seikkula, Jaakko, Aaltonen, Jukka, Alakare, Birgittu, Haarakangas, Kauko, Keränen, Jyrki, & Lehtinen, Klaus. (2006). Five-year experience of first-episode nonaffective psychosis in open-dialogue approach: treatment principles, follow-up outcomes, and two case studies. *Psychotherapy Research, 16*(2), 214–228.

Szalavitz, M., & Perry, B. D. (2010). *Born for love: why empathy is essential – and endangered* (1st ed.). William Morrow. Contributor biographical information www.loc.gov/catdir/enhancements/fy1011/2010280500-b.html; publisher description www.loc.gov/catdir/enhancements/fy1011/2010280500-d.html

Sørensen, T. H. (2012). *Når forældre og netværk skaber sikkerhed for barnet.* Copenhagen, Københavns Kommune.

Turnell, A., & Essex, S. (2006). *Working with 'denied' child abuse. The resolutions approach.* Open University Press.

Van der Kolk, B. A. (2015). *The body keeps the score: mind, brain and body in the transformation of trauma.* Wellbeing Collection, Penguin Books.

Waldinger, R. (2015a). *The Harvard study of adult development.* Harvard University.

Waldinger, R. (2015b). What makes a good life? Lessons from the longest study on happiness. TEDxBeaconStreet.

Werner, Emmy E., & Smith, Ruth S. (1992). *Overcoming the odds – high risk children from birth to adulthood.* Cornell University Press.

Chapter 8

The Circle of Safety and Reconnection, Step 6

Assessing the adequate care and protection of the child by parents and other significant adults and the positive impact on the child's health, well-being, and development

A balanced perspective as the foundation of the risk assessment

Chapter 3 underscored the significance of a balanced risk assessment to ensure children's safety and well-being, and maintaining a balanced viewpoint when working with vulnerable, traumatised, and at-risk children is critical. This involves evaluating the care and protection provided by the parents and other adults in their lives, along with signs of resilience and well-being, while also considering indicators of danger, neglect, trauma, and impairment of their development.

In family observations, we aim to identify safety, secure attachment, and effective parenting while remaining attentive to the opposite traits to enhance child safety. This also goes for observations in contexts other than the home.

When assessing parental skills, it's vital to recognise that there is no such thing as a "perfect parent". Rather than striving for an unattainable standard, we should focus on identifying good enough parents who can provide their children with sufficient care and protection (Van der Kolk, 2015). Also, parents aren't supposed to provide their children with everything on their own: it's natural to rely on other adults to support them in this task (Perry & Winfrey, 2022). Thus, assessing adequate care will take into consideration four perspectives: those of the parents, the private network, the professional network, and, lastly, the healthy development and well-being of the child. To elicit information about these aspects for the risk assessment and create changes at the same time, the solution-focused approach is the most appropriate to use. This approach helps elicit strengths, resources, and skills that parents and other caregivers possess and can utilise, creating a safe and nurturing environment for the child. It also highlights the child's strengths, resources, skills, and well-being across various contexts.

Following the initial five steps of the Circle of Safety and Reconnection, in this chapter, the balanced risk assessment for the child can now be concluded by adding specific details of adequate parenting and care, as well as signs of the child's

DOI: 10.4324/9781003322672-8

healthy development and well-being. After the last information is added, the final balanced risk assessment can be illustrated by a given number on a scale of 0 to 10 to clarify your level of worry for a particular child.

In general, when doing risk assessments in case consultations, 10 is defined as safe and adequate care for the child, and the case is closed; 0 isn't safe at all, and the child must be secured immediately. In other contexts, the scale can be defined accordingly. Whatever number you choose to illustrate your level of worry at any given time is only a snapshot that will change as situations evolve, change happens, and more information is generated. In Chapter 9, I will go into further detail on how to use the scale in a more personalised way when engaging the family and network in the process of creating change and defining the parts of the scale.

During my social work studies, in the subject called "systematic case management", we would learn how to systematically describe, analyse, and assess a case in the correct order and not mix the three steps (Caspersen & Laustsen, 2009). The scaling process mirrors this methodology, using the scale to maintain the discipline of separating these stages. First, describe all the information you have gathered in concrete and detailed ways on worries, risk factors, safety/exceptions, and protection factors. Then, analyse this information, reflecting on what you as a professional consider relevant from your knowledge, experience, and methodology; finally, you select a number on the scale representing your balanced risk assessment of how worried you are about a child. So, whenever someone asks the reasons for your choice of 5 on the scale, you can easily share your analysis with them based on your professionalism, skills, and clearly described information.

Diverse assessments of the same information are common owing to people's backgrounds, experiences, and viewpoints. I always welcome bringing diverse perspectives to the table: it's valuable to learn from each other, and it also enhances the children's safety as we consider more factors and details than we would if we all agreed.

This chapter will describe more elements of what children need from their parents and carers to thrive and develop than the book has already covered and will also describe how to use the solution-focused approach to assess and develop adequate care for a child in their different contexts.

Different aspects of adequate care, connection, and protection

Adequate parenting

To ensure children's well-being through adequate care, primary caregivers must provide them with adequate connection, protection, support, and coverage of their basic, emotional and mental needs. This section briefly recaps and expands upon this topic, building upon insights from Chapters 1, 3, and 5.

Earlier chapters highlighted that children generally need calm, regulated, attentive, attuned, stable, loving, and caring caregivers who provide them with a safe home, safe attachment, good mentalisation skills, and adequate stimuli – adults who take full responsibility for providing what is needed to secure children's growth, healthy development, and well-being (Hejlskov Elvén et al., 2012; Hart, 2009; Siegel, 2020; Struik, 2019). These adults must also communicate clear and healthy boundaries to the child to establish a sense of safety in the child across all arenas where the child is present (Juul, 2016). Additionally, children need to feel seen, heard, understood, and accepted for who they are at their core, which helps them not to compromise their authenticity, validates their importance to others, and establishes a sense of love and belonging (Siegel & Bryson, 2020).

Timing significantly impacts the assessment of appropriate care and nurturing for a child, as the level of care required to promote healthy development depends on the child's age. The first 2 months are particularly critical owing to the child's high vulnerability and rapid brain growth (Perry & Winfrey, 2022). Research in 2022 showed that teenagers' brains are equally as sensitive as infants', and a single incident during adolescence can cause more damage than an equivalent event within the first 1,000 days of a child's life (Andersen, 2022). This groundbreaking finding will have significant implications for trauma-informed work with adolescents in the future and underscores the importance of age-appropriate care in promoting healthy brain development and restoring and rebuilding the brain after trauma. Specifically, it highlights the need for stability and nurturing care, particularly in the formative years when the brain is most vulnerable.

Children and adolescents need relational consistency and stability in their care, including repetitive patterns, a clear structure, and predictability in their daily routines. Repetition over time is necessary to develop basic capabilities and build the foundation for healthy relationships. As stated in *What Happened to You?*, "The key to having many healthy relationships later in your life is only to have a few safe, stable, and nurturing relationships in your first year" (Perry & Winfrey, 2022, p. 164).

Emotional attunement between adults and children is vital to establish safe attachment, which is critical for healthy development. As Bessel van der Kolk and his colleagues note, "the process of establishing safe attachment isn't pure bliss 100% of the time but also involves disruption in the contact followed by a re-establishment of attunement" (Van der Kolk, 2015, p. 114). Disruptions in a relationship are inevitable and offer learning opportunities for both the child and the adult. The adult is always responsible for repairing the relationship after a disruption or conflict because studies have shown that emotional distance and role reversal can have a profound and long-lasting impact on young adults, mainly linked to aggressive behaviour (Van der Kolk, 2015).

Dr Ed Tronick's "Still Face Experiment" demonstrated how disengaged, passive, and cool responses from a parent to a child's attempt to connect can leave the child distressed and withdrawn (Save the Children's Resource Centre, 2022). In contrast, attuned, caring adults nurture feelings of love and being good enough, which are crucial for healthy development because it's vital for children to feel loved and valued rather than growing up with feelings of inadequacy.

According to Donald Winnicott's research, most mothers provide sufficient attunement and adequate care, and this does not require extraordinary talent, but it's crucial to be aware of whether a child has these attuned, caring adults to connect and reconnect with after disruption (Van der Kolk, 2015).

Case example: Julie

While working with Julie and her family, I faced a challenging situation when the 8-year-old girl was angry with me for saying no to something she badly wanted. She threw a heavy rollerblade at me with such intensity and speed that it almost knocked me out. The pain was excruciating, and I couldn't help but scream at her to go to her room. I have neither done this before nor later in my care of children. However, the pain caused my windows of tolerance to shut down, and my mentalisation skills went down the drain. I needed a short break from her to regulate myself and become the safe, calm, and collected adult she knew.

After a moment, I went to her room and knocked on the door. "Can we talk?" I asked. She was reluctant, still overwhelmed by the incident. As I was responsible for the repair part, I said to her, "I am sorry that I lost it, and we need to talk it through – can I come in?" She agreed, and I sat down beside her. "I was not supposed to act like that, and I am sorry", I told her. "It hurt so much, and I couldn't control it. Though, I must say that I don't think it was OK to throw it at me." "You were an idiot", Julie replied, still angry, but I could see that she was slowly engaging with me again. So, I said jokingly, "Now we both know how ugly I become when hit by a rollerblade – let's not try that again?" When she looked up and saw the expression on my face, she started laughing, and I laughed too. Our relationship was restored.

The benefit of this incident was seeing both Julie's and her mother's trust in me grow from this moment, as we all learned from it. Her mother had overheard the incident from the living room and said, "Thank God, it showed me that you can make mistakes as well".

There are various approaches for disciplining children and many opinions about it, and I will highlight the approaches most aligned with my mindset and methodology. Safely demonstrated and communicated boundaries of what behaviours are tolerated form one key aspect of disciplining children, and it represents a tricky balancing act that requires finding the right mix of emotional, social, and cultural support to help them grow and develop while avoiding the trap of making them feel wrong when they fail. One approach to parenting that seeks to strike this balance is called "gentle parenting" (Ockwell-Smith, 2016).

At the core of this approach is the belief that children learn best when calm and not upset, which means discipline should focus on helping them calm down before attempting to teach them a lesson. Once children are calm, parents talk to them about what happened and explore what might have triggered their behaviour so that they can avoid similar situations in the future (Ockwell-Smith, 2016). The key to gentle parenting is treating children with respect, providing them with connection and structure, and setting age-appropriate and realistic expectations to either support their healthy development or heal them if they are vulnerable and traumatised. This approach can be used by caregivers at home, in school, and in day care, combined with a low arousal approach that aligns with the earlier co-regulation and regulation aspects. The low arousal approach will be described in more detail later.

Finding a balance between structure and connection is essential for raising emotionally healthy and competent children (Juul, 2016; Jørgensen, 2017). Demanding something from children and involving them in the family community help them feel valued and respected, while setting personal and individual boundaries can help create a sense of authentic authority. By practising these principles, parents can help their children develop the skills they need to thrive. Research conducted in Denmark in 2012 found that families that strike a balance between connection and structure are relatively rare, making up just 39 per cent of families studied. Of the remaining 61 per cent, 26 per cent don't have any connection or structure, and 34 per cent have a lot of structure and only a little connection (Dahl, 2012; Jørgensen, 2017). Some aspects of a good structure include, for example, the predictability and stability of daily routines and rhythms of the day adapted to the child's age and development.

In Denmark, all newborns and their parents are supported for the first couple of years by health nurse visits at home; they guide parents and follow the development of the child, which is very beneficial for the prevention of vulnerability and traumatisation of children. As it's difficult to find the balance, Bruce Perry highlights local community initiatives that also support parents from when children are born onwards, providing the necessary guidance, knowledge, and support to raise healthier and more resilient children (Szalavitz & Perry, 2010). This demonstrates the importance of societies' investing in preventive support. Again, it takes a village to raise a child, and, when you assess adequate care, it's important also to be mindful of seeking information and details on what the help and support look like that are provided by the people in the network identified in the previous exercise.

Concerning safely demonstrated boundaries and authority, Danish family therapist Jesper Juul stressed the significance of redefining healthy boundaries. Rather than generally formulating commands to make the child behave the right way, according to the family, it works better when boundaries are expressed personally and individually. For instance, transform the general "you don't put your feet on the table" to "I do not want you to put your feet on the table". This would help the parent get a sense of authentic authority that resonates more deeply with children and helps them respect the boundaries much more easily as they wish to collaborate when met in this way (Juul, 2016).

Jesper Juul's approach to healthy boundaries stems from the belief that children are competent individuals who need to feel valued and respected. This approach helps children understand that their behaviour affects others, and that they must be mindful of their actions. Juul also emphasises the importance of giving children tasks and responsibilities to build their self-esteem and sense of competence. Children also learn to take themselves seriously and develop their inner authority, resilience, and robustness by being involved in the family community and treated as equal members (Jørgensen, 2017).

Care for children with special needs due to trauma and diagnoses

My experience as a caregiver for children at risk in a residential home and as a consultant in high-risk cases working to help parents care for children with special needs has shown me the importance of all the topics covered above. For children with special care needs due to trauma and diagnoses such as autism and ADHD, their importance is even more pronounced as we support their health, development, and well-being in the best way possible. Traumatised children require extra support to heal the damage that has been done to their development, and this might be difficult because their behaviour often challenges adults and their nervous system, demanding too much from the parents and professionals around them with the resources available.

Being an authoritative, caring, calm, and collected adult for them and engaging them in decision-making and problem-solving as much as possible, to ensure they have as much control over their life as possible, will create changes faster than you often expect. We must look behind the behaviour and understand what happened to them and what they are reacting to and remind ourselves that our way of approaching them will determine the outcome. This process may involve providing additional resources, such as training in parenting, teaching, and behavioural guidance, to help caregivers engage with the child most effectively.

One helpful approach is the low arousal approach developed by Professor Andrew McDonnell, which can be particularly effective for children with challenging behaviours (McDonnell, 2010). Customised practices developed for working with children with autism and ADHD can also prove beneficial. The low arousal approach builds on professionals' self-awareness concerning their interactions with children, as a state of low arousal requires a high level of reflection on professionals' own behaviour and how they are moderating their own arousal levels to become better at co-regulating children (McDonnell, 2010). Children's heightened sensitivity to emotional affect in other people demands that professionals be much more aware of emotional regulation than usual when affected by emotions and sensations. Otherwise, the children will be affected. The adults are responsible for the children's behaviour.

Another key aspect is how to help the children we work with experience a sense of self-control and self-agency to support their self-regulation. Quite simply, during escalating conflicts and emotional stress, our responsibility and task as adults are to guide and support the child to retain a sense of self-control and stay within the windows of tolerance described earlier, to prevent a chaotic sense of overwhelm in their system (Hejlskov Elvén et al., 2012). When in a situation of escalating conflict, there is a need to remind ourselves and each other that the child wouldn't react with such emotional affect if not overwhelmed by circumstances. Often, this stems from not being capable of meeting the demands of the surroundings, and adults need to understand the triggers behind reactions and how the child can meet them differently to help them feel safe and in control. When I am curious about how the child perceived the situation and what caused the reaction, and then consider this in relation to their special needs and trauma, their response always makes sense to me.

The low arousal approach offers diverse strategies for managing highly aroused children.

Our focus must be on changing their context regarding the demands we set and the way we communicate them, not necessarily reducing them but noticing if they are the right ones and if they can meet them, or if there is something we can do to communicate these demands in ways they will accept and say yes to them. Often, the conflict doesn't arise from unreasonable demands but from the adults' communicating them in ways that don't work for the children (Hejlskov Elvén et al., 2012).

Other strategies include making them laugh, distracting them, and not maintaining eye contact for too long, as more than a few seconds of eye contact in times of conflict and demand will likely escalate the conflict. When there is a team, you can also make a change in the adults working with the child to make a new start because, in these situations, it's not about winning and losing but about creating a safe and regulated child in control of themself and not causing stress and further traumatisation (Hejlskov Elvén et al., 2012). It's all about demanding the right things at the right time so that they will succeed, build strength, resources, and skills, and develop in the safest and most healthy way for them.

The reason for bringing this into this chapter is to highlight that vulnerable and traumatised children have special care needs, and meeting these needs will change their everyday life in ways that are very much demanded. Research shows that more than half of all conflict between children and professionals working in caring contexts outside the home arises in demand situations, and that the level of conflict can be diminished by changing things in their surroundings (Hejlskov Elvén et al., 2012).

Chapter 7 investigated the importance of high-quality day care and schools for the child's health, well-being, and development, and one of the essential professional tasks in the modern world generally has become to develop relational competence (Klinge, 2018; Detlevsen, 2022). Globally, it has become increasingly evident that children with autism are suffering in neurotypical settings, ending up with severe trauma and a huge impact on their self-esteem, self-advocacy, and self-confidence if we try to make them fit into these contexts without any support. This could have been prevented if we were adapting the demands to the special needs of these children and supporting them, instead of requesting of them things they cannot provide, correcting their behaviour, and putting them in the wrong (Gillespie-Lynch et al., 2017).

As previously mentioned, the same goes for children with undiagnosed ADHD, who experience 20,000 more reprimands than other children by age 10 (Jellinek, 2010), influencing their self-esteem, self-advocacy, and self-confidence and leaving them at risk of being severely traumatised (Furukawa et al., 2017). Thus, we must use this knowledge to assess whether they are being provided with adequate care at home and in other areas to avoid further traumatisation and vulnerability.

Case example: David

When David, a 7-year-old, began school, his father had a mental breakdown and left him alone with his mother, a mother he generally felt safe with and who possessed some adequate parenting skills but struggled with structure, stability, daily routines, and disciplining, leaving David somewhat dysregulated. At school, he couldn't necessarily concentrate and regulate himself in class. His class generally had a high level of conflict, some classmates started bullying him, and his teacher was annoyed by him, which left David as the scapegoat of the whole situation. Altogether, the absence of his father, his mother's instability, and the crisis at school disturbed him in ways that left him with symptoms of ADHD, making the situation worse.

Working with the family in their home, I advocated that all the adults around David get together and find the right way to help him. Instead of thinking he needed to be fixed, we should find ways to change the situation at home with his mother, the relationship with his father, and the problems in school. Then, when stability had been established, trauma therapy should be considered.

The most challenging thing to change was at school, and I assumed it would be better for him to change schools. However, it turned out that there would be a shift in teachers after the summer holiday, giving him a window of opportunity to start over and get a second chance. As a part of the collaboration, I had the opportunity to explain to the new teachers about the situation, his condition, and what we aimed to achieve. They engaged in the collaboration enthusiastically to make it work, and we slowly succeeded, one step at a time. After some time, there were still triggers because he felt unsafe at school owing to incidents with the previous teacher, but the situation became so stable and safe that the traumatic incidents belonged in the past. Then, he could finally start processing the trauma from the first, challenging school year. For David, this intervention at a critical time in his life changed the downward, negative spiral into an upward, positive one. So it can be for many children when the adults around them collaborate on all levels.

The above stresses the importance of cultivating more relational skills and gentle caring in professional contexts and why assessing the level of adequate care vulnerable and traumatised children experience outside their homes is essential. This is to make sure that important information and aspects are not left out of our final balanced risk assessment. It also demonstrates the importance of engaging all the resources available, including the child themself, to build a holistic solution to the challenges the child is experiencing, making sure that changes happen in all arenas and resources are used well. This can be done by sharing knowledge and expertise to create the solution that works best for the individual child.

The engagement and involvement of individual adults and children are fundamental principles of working with the solution-focused approach, making it very helpful and influential in work done with vulnerable and traumatised children. From my understanding, it's an illusion to believe that we can create any form of lasting, sustainable, meaningful change for the people we work with without engaging them in building the solution. Yet, many children and parents experience a lack of this engagement in the different professional support systems around them, and this is why I find the solution-focused approach so important and useful to help change this experience and provide a different outcome when both assessing the risk and creating change.

As the low arousal approach reminds us, as professionals, we must be aware that, when we work with a family, we become a part of a system. According to systems theory, the whole is greater than the sum of its parts, and every time a person joins or leaves a system, it changes (edX.org, 2020). This means that our presence in the family can either make its members do better or be more stressed and can influence the assessment profoundly without us recognising this.

To ensure children's safety in high-risk and high-complexity cases, it isn't possible to use the solution-focused approach in the same way as it is used in the therapy setting. It must be adapted to the high-risk context, combining the two tasks of creating change and making risk assessments concerning children's safety, health, and development (Parker, 2011; Turnell & Edwards, 1999). Before going into this in more detail, I will continue with a general introduction to the solution-focused approach.

An overall introduction to the solution-focused approach

Solution focus brief therapy (SFBT) is a therapeutic approach initially developed by Steve de Shazer, Insoo Kim Berg, and their team, in the 1980s (De Shazer et al., 1986). Besides the therapeutic setting, the approach is successfully used in coaching, mentoring, counselling, supervision, child protection work, and other areas where professionals work with people to create change. In this section about solution focus brief therapy, I will use the term client when referring to the therapeutic setting, where I normally use such terms as parents, children, families, and so on.

SFBT is based on a belief that clients are experts on their own and their children's lives, with the ability to construct their individual solutions to their problems, and they already carry the knowledge inside themselves to solve the issues that led them to become engaged with professionals. Therefore, the professional's job is to ask questions that help the clients to elicit this knowledge to create the needed change and find unique solutions to their problems. These solutions are built on actions that will be useful to undertake towards achieving a more preferred future and are always based on the clients' skills, resources, and strengths (George et al., 2017; Ratner et al., 2012).

By stepping back from the expert position, the professionals are leading from one step behind, facilitating a process where clients and professionals are co-constructing solutions in collaboration rather than the professionals solving the problems or finding solutions for the clients (De Jong & Berg, 2006). For this to happen, the professionals must be sincerely curious about the clients' perspectives and carefully select the questions that will be the most helpful to elicit useful, detailed descriptions of actions and behaviours that could lead to change (De Jong & Berg, 2006; Ratner et al., 2012).

We must listen carefully, with a constructive ear, to the openings, resources, strengths, and skills that a client demonstrates in conversations. This focus supports asking questions about resources, skills, and strengths for the client to use to create the change they want to achieve, helping them reflect on this change and their preferred future (Iveson et al., 2012; Ratner et al., 2012). Another aspect of this way of listening involves registering the client's words and then using the same wording in the conversation (Ratner et al., 2012).

Solution focus fundamentally differs from other therapeutic approaches in that it doesn't need to understand the problem and its causes to solve it (De Jong & Berg, 2006; O'Hanlon, 1987). Solution-focused practitioners aren't problem-phobic, and it's essential to be attentive to and acknowledge the client's difficulties (Ratner et al., 2012), but SFBT therapists don't solve problems (McKergow & Korman, 2009). Nor, in conversations with clients, do they focus on talking about the past, diagnosis, getting detailed descriptions of the issues, or seeking to understand why things evolved as they did, as this could turn out to be unhelpful (Ratner et al., 2012). Instead, it's believed that the solution isn't necessarily related to the problem (De Shazer et al., 2007; De Jong & Berg, 2006), but the solution-building process will always focus on the client's preferred future for themselves and instances of success (McKergow & Korman, 2009; Ratner et al., 2012). This process helps the clients describe their preferred future, and conversations should aim to find the quickest way for them to achieve this.

Other basic principles of SFBT are "don't fix it if it's not broken", "if it's not working – do something else" (De Shazer et al., 2007; Ratner et al., 2012), and "the solution is in the detail", referring to the understanding that solutions are found in the detailed description of actions and behaviours, not by talking about emotions. Therefore, the professional's questions must aim to get as many details as possible on specific actions and behaviour that will be helpful to achieve the client's preferred future. It will help them think about what to do and how to do it and investigate past or present successes. The belief is that, if they have done it once, they will be able to do more of it when becoming aware of what they did and how they did it, and what they drew upon in themself to accomplish it.

As it's essential for the effectiveness of SFBT to have a clear picture of the outcome that the client hopes to achieve from the sessions (Shennan & Iveson, 2012), the opening question in the first conversation at the solution-focused training centre, BRIEF, is the best hope question (Ratner et al., 2012). It serves to establish a contract with the client and will help the client get straight to talking about the hoped-for outcome instead of elaborating on the problems (Iveson et al., 2012). When asking the best hope question, it's essential to be aware of whether the client's answer is oriented towards the outcome or the process and the content of the therapy, because we must know where to go before we talk about how to get there (Iveson et al., 2012). Once we know where to go, there are many ways to get there, and possibilities for change open up (Ratner et al., 2012).

After the best hope and contract have been settled, the preferred future will be explored in the conversation, and both will be described in more detail in Chapter 9. Realising how a family will achieve this lies in the solution-focused conversations with families and their network, and this is applicable not only in the child protection context but in all areas where professionals are working with children and adolescents and collaborating with their parents and network.

Being clear about where to go helps bring hope and perspective for change as we can start to investigate all the recent or past times in their everyday life where they have succeeded in achieving this by behaving in a particular way and carrying out specific actions. However, vulnerable families are more likely to need a combination of thinking through the problems and finding the right solutions through the questions asked themselves and getting the necessary professional guidance to develop their parenting skills.

The solution-focused conversation

The structure of the SFBT that I have been taught at BRIEF has one frame for the first session, with three key questions that go like this:

- "What are your best hopes?"
- "What will be different in your life if these hopes are achieved?"
- "What is already in place that will contribute to these hopes becoming a reality?" (Ratner et al., 2012, p. 31).

The structure for the subsequent follow-up sessions is to ask, "What's better (De Shazer et al., 2007; Ratner et al., 2012), helping the clients to direct their focus at the progress since the last session, based "on the assumption that there are always times that the client does something they are pleased about" (George et al., 2017, p. 24). The elements of the follow-up session are covered in Chapter 10.

SFBT has a core belief that problems aren't present 100 per cent of the time, as there will always be times when the issue is absent or less apparent (De Shazer et al., 2007). These moments are called exceptions (De Shazer, 1988) and are considered very important for the clients finding their own unique solution to the problem: what is already working well must be investigated, and as many detailed descriptions as possible of what the client has done to make this happen must be obtained (De Jong & Berg, 2006). I will return to the exception questions later and, instead, engage now in a similar yet different question about what's already working well. One basic principle of SFBT is "if it works, do more of it", and so, to build solutions, the therapist's role is also to encourage clients to do more of what is already working (De Shazer et al., 2007). Realising what they are already doing or have done to conquer the present or former obstacles helps them become conscious about resources, skills, and strengths to use to create further change.

These are some of the important questions we can ask to assess the adequate care of the child and they can also be asked concerning situations in the child's other contexts to help secure their well-being and development in these contexts. Besides providing important information for the balanced risk assessment, they will reconnect the people involved to their sense of self-advocacy, self-esteem, self-confidence, and hope that things can and will get better again. Regarding the positive impact on the child stemming from adequate care, it's important to remember to ask questions about this impact and signs of healthy development and well-being that the child is presently showing or did show previously, to assess how worried to be.

Box 8.1

- What are you already doing that is working well in the care of your child?
- What have you already done recently that aligns with your best hopes for the future?
- How did you do it?
- What difference did it make?
- How did your child respond to this?
- How was it good for your child – and how was it good for you?
- What else have you done?
- What have others seen you do?
- What does it say about you that you were able to do that?
- What does your husband/wife/daughter/son/foster child/pupil do when you do that?
- Are you pleased with that? And what do you then do?
- What signs of well-being and healthy development is the child showing now?
- What else? What more?

Case example: Victor – continued

While working with Victor and his mother, mentioned earlier, this conversation took place to elicit the details about what the mother was doing well in the care of Victor when she dealt with his tantrums safely and calmly, instead of ending in an escalating conflict situation.

Rikke: What are you doing when dealing with the conflicts in a good and safe way for Victor?

Mother: I am feeling more grounded, taking it easier with him, talking more calmly and reasoning with him about how shorts and summer shoes aren't the things to wear when it's snowing outside – somehow he accepts better the things I say when I am more grounded and our behaviour towards each other is more harmonic and balanced somehow. It's just better mornings when we can talk to each other instead of being screamed and shouted at. It's sucking all the energy out of me when he is screaming at me.

Rikke: What does Victor do when you are more grounded, calmer and at ease and reason with him in this situation?

Mother: He still tries to get things his way, but when he senses that I have more energy and am more grounded and relaxed, it's easier to get through to him – I only need to repeat myself a couple of times instead of him keeping going – somehow it seems easier for him to see things more from my perspective – that it's not reasonable to have shorts and summer shoes on in the wintertime.

Rikke: So, how else does it show in the way you behave when you have more energy and are more relaxed and grounded?

Mother: I guess, I am being calmer and more regulated myself to embrace him and contain his tantrum and crisis, so I am *not* losing it myself and won't shout at him. (Mother laughing a little)

Rikke: (Laughing a little with the mother) What are you doing that tells him that you are embracing him and are containing his tantrums in a calm way?

Mother: I have a completely different energy, both mentally and physically, to be able to contain him – somehow, it shows in my voice, body language – That my words and body language match – and his tantrums can't shake me – and he finds calm in this.

Rikke: Yes – and when he is calmer, what does he then do?

Mother: He follows our structure better in the morning and lets me guide him more easily without rejecting every little thing I tell him to do, for example, to brush his teeth, eat his breakfast and get out of the door in time.

From this little sequence, you can see how I am carefully choosing to ask about the details of the exceptions and what's working well in relation to the overwhelming level of conflict they experienced previously and that occasionally still occurs. At the same time, the mother becomes aware of what she is doing that is impacting Victor in a positive way and helps him to react differently. When she becomes aware of this, it leaves her conscious of what she can do and how she can handle things in the future, using this for sustainable solutions and leaving her less powerless in future conflicts. These kinds of conversations are beneficial to investigate the details of the present but also past actions and behaviours and can create immediate change as the clients become consciously aware of how to handle things to overcome obstacles in the present.

The same kinds of conversations are helpful with other professionals and the private network and will help generate shared knowledge and experience at network meetings. What might help a child calm down with one person in one context might help them calm down in a different context with another person too. Thus, it's worth trying to see if we can build solutions on what is already working.

As solution-focused practitioners, we believe change happens in interaction with other people. Aiming to empower people, we focus on helping clients take responsibility for their actions and behaviours, which means solutions are based on activities they can undertake themselves, leaving them more independent of others to change their behaviour. Still, when the clients start to change, their relationships and environments will most likely react to this in a way that will stimulate further change, which is based on the systemic approach mentioned earlier, positing that, when one person changes behaviour, it will lead to whole-system change (edX. org, 2020).

The preferred future and also what's already working should be described from the client's own perspective, other people's perspective, and an interactional perspective (De Jong & Berg, 2006; Ratner et al., 2012). Interactional descriptions have power to make the hoped-for change happen and will influence others to fit in with our hope and plans (Iveson et al., 2012)

The mindset of the solution-focused approach is what really matters in solution-focused work with vulnerable and traumatised children and youth. Seldom will you be able to lead conversations strictly following the structure of the conversations shown above outside the therapeutic context, but using the mindset in action is what we are aiming for, moving back and forth between risk and safety or overwhelming emotion and detailed descriptions of behaviour and actions that highlight the client's strength, resources, and skills to create change and leave them more hopeful, regulated, and empowered after a conversation with us. Now, it's time to investigate a bit more about how it can be applied to the high-risk, highly complex context of working with vulnerable, traumatised, at-risk children and young people.

The solution-focused approach to working with vulnerable and traumatised children

Working with children, parents, professionals, and the private network in collaborative processes can be a challenging task if a structured framework and a solution-focused approach are not used, because there is a high risk of discussion rather than reflection, problem focus instead of solution focus, and a blame game more than a collaborative, respectful process. The solution-focused conversation is a powerful tool to make the process well structured, engaging, and effective, and different frameworks have been developed for this purpose, such as the Signs of Safety framework or the Family Roadmap process that Sonja Parker has developed. I will introduce this in more detail in Chapter 9.

The structure of the conversations developed in these frameworks is slightly different to the one described above:

- Worries.
- Exceptions and descriptions of demonstrated safety and protection.
- Goals.
- Next step towards the goal (Parker, 2011; Turnell & Edwards, 1999).

Between the two ends of the scale, consisting of the worry statement at one end and the safety goals or goals statement at the other, lies the building block to the solution based on exceptions, what's working well, or what has worked well in the past that people can reconnect to and use to create the needed change. So, the questions gathered in this chapter will most likely both support the children and families to solve their problems and help professionals be more precise in the risk assessment for any given situation.

Before assessing the goals to collaborate on concerning vulnerable and traumatised children, all the needed information on worries, exceptions, demonstrated safety and protection, and the child's well-being must be gathered to do an in-depth analysis and assessment of the child's circumstances. In previous chapters and exercises, we have investigated the present risk in the child's life, the past harm done to the child, the damage it has done to them, and the future risk if nothing changes. We have also been looking into the protective factors, particularly networks and signs of resilience. The last piece of the puzzle of what we need to address involves describing all that works or has worked in the past when it comes to the parents, the private and professional networks, and the well-being and healthy development of the child. Again, it takes a village to raise a child, and, if risk is present outside the home, it's crucial to view the situation in this context and at home.

This part of the process is mainly about engaging children, parents, professionals, and the private network in conversations, getting important information on both the present moment and past successes, exceptions, and coping strategies. We have previously discovered there will be different concerns if the child has never been safe and well cared for or if it has "just" been in the last 2 years of a 12-year-old's life that they have been experiencing adversity and harm. The information also gives us a lot of actions and behaviours on which to build solutions in the future. When we look into present and past exceptions and engage with the network, we use exception questions such as the ones in Box 8.2.

Box 8.2

- Describe episodes where the concern is/was not present, and you dealt with them appropriately. What did you do? What did others help you do, and what did the child then do for you to succeed in doing this?
- How often has this happened? What did it take for you to succeed with this?
- What have you or others done that has created safety for the child at home/school/day care/or other?
- When, in the last couple of days, have you done – even in a small way – the things you hope to do in the future? What might others have seen you do?
- Do you know of a time in the past when things have been better? When was this?
- Back then, what did you or others do that was consistent with the child's needs according to the child's age? For how long did you/they manage to do this, and how did it impact the child?

- Who helped the you/the parents/carers to provide adequate care back then?
- What did they do, and how was this helpful for the parents?
- What difference did it make concerning the parenting situation?
- How did it impact the child, and what signs of well-being was/is the child showing?
- Have there been times when you protected your children from experiencing these conflicts between you as parents? What did you do to protect them, and who/what helped you?
- Tell me about times you have been able to look after your children well enough and meet their needs or able to keep your children safe in relation to the things we are worried about now.
- Have there been times when you controlled your anger and stopped yourself from hitting your kids and you did something different? Then, what did you do? Who/what helped you?
- Are there times when you have been able to stay sober and care properly for your kids for a period? How did you do this, and who/what helped you succeed with this?

Information on how much safety, protection, and adequate care there has been over time can help us understand how severe the neglect and risk have been. This brings practice depth to our reflection and balanced risk assessment in the present moment. Another kind of question that helps support this practice depth and also helps create empowerment for the people engaged in the processes is the coping question, which is very similar to the questions already covered. However, these are primarily used when clients express that things are worse instead of better or if they are overwhelmed by challenges, can't see any light, and may have lost hope. This I will return to in Chapter 9 when addressing hope as life-saving.

All the different questions we have covered in this chapter and variations on them are questions we can ask ourselves and our colleagues in case consultations using the Circle of Safety and Reconnection, assessing the present and previous care and the child's well-being and healthy development. I usually structure it by categorising the information gathered on this topic, looking at information about (1) the care given by the parents, (2) the private network, and (3) the care given in professional arenas. Lastly, (4) I describe the signs of well-being and healthy development of the child, making sure to cover all the details needed. This is what you will do in this chapter's exercise, but, first, a little about children's engagement.

Engaging children in building the right solutions for them

Usually, when working with parents and professional and private networks, I talk to the child first and get the child's perspective on everything we need to cover in the collaboration. With reference to safety issues, I have already introduced Sonja Parker's Safety House. Concerning more general views on the child's life, I use the Three Houses tool developed by Nicki Weld and Maggie Greening (Weld & Greening, 2004). This is a tool to incorporate children's voices in the balanced risk assessment in a safe way for children.

The Three Houses represent the three columns in the Signs of Safety framework describing, respectively, what we are worried about, what's working well, and what needs to happen (Turnell & Edwards, 1999). They are adapted for talking to children in a more age-appropriate and creative way with drawings of the House of Worries, the House of Good Things, and the House of Dreams (Weld & Greening, 2004). Just like when we talk to their parents, we talk to the children about what they have experienced as being difficult and harmful to them and how they feel about it. We also talk about all the good things and exceptions to the difficult things and how they think and feel about them. Finally, we talk to them about what they wish to be different in their lives for them to feel better and for life to become better. What are the things that they would like to be different, and what would it look like through their eyes when things are safe and well in their life? This also elicits information about all areas of the child's life, such as home, school, friends, network, and so on, and has a broader perspective than the Safety House.

Other times, I make a list with children about what they are good at, their strengths and resources, or what they have succeeded in doing since a given date or situation, using the same types of questions as we covered above or asking them about what they are proud of doing. I am always aware of empowering and engaging children as much as possible in safe ways so that they can take an active part in the solution-building process and not just provide us with information. However, I must still get the adults to take responsibility for the process and results. Therefore, I always put the child at the centre of attention, talking to them first, using creative items and toys according to their age, before engaging all the adults around them. For this, I have put together a small suitcase with different kinds of toys, Playmobil toy figures, and colours to draw with.

Teenagers, in particular, must be engaged in the solution-building process as they have a will of their own and will go their own way if we don't make engaging in the change process meaningful and worthwhile. Being in the process of becoming adults, they must take on a greater part of the responsibility for solutions when it comes to changing their own destructive or self-destructive behaviour over time. But again, at the end of the day, adults need to take responsibility for providing the right support and context for them to succeed.

Through our conversations with children, it's crucial to gain in-depth insight and description of the child's perspective on their care situation and their actual health, development, and well-being, together with signs of resilience and details of their resources, strength, and capabilities, as it will help qualify the balanced risk assessment of the child's situation. It's widespread that vulnerable and traumatised children and young people resist talking to professionals. They might often answer our questions in ways such as "I don't know", "I don't want to talk to you", or "When are we done?" or not say anything at all but hide in their hoodies.

Inspired by the American psychologist Paul Watzlawick (1921–2007), my understanding is that all behaviour is communication, meaning that it's impossible for us as humans not to communicate (Watzlawick et al., 2011). Thus, I am curious about what the child is trying to tell me through these replies. I allow them not to say anything and will not force them to engage with me, as they have a right to be heard and engaged in the work, but they also have the right not to use this right. Even though we want to engage with them, they might not want anything to do with us, because they don't know us, don't trust us, or for some other reason. We must see and respect their boundaries when they can't communicate them verbally.

Often, I experience professionals getting stressed about not getting anything from a child to use for their risk assessment. They might feel that they have failed to connect with the child, but, often, this couldn't be further from the truth. It's the nature of the work with vulnerable and traumatised children that they protect themselves by not engaging, and, if we push them, they are more likely to close down and disengage even more than if they feel safe, and we respect their boundaries. This kind of relational work takes time, no matter the context and profession, and, if we keep showing up and letting them know that we want to engage with them, slowly, they might open up and let us into their inner world at their own pace.

My general rule is always to show up and explain to them who you are, why you are there, and what you would like to happen in the meeting. You might tell them about your conversation with their parents and teachers and give them something from you to connect with. Then, let them know that it's vital to you to hear what they have to say as well, and that you have learned from talking to many children and young people that it might be challenging to talk about such things with a stranger like you. So, it's perfectly okay to tell as much or as little as they like. One way to give them control and power in these vulnerable processes is to give them choices – as many as possible. I intend to leave them in control, with a sense of safety and power in these processes concerning their lives, and to let them know that I see, hear, and understand where they are at, and that it's okay to be them.

Then, introduce the Three Houses, the Safety House, the Safety and Support Circle tool, or any other tool you use and give them choices throughout the conversation, such as, which of the three houses do you like to start with? Will you write or draw, or should I? What colours do you want? Use toys and make them choose from different toys and so on. If they are young people, and you don't draw, ask them if they would like to start by saying something about school, friends, family, or something else? When giving them choices, you give them control, and they are more likely to feel safe with you, if not the first time, then, over time.

If they aren't engaging in any of this, you could sit with them for a little while or give them something to reflect on rather than trying to get something from them. You can explain the situation from your perspective and give small psycho-educative talks about their symptoms or pass on some compliments that you have heard from their parents, teachers, or similar.

Listening with a constructive ear and talking with adults about the child's strengths, skills, resources, and interests might elicit much information that you can use to warm up the conversation in a safe way and then use patience as your most powerful tool, as it will most likely be rewarded when the child starts to get to know you and feel safe with you. Through your consistency, trustworthiness, and patience, they are most likely to engage with you in time, and you will be able to help them better in the long run.

Case example: Shannon

Shannon – a young teenager – didn't want to engage with me most of the time while I was working with her parents to support them in caring for her and her siblings. They all had multiple diagnoses and trauma with severe symptoms, almost leaving them in total isolation at home. One time, I insisted on having a conversation with her to explain the connection between her challenges in the present moment and the trauma she experienced owing to surgical procedures in her first year and some very traumatic experiences in her time in day care and school. While I explained this to her, she didn't say anything. Still, I could see that she was listening to me intently and nodding her head when I put words to how children feel when experiencing things like this. It showed me that it was beneficial to her to get this information, and that it had been the right thing to do, and so I continued giving her all the information I thought might be helpful to her as psychoeducation. During this conversation, she didn't comment on anything but just asked me a few questions. Later, she used it to explain something about her reactions to her parents, helping them to understand her better; so, through my providing her with this information, she became better equipped to understand and help herself. She even helped her parents to support her better. This is also a way of engaging children in the solution-building processes.

Summarising briefly, it's important to highlight the description and assessment of the care situation for the child from details of the adequate care and support of the parents, the private network, and professionals around them in all their contexts, and how this helps the child thrive and develop healthily. From the completed balanced risk assessment, we can now determine and prioritise the goals to collaborate on, which we will continue with in Chapter 9.

Exercise

To adapt this to your specific context, you can replace or supplement information on the parents with information on other adults' and peers' behaviour of relevance to the child's challenges.

Gather the different papers from the last exercises and, to start with, focus on the ones from Chapter 3 on the child's immediate safety and Chapter 7 on protective factors and resilience. Now, beneath the safety descriptions, start filling out the detailed descriptions with as many details as possible about the adequate care for the child at home and in other areas and finish with the description of the child's health, well-being, and healthy development. Be sure to include information about the parents and the professional and private networks.

Now, for the last time, with the additional information and with all information available to weigh up, assess the scale from 0 to 10, where 10 indicates the child is completely safe, you don't need to worry about them, and no help is needed. 0 is the opposite: it's the most unsafe possible, and the child must be secured immediately.

Assess this information against your reflection about your overall balanced risk assessment in the last exercise, consider if eliciting this information might have made you more worried or less worried about the child, and reflect on which of the people you would like to engage in the further process.

Also, be aware of questions that arise from going through this that you would like to know more about and make a list of them to ask everyone involved with the child.

References

Andersen, S. H. (2022). Mit store spørgsmål (Season 2; Episode 7). In *Hvorfor er teenageårene essientielle for et godt voksenliv?* Podcast publishing science report for Danmarks Frie Forskningsfond, on Spotify and Apple.

Caspersen, Marianne, & Laustsen, Charlotte. (2009). *Systematisk sagsbehandling i børnesager - principper og arbejdsgange.* UC Vest Press.

Dahl, K. M. (2012). Følelser og autoritet – familiepraksis i de 15-åriges familier. In M. H. Ottosen (Ed.), *15-åriges hverdagsliv og udfordringer: rapport fra femte dataindsamling af forløbsundersøgelsen af børn født i 1995* (pp. 105–135). SFI – Det Nationale Forskningscenter for Velfærd.

De Jong, Peter, & Berg, Insoo Kim. (2006). *Løsningsfokuserede samtaler.* Hans Reitzels Forlag.

De Shazer, S. (1988). *Clues – investigating solutions in brief therapy.* W. W. Norton.

De Shazer, S., Berg, I. K., Lipchik, E., Nunnally, E., Molnar, A., Gigerich, W., & Weiner-Davis, M. (1986). Brief therapy: focused solution development. *Family Process, 25*(2), 207–221.

De Shazer, S., Dolan, Y., with Korman, H., Trepper, T., Mc Collum, E., & Berg, I. K. (2007). *More than miracles.* Routledge.

Detlevsen, L. (2022). Pædagogisk relationskompetence påvirker børns livsmuligheder. EVA. www.eva.dk/dagtilbud-boern/paedagogisk-relationskompetence-paavirker-boerns-livsmuligheder

edX.org. (2020). Introduction to systems theory in social work. Author.

Furukawa, Emi, Alsop, Brent, Sowerby, Paula, Jensen, Stephanie, & Tripp, Gail. (2017). Evidence for increased behavioral control by punishment in children with attention-deficit hyperactivity disorder. *Journal of Child Psychology and Psychiatry, 58*(3), 248–257.

George, E., Iveson, C., & Ratner, H. (2017). *BRIEFER – a solution focused practice manual.* BRIEF.

Gillespie-Lynch, Kristen, Bublitz, Dennis, Donachie, Annemarie, Wong, Vincent, Brooks, Patricia J., & D'Onofrio, Joanne. (2017). "For a long time our voices have been hushed": using student perspectives to develop supports for neurodiverse college students. *Frontiers in Psychology, 8*.

Hart, S. (2009). *Den følsomme hjerne: hjernens udvikling gennem tilknytning og samhørighedsbånd* (1st ed.). Reitzel. doi.org/9788741253428

Hejlskov Elvén, Bo, Veje, Hanne, & Beier, Henning. (2012). *Udviklingsforstyrrelser og psykisk sårbarhed.* Dansk Psykologisk Forlag.

Iveson, Chris, George, Evan, & Ratner, Harvey. (2012). *Brief coaching – a solution focused approach.* Routledge.

Jellinek, S. M. (2010). Don't let ADHD crush children's self-esteem. *Clinical Psychiatry News*, May, 1.

Juul, J. (2016). *Dit kompetente barn.* Gyldendal.

Jørgensen, P. S. (2017). *Robuste børn.* Krisetligt Dagblads Forlag.

Klinge, L. (2018). *Relationskompetence.* Aarhus Universitetsforlag.

McDonnell, A. (2010). *Managing aggressive behaviour in care settings.* John Wiley.

McKergow, Mark, & Korman, Harry. (2009). Inbetween – neither inside nor outside: the radical simplicity of solution-focused brief therapy. *Journal of Systemic Therapies*, *28*(2), 34–49.

O'Hanlon, W. H. (1987). *Underlying principles of Milton Ericson's therapy and hypnosis.* Norton Books.

Ockwell-Smith, S. (2016). *The gentle parenting book: how to raise calmer, happier children from birth to seven.* Little, Brown.

Parker, S. (2011). *Partnering for safety case consultation process: a process for consulting on child protection cases using the partnering for safety risk assessment and planning framework.* SP Consultancy. www.partneringforsafety.com

Perry, D. B., & Winfrey, Oprah. (2022). *What happened to you? Conversations on trauma, resilience and healing.* Bluebird.

Ratner, H., George, E., Iveson, C., & ProQuest. (2012). *Solution focused brief therapy: 100 key points and techniques.* Routledge.

Save the Children's Resource Centre. (2022). *Tronick's still face experiment.* YouTube.

Shennan, G., & Iveson, C. (2012). From solution to description. In C. Franklin, T. Trapper, W. Lingerich, & E. McCollum (Eds), *Solution focused brief therapy – a handbook of evidence-based practice.* Oxford University Press.

Siegel, D. J. (2020). *The developing mind* (3rd ed.). Guilford Press.

Siegel, D. J., & Bryson, T. P. (2020). *The power of showing up: how parental presence shapes who our kids become and how their brains get wired.* Scribe UK.

Struik, A. (2019). *Treating chronically traumatized children: the sleeping dogs method* (2nd ed.). Routledge.

Szalavitz, M., & Perry, B. D. (2010). *Born for love: why empathy is essential – and endangered* (1st ed.). William Morrow. Contributor biographical information www.loc.gov/catdir/enhancements/fy1011/2010280500-b.html; publisher description www.loc.gov/catdir/enhancements/fy1011/2010280500-d.html

Turnell, A., & Edwards, S. (1999). *Signs of safety: a solution and safety oriented approach to child protection casework.* W. W. Norton.

Van der Kolk, B. A. (2015). *The body keeps the score: mind, brain and body in the transformation of trauma.* Wellbeing Collection, Penguin Books.

Watzlawick, P., Bavelas, J. B., & Jackson, D. D. (2011). *Pragmatics of human communication: a study of interactional patterns, pathologies, and paradoxes* (First published as a Norton paperback; reissued in 2014). W.W. Norton.

Weld, N., & Greening, M. (2004). The three houses. *Social Work Now*, (29), 34–37.

Chapter 9

The Circle of Safety and Reconnection, Step 7

Setting the right goals to create safety, health, development, and well-being for the child

How to use the balanced risk assessment as the basis for setting goals

When you and your organisation are clear on the worry statements from Chapter 6 and the balanced risk assessment in Chapter 8, then you can clearly identify what changes you need to see in the care of the child and in the child's development. Afterwards, you can engage children, parents, private networks, and professionals in the goal-formulating process and add their perspectives to find a common project for collaboration.

Honest collaboration implies that parents know how serious child protection assesses the situation and the reason for the level of concern to create a partnership around creating safety and well-being for their child (Turnell & Edwards, 1997, 1999). Concerning communication, professionals must be very clear about what they need to see happening in the care of the child for the child to be taken care of appropriately and to feel safe (Parker, 2011; Turnell & Edwards, 1997). Realising how the family will achieve this lies in the solution-focused conversations with families and their network.

Professionals being experts on families' lives and telling them how to solve their problems aren't helpful for those families. Still, we are experts in children's development and child protection work and must use this knowledge to inform them precisely about the changes required to keep their children safe and well in their care. Therefore, we must be as clear and specific about the goal statements and safety goals as we are about the worry statements. In the following, I will refer to goal statements unless the context is safety planning processes, where I call them safety goals.

Goal statements and safety goals

Just like the worry statements, the goal statements also need to be written in ordinary language that children, parents, and private networks understand, instead of the professional language we normally use, which they might need help understanding. Involving everybody of relevance in collaborating around the most

DOI: 10.4324/9781003322672-9

important, relevant, and appropriate goals according to the child's needs is a powerful tool (Parker, 2011; Turnell, 2010). These goal statements must be formulated as mirrors of the worry statements, containing descriptions of the direct opposite behaviour of what the worry statements have highlighted as harmful and risky for the children to experience and its impact on them (Parker, 2011; Turnell, 2010).

The questions we need to ask to formulate these goal statements are (Parker, 2015):

- Who wants to see the change?
- What do they want to see the parents (together with a network) do that addresses the worries and creates safety and good enough care for the child?
- What will the child then do differently that will tell us that the parents have changed behaviour and the child is thriving and developing healthily?
- How long do we need to see the parents and child demonstrate this changed behaviour before we can close the case and entrust the ongoing work to the parents and network?

After formulating the goal statements, it's crucial to reflect on them with everyone involved in ways that makes sense and bring all perspectives into play. This process creates a high level of involvement from children, young people, parents, and networks, whether the issues are acknowledged or we are working around denied child abuse (Parker, 2011; Turnell, 2010).

Sonja Parker taught me to formulate both the worry and goal statements from the initial information, before the first meeting with the family, as preparation for the whole process. This helps me articulate them precisely, leaving the family members with no insecurities about the intention of the collaboration. However, I have also learned from her to "leave them in my bag", so to speak. I intend to wait to show them to anybody until, in one way or another, everyone has articulated their best hopes, preferred futures, and worries, so that I can adapt both worry statements and goal statements to the family's and networks' words and they can see themselves in them. In this way, it becomes more of a joint project and a common ground on which to collaborate, which is crucial to succeed in getting everybody on board in the collaboration.

Focusing on being clear on the goals first has helped me find some common ground on which to collaborate with all the families I have worked with since I started using the solution-focused approach. Despite the danger, harm, and disagreements, in general, the families and professionals I meet want the children to be safe and well and show that they care well for the children, and I use this motivation to build and sustain the collaboration. There are often different perspectives and conflicts about what is good enough care for the child to be safe and well and how to get there, and we might not get to a point where we can agree on everything. However, engaging in honest, open-minded, respectful, collaborative dialogues, with a focus on the goals for the child's safety and well-being, and then adding the parents' and networks' own words to the goal will be the most likely way to engage them in finding the appropriate means and plans to move towards it. It's particularly compelling and helpful when the child's voice is the centre of attention and is incorporated into the safety goals that will help the parents and networks take responsibility for the child's safety and well-being, leaving us as social workers and professionals to play a more supportive role (Berg & Kelly, 2000).

In situations where there is denial, there are still ways to work around it, creating meaningful common goals by using the solution-focused approach as our methodology. Often, the denial and disagreement regard the concerns. Still, we can almost always find common ground in collaborating to demonstrate that the things parents are alleged to have done to their children can't happen in the future. By securing this, the children will be safe, and the parents will also be protected from future allegations. Our focus is to collaborate around the fulfilment of goal statements, with the aim of ensuring that all concerns will be handled in a relevant, safe, and secure way for the children in the future.

The worries aren't up for discussion, but we don't have to agree on them or discuss whether something happened or not. Considering the wall of denial mentioned in Chapter 3, it would be a waste of important time to argue whether it happened instead of working to ensure it can't happen in the future. Professionals possess the information, and so worries remain and don't go away because someone tries to disprove them. If people don't engage in formulating the worry statements, it's not a real barrier to nevertheless facilitating the needed change, but, in some way, everybody needs to be engaged in formulating goal statements to help create direction and meaning for all people involved.

This discipline provides hope both in terms of healing for the children and for the collaboration to succeed. I have not yet been unable to reach agreements on a common project with parents and network when focusing on the goals and meeting them from a "not-knowing" position. If we can't agree on anything else to collaborate on, we agree that they want me and child protection out of their lives as soon as possible. This is sufficient and all right, because child protection only disappears if parents demonstrate protection over time.

My stance in the not-knowing position is that I wasn't there in the past, but I am there in the present to be helpful in transforming some serious worries into a sense of safety. If parents and other carers claim they are already doing what I initially formulated as goal statements, I acknowledge this and won't argue with them about it, but I will let them know that words aren't enough for me to assess the situation as safe. Instead, I also need people around the child, such as a reliable private network and professionals, to document this and I need access to the children to talk about how the situation is from their perspective but also to see it demonstrated myself, which means I need to be able to observe children and parents together.

At the end of the day, this is the only approach to make worries go away, and, when adults realise this, they are very likely to engage in the process of getting the professionals and worries out of their way as fast as possible. It's perfectly okay for them to be motivated by this as long as they do what it takes and provide the children with everything that is needed to secure them, both in the short and long term.

In my many processes of engaging people around the children, I am always hopeful that we will succeed in helping the children through the facilitation of a goal-formulating process using solution-focused questions and being aware of separating the ends from the means. Many times, conflicts arise about the concerns and the "means to the end" and not the end itself. So, before we start talking about the support needed and wanted, we must be clear about the goals and also be open to the idea that there are many ways to reach the same goal, leaving us with multiple choices and ways to succeed.

From my solution-focused work with vulnerable children, I have discovered that professionals and families often exchange means for ends. They identify a problem and consider the best means to solve the problem as the right solution – for example, thinking that foster care is the solution to create safety for the child – leaving out all other possible ways to create safety. To consider foster care to create safety for children is definitely okay. Still, this is only one option out of more possibilities, and it doesn't necessarily create safety for the child. Sometimes, it's impossible to find an appropriate foster carer, or the child protection worker's assessment of the child's needs is different from that of the families, networks, and professionals, causing a massive conflict. These conflicts leave the child at more risk without the problem being solved, as the focus shifts from the safety and well-being of the child to the material conflict between the adults. Again, the assessment might be correct, but the issue is that we focus on *how* to solve the problem before considering and agreeing on *what* change we need to create. By leaving out these crucial reflections, we miss out on finding more possibilities and ways to reach the same goal and might be left powerless if foster care isn't an option for the child.

A deep-rooted assumption I carry with me when working with families is that parents always do their best. They strive to do their best to have good relations with their children, giving them a good chance of success and a better future than their own (Berg & Steiner, 2009). However, sometimes their best isn't good enough for the child, and they need help to create the necessary changes for the child to be safe and well. So, whenever things are difficult in the collaboration, I return to this assumption and put words to it. I have found that acknowledging this verbally in my communication with parents allows me to have honest and often difficult conversations with them about what is best for the child and what needs to be different in the parents' care.

The same applies if the child's issues are related to the professionals' context. I also have a deep-rooted belief that all professionals working with children want to be helpful and make a difference for the children. When I teach and supervise professionals, I often help them acknowledge the same in situations of conflict with other professionals, which will help them see things differently and, thereby, approach things differently.

Case example: Alma – continued

Remember Alma's worry statement and trauma-informed worry statement from Chapter 6.

If needed, go back to the last part of Chapter 6, just before the exercise, reread the statements, and see how the safety goal and trauma-informed safety goal mirror them.

Safety goal: Alma

Her mother and father will work together with child protection and a safety network to develop a safety plan that will show everyone around Alma that:

> Alma will always be cared for by safe adults who can protect her from violence and violent conflicts so that she will experience home as a safe place to be, and the adults are responsible for looking after the children. When this happens, Alma will feel safe in both her homes, giving her the energy to participate more actively in family life by doing activities with the other family members in a good and calm way, without conflicts. In addition, Alma will experience a feeling of trust in her parents and her own worth, believing that she is good enough as she is and trusting the adults that she can count on them to protect her and care for her.

Trauma-informed safety goal: Alma

Her mother and father will work together with child protection and a safety network to develop a safety plan that will show everyone that:

> Alma will get the necessary safety, care, connection, attention, stability, love, and sense of belonging from her parents and other family members to be able to heal and process the trauma that has caused severe harm to her development and well-being. This will enable her to safely attach to her parents and other significant people and help her become fundamentally happy, calm, and more easy-going.

The child protection case can be closed when the family has shown that they can provide this and the other safety measures for 6 months.

These statements were produced by mirroring the worry statements after going through all the case files and then adjusting the language to that used by the parents and Alma when we talked to them about their best hopes. I will introduce the best hope question below. After including everyone's perspectives, we started the solution-building process.

Through this process, all involved agreed it was much better for Alma to go and live with her uncle and aunt as they had been the safest adults for her throughout childhood. Everybody acknowledged their unique bond and that they were the last adults she still trusted. As they didn't live far away, she could easily visit her parents and leave when she had had enough. In this way, her mother and father were also able to create a safe home for her siblings and stepmother's children, and contact arrangements were agreed upon to make it safe for everybody to be together when Alma was visiting. Through this process, slowly, all the family members started to restore their relationships with each other. In this way, the parents and a safety network did reach the goal, but in a different way to what was expected by the social worker who hired me to do the safety planning process. However, he also agreed that this was the better solution when I presented it to him.

The in-depth details of the contact arrangements were qualified by having conversations with the whole family about the preferred future and what their family life would look like when the safety goal was reached. From there, we could find inspiration for how they could be around each other in a different way, without conflict and violence, and could also agree on what to do in case conflict arises. Who knows if this would actually lead to Alma coming home to stay with one of her parents in the future because relations were re-established at a safe pace and in a safe way, with everybody engaged?

The best hope question, preferred future, and next steps

The best hope question and preferred future

The best hope question mentioned in Chapter 8 is the first question I ask everybody I engage with, no matter what context. It's my attempt to invite others to describe what they want from working with me and, from this, create a sense of direction to where the collaboration should bring them.

We aim to get a response describing something (1) the person wants, (2) that must fit with something that you can help with, and (3) that it will be possible to achieve during the collaboration (Ratner et al., 2012). For it to be a common project, we must be able to summarise what the client wants in a few sentences; it has to be important to the client, realistic in the client's present life situation, ethical, and within our remit (Korman, 2004). The question is formulated something like "What are your best hopes from this conversation/therapy/collaboration?" It is followed by more questions, as shown in Box 9.1, until the contract has been established.

Box 9.1

- What is your best hope from this conversation/this meeting/our collaboration?
- How will you know it has been useful for you to come here?
- What will it take for you to say that this has been worthwhile?
- What difference will it make if this happens?

After the contract has been established from the best hopes, the conversation will lead to talking about the family's preferred future. This must be formulated as positive and something they want to achieve, with detailed descriptions of behaviour leading towards change, such as the first small, realistic step, within a time, place, and context, and with concrete and observable action and interactive descriptions of how it will affect others and then reflect back on us (George et al., 2017).

Box 9.2

- Imagine that, tomorrow, you wake up, and your best hopes have been achieved. What is the first sign that this has happened?
- What will you do differently tomorrow that tells you that the change has happened?
- Who will be the first to notice the change?
- What will he/she notice?
- What difference will it make to him/her, and what will he/she be doing then?
- When she/he does that, what will you do differently?
- And, again, what will that lead her/him to do?

In solution-focused brief therapy, the power of change lies in the details, and it might be a small thing in the bigger picture that leads to important changes. This leads me to another principle that it is good to be aware of in a field where things can be overwhelming: "Small steps can lead to big changes" (De Shazer et al., 2007, p. 2). The belief is that, once a small change has been made, it will lead to further changes, which in turn lead to others, gradually resulting in a much larger, systemic change (De Shazer et al., 2007). These dialogues with people will help them experience a sense of control over external events and also gain ownership of the goals and the plan. This is what Øyvin Kvello has found to be closely linked to gained confidence in one's own coping skills and a higher level of motivation to achieve goals (Kvello, 2020).

Next steps as short-term goals

In the solution-focused approach, the part where the scale is used to assess the current situation at any given moment is followed by questions about the next steps in the process of moving towards the preferred future. This helps people reflect on and be clear about the most beneficial small action and behavioural change for them to create the necessary and hoped-for changes in their lives. Used with vulnerable and traumatised children, these next steps can become the short-term goal in the action plan or treatment plan to support our focus on the small changes that, one step at a time, will lead us to reach the goal statements and safety goals.

Box 9.3

- What do you need to do to get one step further up the scale?
- What will tell you that you have moved one step up the scale?
- What will be the signs that you/they have moved one step further?
- How will you know that you/they have moved one step further up the scale?
- How will others know that you have moved one step further up?
- What will you be doing that will tell you/others that you have moved up the scale?
- As you rate the situation 4 out of 10 on the safety scale, what needs to happen for the situation to move on to 5?
- From now, looking at the safety goals, what do you think is the next small step that will help the family make it happen all the time?
- What would the mother/father/child/grandfather/teacher say is the next step?

Connecting the different parts through scaling questions

The previous chapter described the scale in a general, non-specific form used in case consultations with professionals. In the more direct and personal work with families and their networks, after eliciting the best hopes and preferred future, you can engage them in the risk assessment and solution-building process by asking the best hopes scaling question. You do this by using the family's description of their best hope and preferred future to describe 10 on the scale, and 0 will represent the opposite. You don't have to define it in words but can name it "the opposite", because family members will know what the opposite has been. This is a powerful way to gather all involved in a continuous solution-building process that will also help you do the risk assessment with their contribution.

The best hopes scaling question is a powerful tool to elicit more descriptions of instances of the preferred future already happening (Iveson et al., 2014). The scale is also a powerful tool to investigate the signs of progress and to become clear about the next step, elicited by asking the various next-step questions in Box 9.3 (George et al., 2017). In this way, the scaling question gathers all the elements of the solution-focused conversation, and, besides the best hopes scale, there are questions for many different scales, such as the confidence scale, the safety/survival scale, and the commitment scale (De Jong & Berg, 2006; Ratner et al., 2012).

Box 9.4

For parents, it would sound like this: "On a scale of 0–10, where 10 represents all the things that you want to see different in the future for you and your children, such as [things described as their preferred future], and 0 is the opposite and the worst it has been, where would you rate the situation right now?"

A different version for professionals from that already covered in the previous chapter would be: "On a scale where 10 is that your best hope for the family/child is fulfilled, and they are able to [things described as their preferred future], and 0 is the absolute opposite, where would you place the family/child relative to your best hope and what they are already doing?"

- What are you/the family already doing that makes you place it on …? What else do they do?
- What else? Is there anything else you/the family do that tells you that you are on …?
- What next small thing will tell you the family has moved up the scale?

By using the scale in this way to express the balanced risk assessment, it's very simple to measure the progress in the child's situation or to see if it worsens instead and address it. The Family Roadmap is built on this structure of a solution-focused conversation.

The Family Roadmap

Sonja Parker has developed several tools I have mentioned throughout the book, including the Family Roadmap, to provide the most qualified, meaningful, and optimal engagement of children, parents, and network in building solutions to their problems and to qualify the risk assessment (Parker, 2013). The process is beneficial both to create change and to investigate the child's life circumstances collaboratively and safely for all involved, and it is helpful to use it in the investigation phase, to create an action or safety plan, or as part of family therapy, having conversations with one or both parents or the whole family, with or without the network present.

As I hold the same intention to engage families and networks in my work, the Family Roadmap has been an obvious choice to use in my work with families, and I have also introduced other professionals to it, with great success. Therefore, I will also present it here. Sonja has developed a booklet called *The Family Roadmap* for in-depth information about using the model (Parker, 2013). The following is based on the content of this booklet and my training with Sonja.

This process aims to engage families and networks in a solution-focused dialogue around the scaling question, using "life at its best" as the definition of 10 on the scale and "life at its worst" as 0 on the scale. The process consists of a series of questions that are strategically arranged to foster a solution-focused dialogue, and the structure focuses first on the perspective of the individual person/people engaged in the dialogue and ends with questions about how child protection views the situation, so that family members are also invited to see things from this perspective. This helps break down barriers and resistance and supports collaboration and a better understanding of why social workers are saying and doing what they are.

The process begins by exploring what life looks like at its best and then continues to explore what life looks like at its worst. If any unaddressed details arise from life at its worst, additional questions are used to gather more information about life at its best. The family's current position on a scale between life at its best and worst is assessed, and the existing actions that help them be as far up the scale as they are at the present moment are identified. This is followed by an investigation into who has helped them achieve this and what they have done to support this accomplishment.

The family then envisions the specific changes that would occur if they were one step further along the road towards life at its best, and all the steps necessary to achieve this desired state are identified, one step at a time, until all the steps are described. Potential support to help the family achieve their goals, including the role of child protection, is explored. Anticipated obstacles, also called roadblocks, are considered, along with the actions or support needed to overcome them. Finally, the roadmap addresses how the social worker will monitor and observe progress.

This dialogue, with everybody involved, captures all the relevant reflections on overcoming the issues that have led to professional engagement with the children and family. Using the terms "life at its best" and "life at its worst" is a very natural and general way to talk about issues that are often difficult to talk about, because every family, per definition, will have times when life is better than others and times when it is worse. Life goes up and down, and it's a question not of "if" it happens but rather "what" it looks like. In contrast, when you talk about worries, it's up for discussion whether there is something to be worried about.

I have also learned from asking these questions in this way that the family and network's description of life at its worst often looks similar to the professionals' worry statement. It becomes a safe way to talk about challenges, and I have even experienced families disclosing things they have never dared to talk about, leading to greater safety for the children. Still, as professionals, we need to be prepared for this, acknowledge the family for doing this, and manage it in a calm and collected way that keeps everybody safe in the process.

Another meaningful thing I have learned from using this tool is to have conversations with the families about how far back along the scale they can go, towards life at its worst, before the situation is critical, and they will need to seek help to support them actively. I continue with a dialogue about the signs that would show other people they are at this place on the scale. Lastly, we make plans for what these people need to do if the parents haven't yet reached out for help. Again, it becomes a safe way to talk about it, and solutions that no one else could have thought of arise from this. This both leads to real empowerment and provides hope that it can be a sustainable solution.

As the tool can be used for different purposes, it's essential to be clear about your purpose in using it. From this, decide whom to engage in the process, whether it's an individual conversation, a couple or family dialogue, or work with family and their network. Depending on this, we need to prepare for this engagement process and decide how to proceed, as it might differ according to whether we are engaging one person or a whole network. This doesn't concern the questions asked but is more about how you proceed with the facilitation of the meeting – whether the roadmap is created on a wall, a large table, or the floor, so that everybody can see everything recorded on the roadmap.

Sonja has developed this into a highly creative process, with posters and stickers in different colours for the various questions asked. All family members are actively involved in writing and creating the roadmap by sharing their different perspectives verbally and in writing on the posters and stickers. No matter how you do it, the conversation has a structure, following the solution-focused approach used in a child protection setting, and it can also be used in a school setting, in a team-building process at work, and in other collaboration settings.

Life-saving hope

As we are touching upon people's best hopes in this chapter, it's obviously relevant to end with a little more on this topic. As mentioned earlier, hope is a critical lifesaver and crucial in suicide prevention, both in the short and long term. In Chapter 3, I mentioned John Henden's work and how asking clients about their best hopes makes a difference. I hosted one training session with John in January 2023, where he shared his experience with suicide prevention, showing that it's impossible for people to commit suicide if there is hope that things will improve and life will get better. Talking about life at its best and life at its worst also makes the current situation more organic, so that, if you are in the middle of life at its worst, it can be life-saving to be reminded through these types of conversations that things have been better, and life can get better if you take one step at a time towards life at its best. Also, the use of solution-focused questions in general, such as coping questions at times of so much pain and suffering that people can barely move on, will be helpful to reconnect them to their power, coping skills, and confidence in themselves with regard to solving their problems, and it brings hope (George et al., 2017).

Coping questions

In conversations, when people express that things are worse instead of better, or if they are overwhelmed by challenges, can't see any light, and have maybe lost hope, there are several questions to ask to connect the person with their resources, skills, strengths, and vision for a preferred future (De Jong & Berg, 2006; Ratner et al., 2012). For example, these could be questions about how they cope or have coped with situations or other areas of life that aren't difficult (George et al., 2017), just as I used the questions in Chapter 2 to elicit all the white around the black dot in the circle to help professionals process difficult situations. This is based on the same principles and types of questions creating the same impact and can also be used to cope in times of crisis, traumatic experiences, and an overwhelmed nervous system. The purpose of the coping questions is to help the person recognise what they do or what has been helpful to deal with a situation so that they can do more of it, but they also help professionals gain much insight about the person that they can use to create safety and well-being for all involved.

Box 9.5

- How have you managed to get through/deal with/handle this?
- What does it take for you to do this?
- What has been helping you to survive?
- It sounds like it's tough now – how do you cope with it?
- How have you managed to stop it from getting even worse?
- How have you previously dealt with/handled situations like this?
- What gives you the strength to get up in the morning/come here?
- What has been helpful for you to keep moving on/dealing with it?
- What have you done not to give up hope?
- What would your best friend say has been the most fantastic thing you have done?

Helping people reconnect to their dreams, hopes, and preferred futures as well as their strength, resources, and coping skills works wonders and is worth trying in critical situations. It is better than being infected by hopelessness and powerlessness as professionals, as mentioned in Chapter 2, and maybe ending up saying to a suicidal person, "Just accept that being suicidal is your baseline, and you have to live with it", as one of my clients was told while enrolled in the psychiatric system to get help for her self-harming and suicidal behaviour.

There is a saying that what we pay attention to grows stronger in our lives, and so we must be careful about how we will affect children's, young people's, and their families' consciousness while working with them. Would you rather live in an organic world of hope and healing or a chronically static world? I have made my choice, and I do everything in my power to help people join me in the world of healing and hope, and this is why my motto concerning trauma healing is "Remember – there is hope for healing".

One type of conversation I have developed in my work with trauma survivors is about whom they have become because of their life stories, instead of always talking about whom people become despite their life stories. This kind of conversation helps people connect to their survivor inside, being aware of all the resources they have developed to survive these difficult times and what strength, virtues, values, and skills they have gained from their adversity. This perspective can also offer much insight into the intergenerational healing they are facilitating in their families as parents today. Many people I have worked with have decided that suffering in the family should end now, with them not passing it on to the children. These are powerful and beautiful, yet heartbreaking, stories about defeat, rising again, and overcoming deep pain and suffering.

Case example: Michella – continued

"I was a child, then I was sick, and now I'm an adult" are words that belong to Michella. A closer review of her childhood revealed several traumatising incidents and life circumstances but also a story of parents who have helped, supported, and been there for her throughout her illness. One doesn't exclude the other. On the one hand, she was surprised to see the significance of the harmful incidents from the past and the connection with several of her challenges. On the other hand, it gave her hope that she might get better after all.

Just getting the perspective turned from "What's wrong with me?" to "What has happened to me?" offers hope for healing, because it opens up the possibility that incidents from the past can be processed and released. This creates relief and changes people's relationship with themself and the world around them, and it also allows the release of a lot of the guilt and shame that many traumatised people carry. So, working on a change of perspective is highly recommended. This release also happened to Michella, and, in the ensuing process, we identified that she had become addicted to her suicidal thoughts as other people get addicted to substances. The trauma she had experienced had left her with a belief that "I am not in control", and she doesn't like to lose control, and so she would never turn to substances. Instead, she turned to the idea of being able to control her exit from life, and it gave her a sense of control that she doesn't experience elsewhere. The contradictory part is that it helped keep her alive but in disturbing ways. At the beginning of our work together, she had constant suicidal thoughts and, often, she felt that the only thing that kept her alive was a list of relatives that she had written to remind herself of whom would be harmed by her actions if she chose to act on her suicidal thoughts.

As with every other suicidal person I work with, I made a contract with her that she would not harm herself while working with me, a contract she wasn't happy to make because she doesn't break agreements, and, therefore, it felt like closing a door that was otherwise wide open. We agreed that she would add my name to the list of people so that she would be reminded of our contract when she got to my name.

Because she is good at lists and had a great desire to find a reason to stay alive for her own sake and not for someone else's, I got the inspiration to make a "bucket list" with her of things she wants to experience in life. Finding the first thing on the list took time, and she was thinking long and hard. Suddenly smiling, she said, "I once talked to some girlfriends about driving around the Italian coast, but is it okay that I don't *feel* the desire to do it right now?" My answer was, "It's perfectly okay that you don't feel the desire because, when you can't feel your body, you won't be able to feel the desire either", leading us to the vital work of getting home to the body again. The process continued with more things being added the bucket list, and she began to plan the trip with her girlfriends for the following summer. She went on the trip and she is still alive, in a long and slow recovery process involving getting back home to her true self one step at a time, taking in what happened to her and how it affected her life so that she could let go of it later.

The list Michella made to remind her about the people her suicide would harm is somewhat based on the same principles as what Yvonne Dolan calls "A letter for the rainy day" (Dolan, 1998). This letter is developed to provide consolation when people most need it; it is a letter from the person to the person themself and includes a list of:

• Activities most comforting to the person.
• The names and phone numbers of supportive friends and family members.
• Strength and virtues to be reminded of on rainy days.
• Unique talents, abilities, and interests.
• Hopes and dreams for the future.
• Advice and other reminders that are important to the person.

A rainy day letter for a child should be made with an adult who sees the child with the most loving and caring eyes. For everybody, it should be made in a time of feeling calm and well and will become a buffer on days when they are upset, overwhelmed, or distressed.

As in a solution-focused exercise, you can always ask people to make lists of things they are proud of, things they succeed with, or details of their personal traits and powers (Ratner et al., 2012). The list is endless. You can decide how long the list is going to be, but I would advise you to go beyond 25 items and make them think harder, because the powerful purpose of the list is to help people connect and reconnect with themselves and their skills, strengths, character traits, resources, talents, and values at the core of who they are – things they are proud of and that are important to them and the people they love. Sometimes, I make it a work in progress over time, where I will facilitate the list growing longer in every conversation I have with them, consciously adding to it from conversation to conversation.

The most impactful action for professionals is to hold vicarious hope in the darkest hours in families' lives, but also to demonstrate skills to make risk assessments and get people reconnected to their strength, resources, and their hopes for the future, believing that there are times when life is at its worst and times when it's at its best, and all in between, but it's never completely static.

Exercise

From the balanced risk assessment carried out in Chapter 8 and by mirroring the worry statement from the exercise in Chapter 6, formulate a goal statement/safety goal by answering the following questions:

- Who wants to see the change?
- What do they want to see the parents (together with a network) do that addresses the worries and creates safety and good enough care for the child?
- What will the child then do differently that will tell us that the parents have changed behaviour and the child is thriving and developing in a healthy way?
- How long do we need to see the parents and child demonstrate this changed behaviour before we can close the case and entrust the ongoing work to the parents and network?

To adapt this to your specific context, you can replace or supplement information on the parents with information on other adults' and peers' behaviour of relevance to the child's challenges.

What change do the child, parents, and private and professional network want, and how can you include this in the goal statement/safety goal to enhance the feeling of a common project? If needed, adjust the safety goal to your context and to the words of the children and families you are working with.

If possible, describe the short-term goals from reflecting on the questions about the next step.

Now, investigate the questions and process that are most appropriate to use to get everybody involved in reaching the short-term and long-term goals.

References

Berg, Insoo Kim, & Kelly, Susan. (2000). *Building solutions in child protection services*. W. W. Norton.

Berg, Insoo Kim, & Steiner, Therese. (2009). *Børn I terapi – Løsningsfokuseret korttidsterapi* (Children's Solution Work). (T. Bøgeskov, Trans.). Dansk psykologisk forlag.

De Jong, Peter, & Berg, Insoo Kim. (2006). *Løsningsfokuserede samtaler*. Hans Reitzels Forlag.

De Shazer, S., Dolan, Y., with Korman, H., Trepper, T., McCollum, E., & Berg, I. K. (2007). *More than miracles*. Routledge.

Dolan, Y. (1998). *One small step – moving beyond trauma and therapy to a life of joy.* Authors Choice Press.

George, E., Iveson, C. & Ratner, H. (2017) *BRIEFER – a solution focused practice manual.* BRIEF.

Iveson, Chris, George, Evan, & Ratner, Harvey. (2014). Love is all around: a single session solution-focused therapy. In Michael F. Hoyt & Moshe Talmon (Eds), *Capturing the moment – single session therapy and walk-in services*. Crown House.

Korman, H. (2004). *The common project*. SIKT.

Kvello, Ø. (2020). *Børn i risiko* (C. Pietsch, Trans.). Samfundslitteratur.

Parker, S. (2011). *Partnering for safety case consultation process: a process for consulting on child protection cases using the Partnering for Safety Risk Assessment and Planning Framework*. SP Consultancy. www.partneringforsafety.com

Parker, S. (2013). *The Family Roadmap. A process to elicit the views and ideas of family members, in preparation for detailded collaborative safety planning*. SP Consultancy. www.partneringforsafety.com

Parker, S. (2015). *Partnering for Safety Collaborative Assessment and Planning (CAP) Framework*. SP Consultancy.

Ratner, H., George, E., Iveson, C., & ProQuest. (2012). *Solution focused brief therapy: 100 key points and techniques*. Routledge.

Turnell, A. (2010). *Effective safety planning in child protection casework – DVD workbook*. Resolutions Consultancy.

Turnell, A., & Edwards, S. (1999). *Signs of safety: a solution and safety oriented approach to child protection casework*. W. W. Norton.

Turnell, A., & Edwards, S. (1997). Aspiring to partnership – the signs of safety approach to child protection. *Child Abuse Review, 6*, 179–190.

Chapter 10

The Circle of Safety and Reconnection, Step 8

Create an action, treatment, or safety plan with clear agreements on following up

The planning processes

When creating an action, treatment, or safety plan, there isn't necessarily a recipe to follow except for clarifying your goal statement in collaboration with the people involved, as seen in the last chapter. Once the end destination is agreed upon, various paths can lead to it. After the goals have been set, all those involved with the children remain active in central parts of the planning and ongoing development processes. As taught by my teachers, safety planning is more a journey and process than a final product (Parker, 2010), which also applies to the other types of plans.

Normally, the statutory worker in child protection handles the action plan, and other plans set up in different contexts must meet the action plan's goals. If a service provider takes the lead in a safety planning process, it must always be with the close and active involvement of the statutory agency since their leverage and authority are critical for a successful process (Turnell, 2010b).

This chapter covers various plans that differ by context, but they all share a common foundation of having a clear purpose, with goals guiding interventions, and engaging children, parents, professionals, and private networks as part of the solution-building to reach the end goal.

Irrespective of the working context, a critical aspect of the planning process involves prioritising goals by assessing the most urgent and significant ones to address initially when there are multiple goals. There are limits to the number of tasks people can handle without becoming overwhelmed, and failure to prioritise goals might end up becoming a stressor, having the opposite effect. Hence, it's crucial to make this assessment and articulate it verbally and in writing to everybody involved, making sure people know your assessment. If possible, the best and fastest results come from inviting people into a dialogue about their assessment of priorities, as this supports the effort to make it a common project and to give as much control and power over the process as possible to the people who are going to implement the plan. However, there are limits to engagement, and, as a professional, you sometimes must state the most important and urgent goal to work on first.

DOI: 10.4324/9781003322672-10

Numerous interventions can be incorporated into the action or treatment plan based on the strategy, family resources and skills, and the professional's background, skills, and available resources. These interventions must always directly relate to the prioritised goals, and agreements on systematic follow-up to measure progression must be clear.

The paramount consideration is that the plan must resonate with the child, the family, and the network surrounding the child. If it doesn't make sense, they are likely to pursue their own paths, resulting in superficial collaboration with limited potential for co-creating the needed change. This form of pseudo-collaboration happens when it seems like we are working together, but everybody goes their own way. This isn't necessarily because the family won't be able to create the needed change, but more often stems from professionals losing them on the way, and the family proceeding on their own. When this happens, there is a tendency to blame families for not engaging enough, but be mindful of this because it will always be the professional's responsibility to engage people in a meaningful and constructive way.

The different phases of trauma work

In trauma-informed work, it's essential to determine whether the child is in the stabilisation, processing, or integration phases after the processing (Struik, 2019). These three phases involve different interventions carried out by different people. If the child is ready to process the trauma without further stabilisation, the treatment involves processing and integration, but severely and chronically traumatised children might require stabilisation before processing can take place (Struik, 2019). Trauma therapists might play a part in all three stages but will always facilitate the processing of the trauma in the clinical work with the child, occasionally also engaging parents or other primary caregivers, depending on the child's age.

Conversely, parents, networks, and other professionals surrounding the child will mainly contribute during the other phases, as there are many things parents, teachers, foster carers, family therapists, and others can do to help support stabilisation before, and integration after, the trauma is processed. Arianne Struik's "sleeping dogs method", described in her book *Treating Chronically Traumatized Children*, was developed to support professionals working their way systemically through the different phases (Struik, 2019).

In the stabilisation phase, we assess the child's overall stability in life in terms of safety, secure attachment, and consistency in various aspects of their life, such as care, school, sleep, substance use, and self-harm tendencies. In this phase, there is also emphasis on providing the child with good enough emotion regulation skills and the ability to make a cognitive shift from, for example, "it's my fault" to "it's not my fault", as described in Chapter 4. This involves parents and other adults taking responsibility and not blaming the child. The use of the Circle of Safety and Reconnection will provide a solid foundation to assess whether the child's situation is stable and good enough for them to process the traumatic experience or if further stabilisation is needed. However, if in doubt or if the trauma is "a sleeping dog", and you need inspiration and knowledge about stabilisation, I recommend you look into Arianne Struik's work on how to systematically eliminate the barriers there might be to processing the trauma. The situation doesn't have to be perfect in all areas; it must simply be stable enough, and the child needs enough skills and resources for there not to be any barriers to the child processing the trauma in a safe way (Struik, 2019).

In the integration phase, following trauma processing, children need to improve their existing skills and learn new ones that the trauma might have hindered them from learning earlier. They must integrate all the lessons the processing has taught them and then react to situations differently. This is a slow and steady process of re-building the brain and filling the developmental gaps caused by trauma, which con-tributes to building resilience and preventing further traumatisation in the future (Struik, 2019). For this, a new treatment plan must be made.

Even before the stabilisation phase, professionals can play a pivotal role in pre-venting a traumatic event from becoming a trauma. A deeper understanding of the nervous system's reactions to traumatic events can assist children and young people in processing the experiences better and help them digest the overwhelming sensations in their bodies as soon as they occur. Providing this across various con-texts would constitute prevention work rather than treatment, and fewer children would need to go through all the other phases mentioned above.

When working with children, solution-focused and strength-based approaches are helpful to build resources in the children so that the "windows of tolerance" become stronger again. Using these approaches helps children to know and under-stand how they are coping and what strengths they are using to cope and overcome; it also helps them build more required skills and strengths (Furmann, 2021; Iveson, 2021; King, 2021). We guide them to become aware of the remarkable survivors they are by investigating how they use their instincts to protect themselves and how their behaviour is helpful from a survival perspective. We also help them under-stand how they can use their strengths differently and more appropriately for their long-term health and well-being. We can specifically work with them to integrate the strengths they need to face challenges, such as courage, and to employ self-regulation skills to become more in control of their nervous system reactions.

The solution-focused and strength-based approach also has power to help chil-dren realise that they have overcome the overwhelming situation and how they might have contributed to protecting themselves, reconnecting them to their power and helping them understand that it's over now in a way that helps them move on in an empowered way. The list mentioned in the previous chapter might be helpful for this. Strength cards made for conversations with children on strengths can be used, and the psychoeducation tools developed by Arianne Struik are also helpful and are available for download on her website.

The child's action plan

The case worker's primary function in developing the action plan (case plan) is to coordinate the collaboration, making sure everybody works on a common project going in the same direction, doing the right things at the right time with the right interventions to reach the goals (Caspersen & Laustsen, 2009). When working primarily with the professionals surrounding a child, this serves as the primary tool, whereas, when engaging private networks, the action plan might be supported by a network plan or safety plan, depending on the child's situation. I will return to this shortly.

Depending on the country, department, and framework used to create action plans, many things are determined in advance by child protection rules and regulations. The purpose of the action plan is to direct the overall work to support the child's safety, health, development, and well-being. It formulates the intervention's purpose, the goals it needs to address, and, from this, specific support and measures are selected. Subsequently, responsibilities are shared among people engaged in the work so that everybody gets one or more tasks concerning the child and their safety and well-being. Also, a time is pinpointed to follow up on progression systematically, in a structured manner, to make sure the collaboration is helpful for the child throughout the whole process (Caspersen & Laustsen, 2009).

In a solution-focused follow-up with vulnerable and traumatised children, the progress is highlighted first, followed by an investigation of whether other risks or harm have occurred, and, from there, the collaborators move on to setting new goals and next steps until the child no longer requires help. This is a continuous work in progress (Parker, 2015).

As you might recall, the solution-focused approach rests on the two core principles of doing more of what works and doing something else if progress isn't being shown. When progress fails, goals and interventions must be changed rather than the professionals being stuck in a belief that the child and family are too bad or reluctant to create change. Often, it's a sign that the professionals are not prioritising the right things first or working the right way with the right intervention, and the professional support is somehow disconnected from the people at the centre of attention – the children and their families.

The closer you follow up timewise, and the more structured the follow-up is, the faster, more effective, and more successful the change, because continuous adjustments to the plan improve practice between meetings. One thing to be aware of is to make sure that the meetings are constructive and meaningful so that people show up and prioritise the time to do follow-ups. Otherwise, it will be a waste of time, and people will start prioritising other things and drop out.

For SFBT follow-up sessions, ask "What's better?" (De Shazer et al., 2007; Ratner et al., 2012). This helps people direct their focus straight at the progress since the last session and is based "on the assumption that there are always times that the client does something they are pleased about" (George et al., 2017, p. 24). There are two different kinds of questions to ask in a follow-up session – either strategy or identity questions (Ratner et al., 2012). Strategy questions help the person think about what they have done to make progress, and identity questions focus on noticing and naming the skills, resources, and strengths the person has used to take these actions.

Box 10.1

- What is better?
- What have you succeeded in doing since the last time?
- What did you do?
- How did you do it?
- What have you been pleased to notice?
- What difference does it make to you and others?
- What else?
- Who noticed it?
- What have they noticed?
- What difference did it make to them – and what did they do then?
- What did that make you do differently?
- On a scale, where are you now? What did you do? What else? How did you do?
- Tell me about the times you moved one point up the scale since last time?

Creating a network plan based on a private network for vulnerable and traumatised children

Returning to "it takes a village to raise a child", a network plan is a powerful tool when a child's safety isn't jeopardised, and yet parents can't, on their own, provide all the essential care for the child to thrive and develop healthily. I use some general guidelines for the work with private networks to become as powerful and harmonic as possible and to avoid family conflict.

First, the network is engaged as a support network, not a treatment, and we must know how to use these people to support the family in the best way possible. What tasks can we give them, and what tasks must be given to professionals? For example, I always consider guiding parents to become better at their attachment and mentalisation to fall within professional treatment. Assigning this role to other family members might lead to conflict in the family and activate the intergenerational trauma running in the family in uncontrollable and unhelpful ways. Furthermore, they might not know the necessary things to guide or how to do so correctly.

Instead, people in the private network can contribute with practical tasks, emotional support, and direct support of the child. If it's safe and relevant, the parents might sometimes turn to network people for parenting guidance too. When engaging someone in the network directly with the child, ensure the child knows or gets to know the person very well so that it becomes a safe experience for the child.

In general, network plans must only consist of agreements made by people present at network meetings, because you can't make such commitments and agreements on other people's behalf. As a rule of thumb, only give tasks to people present at meetings that they suggest themselves and accept as tasks they can fulfil. Everybody should only offer what they believe is realistic to provide for the child and family to ensure the family is covered as much as needed. Forcing tasks on people that they don't agree with or have time, resources, or skills to perform could lead to failure and unintentionally end up letting the child down.

Next, arrangements should be exact and detailed, outlining what, when, and sometimes how to carry them out. The more precise and clear the agreements, the more effective and successful the collaboration will become, and the easier it will be to follow up on whether everybody has done what they promised to do in between meetings. Giving private individuals part of the responsibility for the child's welfare demands a closer follow-up than if solely relying on professionals. Although networking meetings take some more effort and preparation, the cost–benefit hopefully shows a good return on the investment through changes happening between meetings, brought about by people around the child in their daily life.

The ultimate purpose is to empower families to activate and use resources in their network to support them in a direct and relevant way at a critical time of their life when they need it. Processes should be well structured, with meetings with specific purposes and agendas and with everybody engaged in building the solution. People don't need to attend again if they leave meetings with no task concerning supporting the family, quite simply because to do otherwise would create confusion, disappointment, and meaninglessness in relation to attending and potential conflict between the network person and the family or the professional responsible for the network plan.

My guiding principle for facilitating network meetings is to avoid setting off emotional bombs during meetings. This means refraining from sharing any new and potentially upsetting information during the meeting, triggering drama and conflict. Instead, participants need to contact me beforehand if anything is making them more worried, so I can talk it through with parents and other attendants beforehand to avoid resistance, disputes, and accusations at the meeting. When new worries must be addressed, good preparation is more likely to lead to constructive collaboration during challenging situations. Generally, prioritising good preparation constitutes the best foundation for the work of engaging people in the solution-building process – most importantly, to have a clear structure and purpose for the meeting, from either one or the other solution-focused approaches mentioned previously.

Another fundamental rule is that disagreements concerning the child are acceptable, but they must be communicated in a nonviolent way. In such situations, I closely guide people to succeed in this. We are supposed to talk to each other in such a way that the child can be present and listen to the conversation, even when they are not. This rule sets the scene for a calm and respectful dialogue and will support communication in general between participants. Sometimes, situations unintentionally get overheated, and, in these situations, it's important to take a break and come back to continue after people have had some time to regulate themselves again.

Many people are afraid of involving children in such meetings, but I like them to attend when appropriate and safe for them, and this depends on the purpose of the meeting and the content shared. I am mindful that, if we talk in childproof ways, we might break taboos and help the healing take place. Whatever we discuss is a part of the child's experienced life and not something that they don't deal with in one way or another. We show the child it's okay for everybody around them to talk about the things happening, and that everybody wants to help to support and protect them.

An old investigation of network meetings showed that, of 130 minutes, 121 minutes were spent talking about worries and problems, and 90 per cent of the time the professionals were talking (Farmer & Owen, 1995). In a solution-focused approach to network meetings, 121 minutes should be spent on taking solution talk rather than problem talk. The meeting's structure can be formed very effectively from the worry statement and goal statement; based on them, everybody can be asked how they can support prevention of the problems and achievement of the goals, either practically, emotionally, or directly. Other approaches could involve using the roadmap described in Chapter 9 or the Signs of Safety framework to support the facilitation of the meeting. Sometimes, I have held network meetings solely based on best hopes, preferred future, what's already working well, and the next step as a solution-focused brief therapy session. All of them work well and are recommendable, and I chose which one to use according to the purpose and agenda of the meeting.

When talking to parents about engaging their network in collaboration, I normalise the use of private networks, emphasising that most families rely on help from relatives and friends in everyday life, such as looking after children when working late and so on. The children and families we work with are also connected to others who can become a support network, even though they might not realise this. So, I am always listening for names and stories that include other people around the child and family and ask curious questions in a solution-focused manner about how these people are or have been helpful, as described in Chapter 8, and how it might be possible to engage them in the solution-building process in the future.

These principles are equally applicable to safety planning. The difference lies in the level of risk and the safety needed to be demonstrated by the parents and their network. A higher risk demands a higher level of intensity and control. Sometimes, despite parents working the hardest they can together with the network, they might not be able to provide the needed care as fast as the child needs them to. Since they have been engaged and trusted and have provided relevant support to make the necessary changes, they are more likely to accept the necessity of others caring for the children when they don't succeed. This ultimately benefits the children, because collaboration and communication become better when parents accept that somebody else needs to care for their children when they have had a fair chance (Sørensen, 2012).

Creating a safety plan for children at risk by engaging the private network

The process of creating, testing, and adjusting the safety plan is based on trust, openness, honesty, and clear communication and expectations. Transparency and openness are non-negotiable aspects of the work, as everybody involved, including the children, must know the details of the worries and talk openly about them in a childproof way (Turnell, 2010b). Also, the family is always informed about my thoughts and assessments, and child protection concerns are also openly addressed, with no hidden agendas. We don't have to agree on the worries or discuss the past and what happened or didn't happen. However, as mentioned before, it's non-negotiable that we agree and focus on the future change that we need to see happening for the children to be safe in the care of the parents (Turnell, 2010b).

These processes are intensive, with close follow-ups, control check-ups, and frequent visits, depending on if the children are still at home or if it's a reunification process. Without a doubt, this is demanding work for them, yet most of the families I have worked with believe their children are worth the effort and would do it again. Sometimes, they feel like giving up or stop engaging in the process, and they might get angry with me because it's too demanding for them to proceed. In these situations, I always leave them with a choice to stop or continue. When left with a choice and the responsibility to choose what way to go, it often helps the parents reconnect to the purpose of the process again and continue moving on. Occasionally, it's also a sign that the parents and network together can't do what is needed, and I need to assess that safety planning isn't an option for them and the child must be secured in other ways.

There are different phases in the safety planning process:

1 You always make sure that there is immediate safety for the children.
2 Engage children, parents, and networks in the co-creation process.
3 Next is the development phase, where you start developing the long-term safety plan.
4 Then, there is a test and integration period, with close follow-up and adjustment of the plan, most likely to be for a period of a minimum of 6 months.
5 The case can be closed at some point, and the family and network will monitor the safety plan (Turnell, 2010a, 2010b; Turnell & Essex, 2006).

The safety plan isn't a static product but needs to be adjustable to changes in life circumstances and children's age and needs in a dynamic process (Parker, 2010). Processes go up and down like life itself. Still, at every step of the way, children must be safe and cared for, and children, parents, and networks must be engaged in building the best possible solutions for the children. The work combines statutory work with a more family-oriented treatment, which is possible because its foundation is solution-focused brief therapy and other treatment elements, such as the use of words and pictures (Turnell & Essex, 2006).

Four options are available for immediate safety to be created when engaging the private network. Either the child moves out, people from the network move in, the suspected perpetrator moves out, or, sometimes, the family moves into a family institution together, if this is an option. Which one of the options is chosen depends on the specific situation, what possibilities are available in the given time and place, and the child protection service in the country and area where the family is living.

As previously outlined, I start each safety planning process by going through all the case files to get a clear and comprehensive picture of all the past and present worries and harm and formulate worry statements. This helps me not to overlook any danger but also to clearly explain child protection worries to the parents and children in a language they understand. Then, I formulate the safety goals describing what the parents and network need to do in the care of the child to ensure its safety, but also the bottom lines that the parents need to agree on for us to begin the safety planning process (Turnell, 2010b).

I teach some general bottom lines for this work. For example, there needs to be an actively engaged and informed private network in the collaboration on safety – typically, a minimum of six to eight people, and, the higher the risk, the higher the number. Therefore, it's always an individual assessment. To be informed implies that all participants are aware of all the details of the concern (Turnell, 2010b). The parents also need to agree on an intensive process with many meetings and home visits, actively engaging the children and making a "words and pictures story" for them to explain openly the concern and the process (Turnell, 2010b). Depending on whether the national law in the respective country allows it, a general bottom line can also be to accept unannounced visits to make sure the children are all right and everybody is following the plan as agreed.

More specific bottom lines are also formulated based on the individual family's situation and according to the law and regulations of the respective country. For example, in cases of violence and abuse of any sort, a condition might be established that the child must not be alone with the alleged perpetrator until a safety plan is in place. This plan should demonstrate safety for the child in actions and behaviour to such an extent that everyone involved with the child and the child themself trust the plan.

The worry statement, safety goal, and bottom lines form the safety plan's foundation, and, when these elements are settled, engaging everybody in the solution-building process can begin. First, after my initial meeting with the parents, I always talk to the child using the Safety House tool explained in Chapter 3 (Parker, 2009). The information I get from the child about what safety and care look like then becomes my North Star and is incorporated into the safety goal. I will also talk to the parents and network about their worries to get everybody's perspectives on the worries and goals before I formulate the final worry statements and safety goals (Parker, 2009; Turnell, 2010b).

Then the process starts to determine *how* the family will meet these goals. The *how* becomes a tailor-made safety plan for each child we are working with, including agreements that refer to both preventing things from happening again and damage control in case a risk situation arises again that needs to be dealt with safely for the child. Construction of the plan involves intensive conversations with children and parents, network meetings with everybody involved, and family therapy if required. It's built on the families' strengths, resources, and skills, which are uncovered by asking the questions they need to reflect on (Turnell, 2010b; Turnell & Essex, 2006).

Throughout this process, we determine the child's designated safety person; they take on greater responsibility for keeping a close eye on the child, being in touch with how they are doing and how they feel, and representing the child's perspective in the safety planning process. In the safety planning process, the child will choose a safety object – this could be their teddy – a nonverbal means to communicate their worries to adults in their safety network (Turnell, 2010b). Everybody knows about their chosen safety object and where it's placed. Then, agreements are made on how the child can use this safety object to let their safety person and other people in the network know that they don't feel safe and they need them to check up on both the child and the safety plan.

The facilitator of the safety planning process has the crucial role of co-constructing the solutions the family comes up with that are safe enough for the child and continuing to make the family reflect and work until the situation is considered safe enough. Using the solution-focused approach helps facilitate a process where they think through all possible and impossible future scenarios where the risk might occur again and where they need to handle it safely for the child. This reflection includes looking at triggers and their previous successes in addressing these triggers and other challenges, helping them create the needed changes in their behaviour and actions so that they can approach situations differently.

After the plan has been developed, there is an integration phase where it's tested and adjusted as much as required to enhance its sustainability over time. It is recommended that there is close follow-up with the network and ongoing family counselling or therapy for at least 6 months to assess and ensure the plan's sustainability. During this period, the plan will also be tested in collaboration with the child to ensure that all the adults act according to the plan. For this test, the safety object and the agreements made around it are used to activate the safety plan, to show the child and everybody around the child that everybody is doing what they are supposed to do when the plan is activated (Turnell, 2010b).

When the safety plan works well, the process is complete, and the responsibility for ongoing monitoring and evaluation of the safety plan rests with the family and the network. Some people need professional support for an extended period after the safety planning ends, such as to enhance overall parenting skills. Therefore, the case might not be closed afterwards; this will also be determined by the threshold of different countries' social security systems.

The development of a concrete safety plan for Sam and Oliver

A child protection office asked me to collaborate with Sam and Oliver's family to make a safety plan for the children to return to the care of the mother. The children had been removed from the home owing to concerns about violence against the boys, and the boys witnessed violent and chaotic conflicts between their parents and suffered massive neglect owing to the mother's and father's substance and alcohol abuse.

Using the roadmap process in our initial conversation to elicit the parents' perspective, it became apparent to me that they largely agreed on the previous circumstances and wanted to prevent these things from happening again in the future. After the children's removal, the parents had separated and now had separate homes close to each other. I formulated the following worry statements and safety goals from my conversations with them, the children, and the network.

Worry statements

Child protection is worried that the mother and father might become so frustrated and angry with each other that the boys risk experiencing violent and chaotic conflicts between the parents, with screaming, shouting, threats, and slamming doors. The boys are also at risk of being hit, grabbed hard, pushed, and yelled at themselves. If this happens, they might be hurt, scared, and sad and feel that home isn't a safe place. They are also at risk of losing trust in their mother and father and feeling that they can't count on any safe adults to care for them, which might leave them in a state of chronic stress and survival that can cause severe harm to their development and well-being.

Child protection is worried that the mother and father will start using drugs and alcohol again and that they won't be able to provide the necessary attention, care, stability, predictability, and routines in the daily care for the boys that they need to thrive and develop healthily. The boys might be left on their own to care for themselves and their parents, with too big a responsibility for their age, causing them to be overwhelmed by their daily lives and creating a risk of their experiencing a sense of being all alone, of not being important and worthy of love and belonging, which can cause a negative view of themselves that in turn can cause a disturbance in their relationships with themselves and others.

Safety goals

The mother and father will work together with Rikke and child protection and a safety network to create a safety plan that will show everyone that:

When the parents are angry or frustrated with the boys, they will regulate their emotions, deal with the boys, and discipline them in safe and regulated ways. Also, when they are angry with each other, they will protect the children from seeing and hearing any violence and will deal with their conflicts in ways that are safe for the children. This will help the boys trust their parents and other adults and feel safe in the care of the parents, allowing them to feel safe, calm, and well in themselves and helping them to develop healthily and according to their age.

The boys are always cared for by safe, sober, and clean adults who provide them with the necessary care, peace, stability, structure, and safety so the children feel safe and that the adults will take care of them and they leave all adult responsibility behind so that they can be children acting their age. They will feel a sense of safe connection to their parents, growing up knowing they are important and worthy of love and belonging, and this will help them develop healthy relationships with themselves and others.

When the parents have shown that they can do this continuously for a period of 9 months after the boys have returned to their mother's care, the case will be closed.

The process of developing the plan

During the first month, there were meetings of several hours per meeting three times a week; this was reduced to appointments twice a week in the following month. After 6 weeks, the newly developed plan was tested for the first time when the mother almost lost her temper with Sam one night when he was at home on a contact visit. After this, we adjusted the safety plan by going through what was working well and what needed adjustment to become safer. After 8 weeks, we had developed a plan for the boys that everybody was satisfied would be safe enough, and the boys came home to stay with their mother. This became the final plan, which needed to be tested and adjusted over a period after the development phase to secure its sustainability. The family was also enrolled in family therapy during this period to support the plan's sustainability.

The final safety plan was presented to the boys at a big meeting with all their safety networks, the case worker, and me present; words and pictures were used to describe the plan's details. It turned out to be a thorough plan, and sections of the full plan is shown here alongside some of the illustrations.

Sam and Oliver's safety plan

Rule 1

If their mother gets angry, she takes some deep breaths and counts to ten to calm down or goes into the garden alone to smoke a cigarette to regulate herself, so she won't take her anger out on Sam and Oliver. If this isn't enough, and she can't calm herself down, she will call her aunt or sister to talk to them about what's making her mad, so they can help her calm down. They will come over immediately if it's required or send one of the other family members to help do what it takes to protect the boys. As a backup, their mother can call her brother, James, who will have his phone on 24/7 and will reach out for help from other people in the network on the mother's behalf. He will notify her if he turns his phone off, so that she can make arrangements with other people in the safety plan during this time.

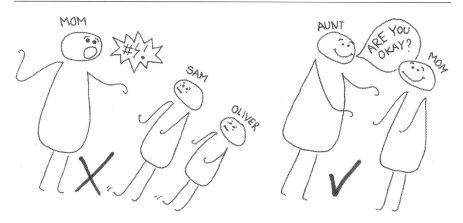

Illustration 10.1 Unsafe   *Illustration 10.2* Safe

Rule 4

Sam and Oliver must always be cared for by clean and sober adults. To prevent their mother from using drugs again, their aunt, uncle, grandmother, and cousin Laura monitor her closely and talk about the difficult issues that tempt her to use drugs again. Laura checks in daily, and the uncle calls once a week to check on how she is doing. If they sense something wrong, they gather all the network at the mother's to create immediate safety for the boys. To prevent her using again, she can do yoga, go for a run or a walk, read books, listen to podcasts, or visit friends and people in the network to talk about things. If this doesn't work, and she has a setback, she will move out of the house, and the aunt or grandmother will move in and take care of Sam and Oliver until she is clean again. If the aunt and grandmother can't look after them, then the plan is for Laura, the neighbours, or James to stay with them until their mother gets clean.

Illustration 10.3 Unsafe   *Illustration 10.4* Safe

Rule 6

Sam has chosen Laura as his special safety person, and Oliver has chosen his grandfather. The boys can talk to their safety person about anything, including all the things that they need to talk to an adult about, and Laura and the grandfather will help them if they need help. They are good at sensing the boys' feelings and promise always to be aware of how they are doing and whether they are all right. If the safety people get worried that everything isn't well, they will take action to gather together all the adults in the safety plan to investigate what is wrong, what needs to be dealt with, and what to put in place to create safety, if it hasn't already been arranged according to the plan. If Laura or the grandfather can't be there, the boys will choose another safety person in the network to do the same things.

Illustration 10.5 Safe   *Illustration 10.6* Safe

When writing about safety planning, it's important to stress that this is such complex and high-risk work that it takes collaborative team efforts for its execution. Effective organisation within the professional offices coupled with required training and supervision is vital to ensure the child's safety and prevent the practice from becoming dangerous. The shared practice also safeguards the workers involved and the organisations implementing the methodology. It takes teamwork in a larger team that also extends to working in pairs during family visits to enhance observation, listening, and critical thinking. Risk assessments should always be conducted jointly with team members and the manager to minimise the risk of errors in the assessments, which requires the entire organisation to be involved and ready. However, there are many things to gain from this.

Given the prevalence of serious and chronic trauma among the children and adults I work with due to their upbringing and violent childhood experiences, it has been imperative to become more trauma-informed in this work, as mentioned in Chapter 5 (Parker & Struik, 2017). Trauma introduces a risk since abuse might be repeated if parents are easily triggered by past experiences or by the children's trauma symptoms. The way trauma-informed safety planning works is by cultivating emotional safety as well, after physical safety has been established, to maintain sustainable changes and create security for well-being and healthy development.

The initial step involves formulating trauma-informed worry statements and trauma-informed safety goals and assessing what kind of trauma-healing interventions might be necessary to sustain physical safety in the long term. Trauma healing potentially has three phases in which different people play different roles at different times. This could be connected to the safety plan process to provide coherent and profound support for the children and families. This way of integrating safety issues and trauma healing is an investment in the here and now that, without a doubt, will be beneficial in terms of costs and change the social and health systems if we dare to do it.

Each safety planning process includes parents developing a coherent and meaningful explanation for their children, in words and pictures, of the difficulties they have experienced in their lives. This explanation is called "words and pictures" and holds significant therapeutic potential for both children and parents (Turnell & Essex, 2006). For children, it fosters a meaningful, comprehensible, cohesive understanding of their past experiences in combination with being told that they are over now and were never their fault. This can help their nervous system to become more regulated. For parents, it supports them to take responsibility for their previous behaviour and deal with shame and guilt but also get closure regarding the past and realise they can help their children heal by doing this process with us as professionals. When listening to the story, the children get the opportunity to ask the parents questions about things they have never talked about before, and this is an in-depth healing process for the whole family. More about the content will be described shortly.

Treatment plans for different contexts

Whether working in the psychiatric system, school system, or foster care system or practising as a family therapist or a trauma therapist working with children in a therapeutic setting, you can make a treatment plan to set the direction for your work with great success. However, the treatment plan should be aligned with the purpose and goals formulated in the social workers' action plan if your intervention is part of a collaboration with child protection. Within your remit, you will most likely have the freedom to decide how you reach these goals and what interventions to use to get there in the best and fastest way with the tools you have available, and this is important to also reflect and decide on before starting the treatment.

Based on your role and the assessment of the child's situation, the approaches to promote the child's safety and recovery will vary. However, being clear on the purpose and goals before deciding the measures and means is equally important when it comes to treatment plans, as mentioned previously. As it has already been covered, I will continue with the interventions immediately.

Interventions

Many traumatised children struggle to connect fully with their bodies and have lost natural contact with them. To some extent, they have dissociated and may not even feel pain when the level of dissociation is high. As mentioned earlier, one of the most crucial tasks across contexts is to re-establish contact between the child and their body. For example, this can be done by noticing bodily sensations such as cold, warmth, thirst, and hunger, or feeling the emotion in the body such as feeling angry, scared, happy, or sad (Struik, 2019). Other suggestions include teaching them relaxation through breathwork, yoga, and safe touch with either other close relations or elements such as water and sand.

One girl I worked with created a small survival kit with sanitiser and sour candy because of her tendency to dissociate in class. As the sharp smell of sanitiser can help people come back to the present, it was very effective for her to escape the dissociative state, just as eating very sour candy was because it stimulated her senses and reconnection with her body. Also, no one would notice her doing this because, with the COVID-19 pandemic, carrying hand sanitiser everywhere was very common.

One of the exercises I practise with children as part of their recovery process is gaining more control over their body and mind. This involves becoming more aware of their triggers and cultivating strategies for immediate management of them. Inspired by exercises I got from John Henden, I help them to say to themselves when being triggered, "This is normal – it happens once in a while and it will pass", or to say, "That was then – this is now" or "this is now June 2023"; the last two help get the person back from the trauma time to the here and now (Henden & Ebscohost, 2018). Additional techniques to help them come back are doing really deep breathwork, counting backwards in threes, or looking around and naming five things they can see, hear, and feel and then naming four more things and then three and two and one. These last exercises demand something of their neocortex that could help them get regulated enough to come back to themselves again. Employing psychoeducation, such as explaining their windows of tolerance or the wave and volcano developed by Arianne Struik, all mentioned earlier, is also a very powerful tool to help children understand better what they are experiencing. When they know this, they might be able to deal with it differently and control themselves better when triggered.

Visualisation to gain more control over one's mind is also an option, with guided meditation/mindfulness and play, as they are also powerful tools. When you visualise with the children that they can place their memories in a bank box and send it to the moon or down to the bottom of the sea, they will also get a sense of self-control back.

Speaking of self-control, this is strongly linked to children's emotion regulation, nurtured and cultivated by guidance from adults around them. Walter Mischel's famous research, known as the marshmallow study, demonstrated that children who could delay gratification by not eating the marshmallow in front of them in order to receive a reward of another marshmallow tended to experience better outcomes in adulthood. They achieved a higher level of education, had more stable family setups, and were less likely to engage in criminal activities. These children showed greater tolerance of frustration, persistence in achieving their goals, and better impulse control. They also demonstrated the ability to stick to tasks, maintain their activity level, think before acting, wait for turns, and act carefully. These skills involve integrating executive functions using integrative functions such as assigning them meaning and emotional significance (Jørgensen, 2017). Other aspects of emotion regulation include training them in coping skills and breathwork and teaching them to count to ten before saying anything. We must also teach them to reach out for help if needed and provide self-care in daily routines that will stimulate the building of stronger positive emotions and greater capacity to regulate difficult emotions.

One helpful thing to work on is integrating the opposite, positive beliefs instead of the negative beliefs that come with trauma – for example, I am not in control, I am not worthy of love, I am wrong, I am powerless, I am in danger, it's my fault, I am stupid. By listening carefully to children's way of expressing these beliefs and taking them seriously, we can modulate a change in them by working on installing a direct opposite, positive belief. Installing a new, positive belief can have a profoundly healing impact on them. We can do this by continuously helping the children to think, "I am in control", when they falsely believe they are not, and, when the danger is over, we can help them understand "I am safe now". Other beliefs to install might be "I am worthy of love", "I am good enough/okay as I am", "I can change things now", "I am smart", and "It's not my fault".

Emphasising these beliefs over time can make them stronger and truer owing to new neural networks being built in the brain. Once they feel true, the power of the negative belief resides, and the trauma will no longer have the same impact on the child. This small awareness is a simple way to create lasting, profound change in a way that feels good. Still, in other contexts than therapy, it will take time to sink in, and so you must be patient and consistent in your effort to help the child believe differently about themself.

An impactful intervention for parents to use with a child is the words and pictures process described above, either as an immediate short story – an explanation of a safety planning process or why child protection is involved – or a longer, coherent story about all the things that the child has experienced in life. Also, like the illustrations above, it can be used to explain the rules of the safety plan in detail. Whatever the expression you choose, the purpose is to provide explanations for the child about their life circumstances that create new narratives internally, replacing the inaccurate and harmful ones they might have told themselves about the situation, which often portray the child as in the wrong and somehow guilty for what happened.

A words and pictures process has the same format, no matter the size and shape, and the story always balances difficult and good times and focuses on creating a safe and hopeful ending. A story starts with something good or neutral from the family's life together and then continues by describing who is worried about what in the child's life. It uses appropriate language for the child's age that is detailed enough to show that the situation isn't normal but not so detailed that it becomes re-traumatising. If there are disagreements on perspectives, it's okay to integrate them into the words and pictures in a neutral way, leaving the child with a sense that it's okay not to agree on this. Finally, the story ends with hopes and dreams. This process helps bring some closure to the traumatic events, supporting the digestion and processing of the event and the child's understanding that it's over now. It also creates a feeling of safety about what the future will bring, making the belief "I am safe now" feel truer over time as the consciousness takes it in.

Nature also possesses remarkable healing potential if we give it a chance. So, you should consciously bring nature into play as much as possible by guiding children into contact with the elements, walking barefoot in the grass or sand, taking in deep breaths surrounded by trees in the forest, petting safe animals, walking by the sea and tossing stones and shells into the water, and so on. It serves as a potent regulator and is always available for us to connect with, and children need it nowadays. Therapies using horses are also highly effective, and dogs are used widely to support people with psychiatric diagnoses in Denmark now.

These are just a few ideas to show that many things can be done as small interventions, in contexts outside the therapy room, and might be possible for you to engage in within your remit without being a trained trauma specialist. You can, nevertheless, use your knowledge about important aspects of regulating overwhelming sensations and feelings and reconnecting children to themselves and safe adults. Sometimes, the intervention will mainly focus on helping the adults to care for the children better and to be safe adults to them.

Exercise

From the goal statements/safety goals you did in the last chapter, choose which one is the most important to start with and reflect on the means to reach them, including how to progress with the involvement of the network in creating a network plan or safety plan. Also, make sure to address how you will follow up on whether it creates change or not.

Then, consider the actions that can be included in a treatment plan to help the child towards well-being and development. Elements of this consideration could concern what interventions would be most beneficial according to goals, such as which positive beliefs should be incorporated, what psychoeducation the child might need in relation to trauma/emotions/triggers, and how to work on emotion regulation.

Lastly, explain to the child in words and pictures why you are involved in their life. This could involve four pictures where the first is neutral or positive, the next explains the challenges, the third describes your role and what you do, and the last provides a hopeful ending.

References

Caspersen, Marianne, & Laustsen, Charlotte. (2009). *Systematisk sagsbehandling i børnes-ager – principper og arbejdsgange*. UC Vest Press.

De Shazer, S., Dolan, Y., with Korman, H., Trepper, T., McCollum, E., & Berg, I. K. (2007). *More than miracles*. Routledge.

Farmer, E., & Owen, M. (1995). *Child protection practice: private risk and public remedies*. HMSO.

Furmann, B. (2021). Kids'Skills – a creative solution focused method for helping children overcome difficulties and problems. In D. Yusuf (Ed.), *Solution focused work with children and young people*. Routledge.

George, E., Iveson, C., & Ratner, H. (2017). *BRIEFER – a solution focused practice manual*. BRIEF.

Henden, J., & EBSCOhost. (2018). *What it takes to thrive: techniques for severe trauma and stress recovery*. World Scientific.

Iveson, C. (2021). There's more to children than meets the eye. In D. Yusuf (Ed.), *The solution focused approach with children and young people*. Routledge.

Jørgensen, P. S. (2017). *Robuste børn*. Kristeligt Dagblads Forlag.

King, P. E. (2021). Yes … and – useful conversations around trauma. In D. Yusuf (Ed.), *The solution focused approach with children and young people*. Routledge.

Parker, S. (2009). *The "Safety House" – a child protection tool for involving children in safety planning*. SP Consultancy.

Parker, S. (2010). *Principles of safety planning*. Aspirations Consultancy.

Parker, S. (2015). *Partnering for safety Collaborative Assessment and Planning (CAP) framework*. SP Consultancy.

Parker, S., & Struik, A. (2017). *Trauma informed safety planning*. SP Consultancy.

Ratner, H., George, E., Iveson, C., & ProQuest. (2012). *Solution focused brief therapy: 100 key points and techniques*. Routledge.

Struik, A. (2019). *Treating chronically traumatized children: the sleeping dogs method* (2nd ed.). Routledge.

Sørensen, T. H. (2012). *Når forældre og netværk skaber sikkerhed for barnet*. Copenhagen, Københanvs Kommune.

Turnell, A. (2010a). *Effective safety planning in child protection casework*. Resolutions Consultancy.

Turnell, A. (2010b). *Effective safety planning in child protection casework – DVD workbook*. Resolutions Consultancy.

Turnell, A., & Essex, S. (2006). *Working with "denied" child abuse. The resolutions approach*. Open University Press.

Chapter 11

Closing the trauma circle and opening a healing circle instead

Recap of the book and how to implement it in your daily practice

As we end this book and the Circle of Safety and Reconnection, a short summary of what we have covered will be provided to ensure a complete overview of this comprehensive and holistic approach to providing practice depth when working with vulnerable and traumatised children. We have covered eight crucial areas of professional work with these children:

1 The current risk to the child's safety, health, development, and well-being.
2 An overview of the child's trauma history, diagnoses, and current state of mind.
3 Parents and intergenerational trauma, diagnoses, and their impact on parenting skills.
4 ACEs and other important risk factors in the child's life.
5 PCEs and other important protective factors in the child's life.
6 The adequate care and protection of the child by the parents and other significant adults and the positive impact on the child's health, well-being, and development.
7 Using the balanced risk assessment to set the right goals to create safety, health, development, and well-being for the child.
8 Creating an action, treatment, or safety plan with clear agreements on following up until the child no longer needs it.

In-depth knowledge is given about various types of risk and trauma that children and parents experience, the impact on the child's health, development, and well-being, and the risk factors on one side of the circle. Then, on the other side of the circle, in-depth knowledge is given about protection factors, adequate care, connection, and attachment, and the impact on the child's health, development, well-being, and resilience. Also, the book promotes necessary knowledge about the healing power of a network and how to engage everybody in collaborative solution-building processes, using the solution-focused approach to make a balanced risk assessment and prioritising the right goals and interventions to work with the action, treatment, or safety plan.

DOI: 10.4324/9781003322672-11

The Circle of Safety and Reconnection

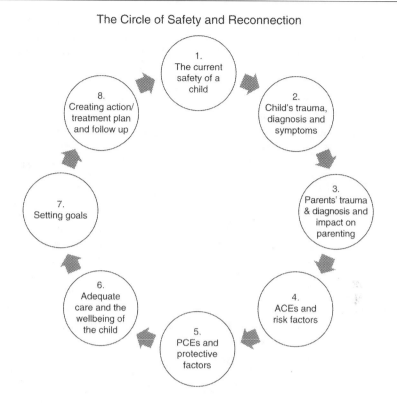

Illustration 11.1 The Circle of Safety and Reconnection

The intention has been to provide you with a simple structure for the complex work of working with traumatised and vulnerable children that will help you reflect on the most crucial aspects of these children's lives. Finding the fastest and gentlest way to safety and recovery after trauma for many children and families is continuous work, depending on how severe the risk and trauma have been. This model will provide the help needed always to be able to assess whether we are doing the right thing at the right time for the children and, if progress isn't being made, to stop and redirect our interventions, if we need to do something different according to their actual situation. As I mentioned in Chapter 10, if progress isn't evident, it's not because something is wrong with the child but because we aren't doing the right things. There might be something we have not yet seen and understood, and so we must know more about the actual harm, risk, or trauma to adjust our goals and interventions.

There is always hope for healing and recovery when it comes to issues of harm, risk, and trauma, and the professional must carry this hope and bring it to the children, their families, and their network. When dealing with children with health issues and disabilities that are chronic, the healing perspective is more one of help-ing them to cope better with their conditions, but also be aware that there might be trauma related to the medical treatment or the diagnosis, as we have seen through-out the book. Providing healing for this can also help these children thrive better, even in a state of chronic disease or disability, and is worth the effort.

The various aspects of this book support the recovery process after trauma, so that all children, regardless of their conditions, can go from victims to sur-vivors and become thrivers. It is influenced by Yvonne Dolan and her impor-tant work with adult survivors of sexual abuse described in *One Small Step – Moving beyond Trauma and Therapy to a Life of Joy* (Dolan, 1998). The three stages represent the professional work in progress, from helping and acknowl-edging victims of traumatic circumstances that have shattered their physical, emotional, and mental health to connecting them with the power to survive the incident(s) and ending at a place where they can live life to the fullest. For this process to be fully completed, the children must acknowledge the different aspects of each stage.

The victim phase is characterised by acknowledging the overwhelming negative feelings and emotions and allowing the children to feel and express them safely. It supports the process of taking in that something that was not their fault happened to them, and they can talk to somebody about it and release guilt and shame through this. In case something happened that was their fault, finding the right proportion of blame is also important.

The process continues into the survivor phase, when they start to understand that the trauma belongs to the past, and they have survived it and will function again in everyday life. We also start to examine internal and external resources that helped them survive. We tend to think and talk about what people have become despite their life circumstances, but, as described in Chapter 8, I always like to talk with children and adults about what they have become *because of* their life circumstances, knowing that it's through hardship that we build our character, re-silience, and mental robustness and gain strength to deal with life. Often, people aren't aware of this, and, therefore, I will bring this perspective into play whenever suitable.

The last stage involves moving beyond survival, thriving, living life to the full-est, and becoming free from the traumatic incident. In this stage of their life, after surviving difficult challenges, the children regain the ability to engage in every-day activities such as school, spending time with their family and friends, pursu-ing hobbies, and participating in community activities. By acknowledging their survival skills, strengths, qualities, and resources, they can move beyond mere survival and strive to thrive. This stage offers more freedom than earlier stages, allowing them to experience a compelling present and envision a realistic and ful-filling future. Despite any physical limitations, they can enjoy life to the fullest. It's worthwhile to explore and pursue the future possibilities and dreams that they cur-rently envision. This stage also provides an opportunity for personal expression, re-warding experiences, and creative endeavours. The children's current experiences and relationships may evoke a sense of immediacy, wonder, and the potential for future growth.

In this sense, the primary purpose of our work using this reflective model, no matter what actions we take, is to reconnect a child to their true being and the sense of love and belonging that we all need to thrive. The model can become a mind map of the way back home for the child – a GPS where the journey ends with the restoration of connection, health, development, and well-being and the child's becoming their true self, expressing themself uniquely. This is the true essence of trauma healing.

To integrate this into your daily practice systematically, I will bring to your attention the exercises completed while reading the book. By going through each chapter and doing the exercises, you have now worked your way through the model with a child. Hopefully, you will now have a structured overview of the most essential information available regarding this specific child that has helped you make a qualified, balanced risk assessment; you will have formulated both worry statements and goal statements for the intervention; and you will have prioritised the most important goal to start with. Your intervention plan is also now explicitly and clearly formulated as the most suitable plan for your work context and the change that the child needs. Lastly, you have decided on an adequate level of follow-ups until the child has started to thrive.

To implement your new knowledge and reflections in your practice with this child, you can use your new ability to understand the child's situation differently and bring this understanding to the table to qualify the excellent work you are already doing, while still following the rules, regulations, and guidelines at your workplace. My advice is always to be aware of doing this in a safe way, for the child and everybody engaged in the case, including yourself. When introducing new ideas and practices, you must have your back covered at your workplace, especially if safety is at stake. I recommend never doing safety planning alone; rather, always do it with a team of people, as described in the previous chapter. Sharing with your colleagues what you now know about trauma-informed work with children and reflecting on this with them at meetings, in supervision, or during training might start a collective journey at your workplace – a ripple effect I hold hope for.

You might be overwhelmed by incorporating all this into your daily practice now. Therefore, I will cite Martin Luther King Jr's famous saying, "You don't have to see the whole staircase; you just have to take the first step". This is how I started my journey working with vulnerable and traumatised children and how I continue the journey. I have never forgotten Andrew Turnell's words about the Signs of Safety being a continuous learning journey. This expression was meaningful to me and has formed my ongoing curious investigation of how I can always do this work better for the children I work with. I hope to bring some insight, knowledge, and experience to your learning journey by sharing my most important findings with you in this book. When I first learned the solution-focused approach many years ago, I chose the three most meaningful and powerful questions for me and started practising them with the children and families. Then, I got familiar with them and saw their effect and I took three more questions and, suddenly, I had learned a new language. From this experience, I recommend you start by picking what is most exciting and important to you and get familiar with this aspect before taking in another part of this book.

In your busy work life, you might not have time to apply this model to every child you work with, but I recommend doing it with children where the progress is somehow stuck, and you can't find the right way. Other suitable situations could be where collaboration is full of conflict, where you might feel insecure about whether you are doing enough or the right things, or where you spend a lot of time with only a little progress. Maybe working through the model using the exercises will help you gain the needed insight. Remember, every time you use it, it gets easier, and one day you might automatically start drawing a trauma line for a child and a parent in a conversation with them or consider working around the PCEs or again asking a best hope question.

Since 2012, I have advocated bringing trauma-informed work to the forefront of the professional field involving children at risk and their families and in child psychiatry fields. In Denmark, particularly in recent years, it seems to finally have had a breakthrough and become what everybody is talking about. As the latest "new thing", some people view it as a passing trend, but I see it differently. Knowing the essence of trauma and how it impacts the nervous system is as natural and important as taking in oxygen to breathe and live. If we don't get the necessary oxygen, it can lead to severe damage to the brain and body, and, in the worst case, we die. With the growing knowledge and learning about the considerable impact of trauma on people's bodies, minds, and souls, ignoring this knowledge during times of suffering is inconceivable. Now, more than ever, in our chaotic world with continuous crises, it's a necessity to use this knowledge more effectively and profoundly.

For my part, in my trauma release work, I still engage in an exploratory learning journey on how to heal trauma in the fastest and gentlest way by combining several functional methodologies that I have investigated in the 20 years since I first read Peter Levine's book *Awaken the Tiger* (Levine, 1998). This led to my method, the "Reconnect Trauma Release System", combining Western and Eastern knowledge and wisdom, which I have tested and adjusted for several years now. For me and the people I have helped to release their trauma, it has been mind-blowing to get to know humans' capacity for self-healing when being supported correctly and bringing body, mind, and soul together. One of the essential aspects of this work is to reconnect people with their body through breathwork while slowly building up resources in their body to deal with the overwhelming emotions from the trauma. As Bessel van der Kolk says, "the body keeps the score", and reconnection to it is vital for all future work with children, both for prevention of and healing from trauma. This message is relevant for all the different professional contexts where people working with children need to be more trauma-informed, from the schoolyard, where outdoor play could be one way of getting them back into their bodies, to the psychiatric ward, where trauma-informed yoga could be a powerful tool to regulate patients in healthier and less invasive ways than traditional practice.

In 2019, I completed a yoga teacher training course in India in order to work with traumatised children and their regulation through yoga, breathwork, and mindfulness. This work taught me that breathwork in any context is a powerful tool, and you only need to be aware of it, as it doesn't cost anything and can be done everywhere and at all times. The strength of breathwork lies in its simplicity and naturalness. Reconnecting to the most basic human needs might significantly impact work involving healing from and prevention of trauma, such as re-establishing the connection to real human contact, touch, breathwork, and emotional regulation by being there for each other. Also, to reconnect people to the broader family, important network, and communities, remember that "We are hardwired for connection", as Brené Brown says in a TED Talk. For a long time, Bruce Perry has raised his voice about relational poverty because he is very concerned, with good reason. So am I, but we can do so many things if we are aware of it.

Also, the toxic impact of shame is significant and must not be underestimated. This is the reason why I am such a huge advocate for bringing compassion into trauma work and social work. Addressing shame and guilt through compassionate practice can profoundly transform the lives of vulnerable and traumatised children and could potentially reduce their reliance on medication for regulation. Again, this is a capacity we are equipped with by nature, and, I guess, in many ways, we must take this path in the years to come – the natural and human way!

All this will positively affect children and their environment and help stop the vicious spiral of intergenerational trauma, thereby affecting future generations in families. The circle ends with the healing of trauma, and a new process of love and belonging can start, and this healing circle is now in your hands. I will end by referring to the Japanese art of *kintsugi* as a symbol of the reconnection and restoration work that the Circle of Safety and Reconnection supports. In kintsugi, practitioners use lacquer dusted or mixed with gold, silver, and platinum to repair broken pottery, turning it into art and honouring its history by illuminating the repair instead of hiding it. Let's turn the world's brokenness into a beautiful piece of valuable art, one child at a time.

References

Dolan, Y. (1998). *One small step – moving beyond trauma and therapy to a life of joy.* Authors Choice Press.

Levine, P. A. (1998). *Væk tigeren – helbredelse af traumer* (Waking the tiger – healing trauma) (F. R. Pedersen, Trans.). Borgens Forlag/Gyldendal.

Index

Note: Locators in *italic* indicate figures, in **bold** tables and in ***bold-italic*** boxes.

Printed in the United States
by Baker & Taylor Publisher Services